Management strategies for maintaining your sanity
while building your company

Business
Black Belt

Develop your strength, flexibility
and agility to run your company.

Burke Franklin

Order another copy of
Business *Black Belt*
$24.95 + $3 Shipping & Handling
Visa • MasterCard • Amex
1-800-346-5426
www.jian.com
Mention Discount Code: 4003

Published in the United States by Business Black Belt Press

Library of Congress Cataloging-in-Publication Data
Franklin, Burke
Business Black Belt by Burke Franklin

Library of Congress Catalog # 96-94833

ISBN: 1-56811-016-2

Business; self–improvement; personal growth; management

Printed in the U.S.A.

10 9 8 7 6 5 4 3 2 1

Dedicated to my grandfather Mason Franklin,
W.W.I. balloon pilot and founder of TubeSales™,
who taught me what really worked in life and business
at the same time he was teaching me good manners.

Acknowledgments

Shelley Beban, our VP of Finance at JIAN, for building our finance department, taking on tough projects and telling me what's on her mind and keeping me informed on more than financial matters.

John Bock, the chairman of my TEC group, (The Executive Committee—I meet with 14 CEOs once a month to discuss management issues and assist each other with problems) is an instrumental coach I call upon for ideas, answers and direction—especially on the tough decisions. You can call John at 415-344-2531.

Lindon Crow & Rick Itzkowich, run a seminar operation called Productive Learning & Leisure where they take busy executives river rafting, skiing, golfing, scuba diving and mountain biking. They weave a variety of compelling lessons into these fun workshops where you can learn much about your thinking and behavior as it applies to your life and business. Call them at 800-717-1817 or contact them at www.ProductiveLeisure.com

Virginia Franklin, my grandmother, who financed my early business ventures. Be very careful when you raise money through relatives. They always remember and you have to face them during the holidays. Nevertheless, she has always been my biggest supporter.

Wilfred T. Grenfell, my Ancient History teacher at Woodberry Forest School in Virginia, who was a fanatic for dates, facts, figures, names, proof, and all-around writing that someone could believe. He ruthlessly graded papers looking for content and quality. I hated him. It's too bad there aren't more teachers like him around because I'll never forget what he taught me about writing good reports. It's much of the magic in JIAN software today.

Barbara King, who made more red marks in this book than anyone. I thank her for her pointed questions and blunt comments—she made sure that I explained myself clearly and didn't make an ass of myself in the process.

Paul Larson, founder of the Summit Organization. What makes you unique is realizing how much like everyone else you are. He didn't care how smart you were, what you looked like, how much potential you had, or about any of your excuses for not succeeding—he expected you to produce results at whatever you did. And he wrote some tremendous workshops that got me out of my own way.

Soojin Lee, my Tae Kwon Do instructor for 6 years who taught me from white belt through second degree black belt. "Get in there, be first, and use combinations. Even if they hit you, make 'em pay for it." Our school won a lot of tournaments so I know he taught us the good stuff.

Darshan Mayginnes of Essence Partners for his incredible ability to be mellow at all times and for his teaching and guidance in ways to have things be easy.

Pat Napoles has edited and desktop published my stuff for years. She understands my good intent regardless of what I actually write or say. She makes all the changes on short notice when I change my mind. I know I'm not paying her enough, but she still takes great care of me. I'd marry her if she were available.

Neal Novotny our VP of Research & Planning at JIAN, for always being the stable, team player. He has the cojones to confront me when he thinks I'm out of my mind and usually has a good reason. I'd want to play rugby on his team and not against him.

Alicia Parnell, originally my assistant at JIAN and formerly our Media Relations Manager, for her constant and patient counsel when it comes to people matters and for talking to reporters, writers, and editors to make sure the story is straight.

Ed Pera, a Director at JIAN, for his "adult supervision" in financial matters and for being there to provide a second opinion regarding our employees' performance and for seeing the invisible in the financial and retail machine.

Erik Pitelka, my assistant, who picked up the ball on this book, put in all the changes, made the arrangements for publishing it and made sure everything was right.

Alison Kaye Rhodes sat for hours as I explained on tape everything I wanted to say and then transcribed the whole thing. She asked a lot of great questions from a "beginner's mind" to make sure that I didn't make any statements that only I could understand. For this effort I am deeply grateful.

David Shohfi, our VP of Sales at JIAN, for his attention to managing people and demonstration of focus, organization, and a great job in making sure that our software is available everywhere on Earth.

Judy and Julian Smith, my parents, who read this book on their ski vacation and provided editing wisdom that made a lot of sense and kept me from pissing off a few people.

Susan Snowe of Essence Partners for her constant observation and accurate comments on my behavior because she wants me to succeed beyond my wildest expectations.

Jerry and Valerie Starr, at Apple Computer for loaning me their Macintosh computer to start my business.

The illustrations in this book come entirely from the Art Parts™ collection of ClickArt electronic clip art available from the T/Maker division of Broderbund Software. For their catalog of these and many other clip art images, call 1-800-9TMAKER

Unless otherwise stated, all quotes in this book belong to Burke Franklin.

Contents

Introduction

We are limited more by our own thinking than by reality.

I've earned a black belt and I've built a business. Coincidentally, I started the process for each at the same time. What's behind the nuts and bolts of success? Much has to do with willpower, luck, and some fortuitous technology, but only a few people have successfully built companies on those things alone. What else does it take, and can that be *learned?* I think it can.

Since 1979, I've participated in over 100 seminars—business, personal, sales, corporate. Some were touchy-feely, some involved screaming, yelling, and crying. I've read many of the popular books, listened to speakers and their tapes and videos, but only after building and running my company could I synthesize them into actual, usable direction for you. I've applied much of this knowledge and experience to building my own company, and I share with you what actually worked for me. I share selected processes that, from my experience, have had a profound impact on the success of my business. You will be more effective with people and your approach to building your company. These concepts will benefit you as a manager of a start-up as well as a mature company. Also, we've built much of this information into the JIAN line of software packages.

The '90s are very different than the '60s, '70s and '80s, but these years are only a warm-up for the coming millennium. Something big but subtle happened when we turned that last corner. Now more than ever, it's crucial to apply new ways of thinking—doing the right thing, being supportive of people's well-being, and paying attention to karma—to business in the '90s. (*I use the definition of karma from Hinduism and Buddhism. Karma is the total effect of a person's actions and conduct during the successive phases of the person's existence that determine the person's destiny.*) No more hype and get-rich-quick schemes. They seem to be back-firing in record numbers. People are smarter and less victimizable. No more anxious pushing to close sleazy deals. They end up costing more in the long run and the lawsuits aren't worth the trouble and the cost. Any form of harassment is intolerable. Crooked financial schemes are unraveling. Anything less than excellent workmanship is unacceptable.

Fear, Uncertainty, and Doubt: The universal sales pitch

Scare the hell out of your sales prospects and they'll buy your product or service. How is your underarm deodorant working today? Are you driving the right car? Are you spending too much money?

It occurred to me that many people around me are trying to scare me. Scare me into buying their product or service. Give me bad enough news and I'll do what they want.

I'm already motivated to take action when something needs to be done. Like most entrepreneurs, I'm not predisposed to sit around, but when I decided not to be afraid, my mind became clearer. I knew what I wanted and how to go about getting it—without being at the mercy of other people's fears or their projections of fear. The elimination of my unconscious *physical* fear on my way to becoming a black belt is largely what led to these invaluable insights.

A black belt for you?

I think everyone should practice a martial art of some kind—even if you don't go as far as black belt. The martial arts are a safe channel for aggression and frustration, to train your mind with your body, and to enhance your skill and mental acuity in every other sport and physical activity. You can practice it for the rest of your life. You also won't be afraid of the dark or anyone in business meetings, big cities, and foreign countries.

You'll find many parallels between the martial arts and business. To earn a black belt, you must train, persist, and be prepared. You must know what to look for, what to do, when to move in, and when to back off. When you apply the martial arts philosophies to your business, you'll protect yourself as you practice a healthier, longer lasting approach to successful business. The world at large may not quite be ready for businesspeople who "do the right thing," so you need to watch out for yourself. But if you do the right thing to make sure that all parties win and generate a nice profit, you can avoid getting beaten up in the process.

Many times in martial arts, the subtlest move can have a major effect. This can be a helpful concept in management, marketing, and sales. Some moves are indirect, some are counter-intuitive. Your opponent zigs, expecting you to zag, but you might zig too. Instead of blocking and moving back, you sidestep and move in. Sometimes you need to be consistent, sometimes you need to be unpredictable. Flow with what's happening at any moment in time and look for the openings, the opportunities. Sometimes you need to do nothing and let your opponents just wear themselves out. A true master is aware of the dirty game and can defend against the cheaters with dignity. In my Tae Kwon Do (tie´•kwon•doe´) school, we were taught to watch our opponent when we bow in the unlikely event that he or she might try to kick us in the face during what is supposed to be a gesture of respect. When you think, feel, and act like a Black Belt, you'll have more control of the game and play it your way.

Compete without fear

When you have the wisdom to do business without fear, you also have much more time to think because your mind is not locked by fear. Why fear your competitors? Instead, use them for training, focus, and motivation. Why try to beat up your competitors? Just have the strength not to get beaten up by them.

What I see in business is very much like what I see on TV. Some guy gets beaten up or a woman is molested before the martial arts hero shows up. If the victim had just known some slick moves, he or she could easily have defeated the attacker. In business, you can get mugged, but why not turn the attack into a victory for yourself?

Everyone is in business one way or another. The insights in this book should help you run your business more efficiently, and be street-smart on the job. This book is dedicated to promoting the idea that people work together and do the right thing. How can that not be successful?

Where the rubber meets the road

This is not a management analyst's look at business from 10,000 feet. Instead, I look at things likely to happen day to day, Monday through Friday (usually Saturday and maybe part of Sunday), that are going to bite you on your butt and cost you a lot of money—if you overlook them. If I'd had this foresight to do some things differently from the beginning, I'd have saved myself thousands of dollars and many headaches.

At the end of the week when I'm signing a pile of checks with hundreds and thousands of dollars going here and there, I know that every one of them is the result of my past attitude and actions—what I was thinking and doing in a previous moment to create that expense. I've enjoyed learning some very expensive lessons. In fact, each chapter in this book cost me from at least $1,000 to as much as $350,000 apiece. After reading all of it, I hope you'll have profited from my investment.

We enjoy the same problems

This book is written from my experiences, from my perspectives and as I perceived them—the solutions I describe have nothing to do with others. What I write and describe are not about them. They're about me and my contribution to the situation—good and bad (if you are making those judgments). This book is meant entirely to assist you (if and/or when you might be in a similar situation) to consider some alternatives to maneuver effectively through potentially painful and expensive situations. The reader (you) must not make any assumptions about who or which company I may have referred to as a source of any wrong doing—I make no accusations. No one person or organization can claim credit for providing the scenario I use as my example. (If you think or perceive that it's you I'm referring to or embarrassing in some way, it's not; however, I do appreciate any contribution to my learning.) Unfortunately, it often took several situations before I got the message.

Business Black Belt is an outlet for me to share the not-so-obvious and the obvious-if-recognized things I've learned or seen in business. I'm going to assume that I'm not much different from you as an ambitious businessperson. I'm sure that my experiences, with variations, will somehow benefit you. To make the most of this book, see how the information, anecdotes, and situations indeed apply to you and your situation.

I'm looking forward to doing business with you some day soon.

All the best,

Burke Franklin
January 25, 1998

All you need is a good idea...
sell it...
and live happily ever after.
— A common belief

White Belt:

The Beginning of a New Way

While practicing the basics of a martial art, your body and mind will be required to accept some things that may seem odd. You learn to move with a lower, more stable center of gravity. This can only be done through your mind. Moves you are asked to perform may seem to have no meaning. They will. Just keep practicing. You must master them.

How I Earned My Business Black Belt

When you know what to do and have the right tools, you can do anything.

☞ This is my brief biography, to give you an idea of who I am, what I've learned, and some of the experiences that have contributed to this book.

I can't tell you how many times I heard, "All you need is a good idea... sell it... and live happily ever after," while growing up. I guess it's the American Dream. I heard it from my grandfather who founded a tubing distribution company after World War II. His company, TubeSales, became a successful worldwide distributor of industrial tubing.

Dinner table discussions were always about the tubing distribution business. When I was six, my grandfather imparted his wisdom to me: "You'll never make any money working for somebody else." He also advised, "Get a product (or invent one) and sell it." I scrounged around the house looking for something to sell. Because my grandmother was on a political election committee, the next day I was in business for the first time, in our driveway, selling *Ronald Reagan for Governor* buttons for 25 cents each.

Skip ahead about 15 years

I was a college junior studying electrical engineering at the University of California at Santa Barbara, but *Nth* dimensional equations were driving me crazy! It was too complicated for a guy who saw the real life applications of high-technology and just wanted to put it to use. So, I switched to business economics to learn about the ebb and flow of money on the planet. It was interesting, but still I yearned to do something on my own.

I borrowed $5,000 from my grandmother and started a *do-it-yourself used car lot*. You know, "Rent a space and sell your car." I developed all the sales promotion materials, advertised in the paper, and plastered my fliers on every car with a For Sale sign in its window. I even did the radio commercials. (When I wanted to sleep in, my clock radio would come on and I'd hear myself, telling me to come to work. Anyway, I was a big hit at school as a result.) Despite angry car salespeople (I assume) who chopped down my sign and a telephone pole, I built the business to display an average of 20 to 30 cars, trucks and motorcycles just about every Sunday. The business wasn't really successful, although I did get an A every quarter from my professor/advisor. I did get my BA degree in business economics from U.C. Santa Barbara. This business experience is a small, but important part of what I learned and contributes much to *Business Black Belt*.

My first *real* job after college

With Texas Instruments in Southern California, I sold electronic components to engineers and corporate buyers. After practically living in my car for two years (in the pre-carphone days), I created a direct-mail and telemarketing program and I was just becoming successful. Alas, my division of T.I. was sold.

During this time, I started reading books on business success and taking seminars on personal development. Although these were powerful eye-openers for me and compelled me to eventually change my ways for the better, I first believed that I could make an end-run to the top. (There *had* to be a get-rich-quick scheme or a deal that would make me a millionaire before I was 25.) I went to work for the seminar company, thinking that total immersion in the information would get me there faster. I didn't do well at selling seminars because I didn't have what they sold. I wasn't sure of the results people would get or how they would feel about it (and me). I learned a lot about myself and human nature but made no money.

One of my better customers from my T.I. days, a distributor of HP–3000 accounting software, needed a director of marketing. The first thing I did was set up direct mail and telemarketing. I was trying to get rich quick here too. I sold a few software packages, but I learned that people want the assurance of functionality and support more than a discount on the software they use to run their business. One day, after a rare sale, I was reading a Sharper Image® catalog and wondered if I could get out of sales and do something more fun.

I knew that I had to go for it

I became the electronics buyer for The Sharper Image Catalog. Wow! There I was with all the toys I ever wanted and more. (By the way, I learned that having these things really doesn't improve the quality of your life—but this would make for a good philosophical talk at another time.) I always wondered how a successful mail-order company worked, and how someone became as successful as Sharper Image CEO Richard Thalheimer. So I watched him, studied how he operated, and I learned a lot. It wasn't rocket science, just the perfect execution of the basics of mail order. Many books on the subject tell you the same things—just do them and keep your foot on the gas. I also learned about karma here. As a salesman-turned-buyer, I must have seen or been the butt of every sales ploy I had ever tried before. Every salesperson pulled something on me! Tactics I'd used before, tried once, or read about, all came back to haunt me. (Every salesperson should be a buyer for a while to learn respect for the sales process and buyers should try their hand at selling—I've known several who have become very successful.) This was a very fast-paced organization; my problem was that although I had the gift of knowing what to buy, I lacked the experience and nerve to purchase quantities worth more than three times my salary—and do it fast enough to keep stock on-hand for the catalog demand. I was a sales and marketing guy pretending to be a *buyer*. However, I showed promise as a writer, so they moved me over to the creative department to write their catalog copy. I love The Sharper Image catalog conversational copy style. Readers feel like they know everything about a product in 50 to 100 words and are compelled to dive for the phone with their credit cards ready.

Next, I found a low-key marketing/advertising firm in Silicon Valley where I could get in on the ground floor, help them grow, and reap big rewards as the manager of new business development. (The get-rich-quick bug still held me.) In less than a year, I established six key accounts. Although I learned much about marketing, unhealthy business practices were going on around me. This experience also contributed much to what I write about here and is valuable to the long-term success of your business. I left being owed several paychecks.

One day I was driving up Highway 101 and passed an 18-wheeler loaded with tubing. The mud flaps read "TubeSales—Worldwide." A reminder of my grandfather. A message.

Whoa. . . I'd better get moving!

1984. I wanted to work again for a solid company that would let me apply what I'd learned so far. Soon, I was working out of a local sales office in Santa Clara, California, for CPT Corporation, based in Minneapolis, selling sophisticated information management systems. These were great systems to sell at the beginning of the personal computer era and I could make a lot of money fast. I was actually starting to do well, but our CEO felt that his $200-million company didn't need to follow suit with the IBM PC and be DOS-compatible. Oops. . .

July 1986, I'm on my own

(In a later chapter I'll describe what happened that got me onto a new track that ultimately proved very successful.) I was tired of all my get-rich-quick attempts. However, I knew that I could make sales materials that would help good products sell and help salespeople in the process. So, I founded Tools For Sales™ to develop sales promotion materials. I didn't want to call myself a marketing consultant because there are too many of those—promoting my specific service to create sales tools gave me an advantage. I produced simple, direct advertisements and brochures providing my clients' customers with complete and clear information. And my clients' sales consistently jumped from 140 to 300+ percent. Finally, I was doing more things right than wrong. And for the right reasons.

I also worked on a variety of business plans and discovered that by applying my marketing experience to the development of a business plan, the result was more descriptive, more concise, and easier to understand. I wrote business plans as if they were an elaborate company brochure to win over bankers, investors, or senior corporate managers. This style of plan was more likely to be read and approved for funding. It's still working.

My first glimpse of daylight

What if I got a hold of a product or invented something like my grandfather had advised? I'd need the *ultimate* business plan myself, and I could really do it right this time. I had enough materials to put one together, so I began to organize and refine them. All I needed was a product. Then it happened. I was standing in the shower sometime between Christmas and the new year in 1987, I was ranting and raving to myself about how pathetic most business plans were. People just didn't get it. How come the plans were so unclear, disorganized, incomplete, non-compelling? These people understand their business, but a lot of them were in a jam trying to write their business plans. It hit me. Maybe they could use the template I'd started for myself from all the work I'd done?!

Not long after, BizPlan*Builder*® was conceived and first published. At about the same time, I began training for my black belt in Tae Kwon Do. This book picks up here, when I finally started to put it all together and do things right. Now JIAN is a fast-growing company whose products help others do the same.

Qualify Your Advice

What You *Get* and What You *Give*

*A big part of listening skills is in your choice of
who you listen to and what you believe.*

☞   I recommend that you qualify the source(s) of your advice and in
so doing, qualify the advice you give.

The cobbler's kids have no shoes

I learned a few years ago never to take advice from someone who hasn't been
there before. You wouldn't hire a fitness trainer who is fatter than you are, would
you? Leaders must set an example in the area they claim as their expertise.

You've heard the saying about the cobbler whose own children have no
shoes, meaning he doesn't practice what he preaches. If the cobbler's kids go
barefoot, obviously he doesn't care about them, so why would he care about
you? And if his shoes aren't good enough for his kids, why should you buy
them? There's a real problem if someone doesn't use their own stuff or follow
their own advice—especially when they're offering or selling it to you.

It's important to get the right advice only from the right people. Unless
you're doing market research, where every opinion contributes, remember to
weigh the quality of your advice according to its source. Ask someone in a

position of leadership—an active expert in that area. Also, ask more than one expert (a second opinion). And whatever information you gain, be sure to filter it through your own experience and knowledge. In other words, don't deny or discount your own direct experience. Often, business leaders ignore their intuition in favor of conflicting opinions and, usually, regret it.

In the past, when I had a question, I would seek advice from everyone, regardless of their qualifications on the subject. For example, I would pose a technical marketing question to lots of people. I would weigh their opinions equally no matter what they knew or how qualified they were. On the other hand, I used to give my opinion about all kinds of things only to be upset when people didn't believe me (even though I might not have known what I was talking about anyway). I should have said, "Look, I don't know about that subject. I'm not an expert. But if you still want my opinion. . . ."

Unfortunately, many people who have no idea what they're talking about are happy to give you their opinions anyway. The ones who really make me laugh are the "consultants" who've just graduated from school but have yet to get a real job. Don't ask everyone for their opinions. Just because someone has a college degree, has written a book, or leads a seminar doesn't mean he or she is an expert. In fact, you may have more expertise than they do!

Asking the wrong people for advice is a *big waste of time*. And if you take their unqualified advice, it will be a *big waste of money* too! The time invested in qualifying your source far outweighs the time wasted in recovering from a mistake made with bad advice.

> *There is a fine line between fishing*
> *and standing on the shore like an idiot.*
> — Stephen Wright, comedian

There's a BIG difference between opinion & experience

You must distinguish between opinion and fact. Often, a person offers an opinion but states it as if it were an experience. Many people give advice without distinguishing its quality. You can determine the quality of the advice you receive by simply asking:

How do you know that?

The explanation should give you a good idea as to where the advice sits between opinion and experience. If someone has been through the same situation and appears to be honestly successful, then you can make a pretty safe bet the advice is based on fact.

Here's how I rate the quality levels of advice

- Direct experience—the advice-giver was successful, has been doing it for years, offers many variations, and can distinguish many nuances in the situation
- They were taught by a known expert
- They talked to someone with expertise who learned through his/her own direct experience
- They observed someone else apply it and succeed
- They read it in a book
- They overheard a conversation
- It seems like a good idea

Above all, the advisor must clearly understand your situation and objectives. A good sign is that he or she takes the time to ask a variety of questions. The ease with which the advisor asks uncomfortable-to-answer questions is a plus. One who leaps to solutions is dangerous.

If they share an experience with you, most people will tell you how well it went. Nevertheless, always ask, "How well did it work for you?" Even if they weren't totally successful, you can still benefit from the experience they did have by asking, "What do you think would have made a difference?" and "Why do you think that would have worked?"

Your ideas will be accepted more readily if you've already demonstrated success by using them yourself

How to offer advice—an investment in credibility

Credibility is one of your most important assets in business and in life. Not only do you need to trust others for the information they give you, it's equally important that others know they can trust you too.

I recommend that when you offer advice, follow it with a statement of how you came by this knowledge. That way, regardless of whether good or bad results come from the advice you give, your integrity is always maintained. "Here's something I learned from my own personal experience and it might work for you." At least he or she knows where your information has come from. If you give advice that is just an opinion or something off the top of your head and it doesn't work, he or she will look at you and say (or worse, think and not say), "Your advice sucks." "You're a loser." However, if you say, "I read this in a book and it worked in this particular context, so it might make sense for you," at least if it doesn't work, in all honesty he or she will know that you read it in a book. You're really not on the hook for this one.

When offering advice, state, "Here's how I know this. . . ." If you don't know what you're talking about, do everyone a favor and keep your mouth shut. Maintain your credibility for the future when it counts. You don't need to be temporarily impressive at the cost of your reputation that follows you forever.

Beware of extremes

In the past, I've often used examples of extreme situations to illustrate a point. The mistake I made was not to state that it was an extreme example of how something is or might be a worst-case scenario that only happens one percent of the time, or has a 1-in-10,000 chance of happening. Instead, I used an extreme example without qualifying it, mostly just to be funny or gross. The problem was that people mistook me or developed a perception about me that I was negative or off the wall.

While we're on the subject of credibility, I'll address sarcasm. You may use sarcasm to be funny. Maybe you think that you're above it all; your off-handed sarcastic commentary demonstrates such mastery of the subject that you can afford to be funny. The danger with sarcasm is that people often cannot distinguish it from your true intent. They may take you seriously, with detrimental implications, or perceive that you're a jerk. I discovered this when someone was sarcastic with me. I wasn't sure what he meant. I didn't get it. From this experience, I realized that I was sarcastic a lot of the time, and I realized why people weren't paying attention to me or understanding what I really meant. If you're always joking, when do people take you seriously? Besides, sarcasm is usually negative and puts people off.

Remember, qualifying your advice will keep you conscious of the quality of the advice you are giving; if you can't qualify it, then it's probably not worth mentioning. This will prevent you from steering people wrong, being taken seriously when you are joking, or being perceived as a fool when you are serious.

Business Black Belt Notes

- Question the source of people's advice. Are they credible?

- Ask, "How do you know that?"

- Choose advice givers carefully. Don't ask everyone for their opinions.

- Did the advice giver have a direct experience? How well did it work?

- Is this person successful in general or successful with the recommendation?

- Pass along the source of your own advice to build and preserve your credibility.

- When you are doing the advising, play it straight.

I Can't Believe You Asked That!

*You can ask or say just about anything
as long as your motive is clean.*

☞ Asking the right questions is the key to getting the most useful information and validating assumptions.

First, let's identify a simple problem most of us are afflicted with: the need to be polite. When I was a little boy, my grandmother told me that there are three things you never ask a woman:

1) how old is she?
2) how much does she weigh?
3) how much money does she have?

I learned then that you never ask people certain questions. Of course, these became the three most important things I wanted to know. The subject probably surfaced when I asked one of my parents' friends how much she weighed. She must have been huge and I just wanted to know. (It's amusing how kids have no problem asking questions, until they get the idea that it's bad.) We grow up learning that there are questions you don't ask and things you don't talk about. In fact, over time you learn that you're better off *not* asking any questions at all for fear of making a mistake, committing some kind of social faux pas, or causing an embarrassing situation.

In business, the inability to ask probing questions can kill you if you don't ask crucial questions for fear of offending someone. You really have to ask the kind of questions that may seem offensive or distrusting:

"What's your experience on this project?"

"How do I know you can come through?"

"What is it about your experience that makes you the best person for this project?"

"How can you prove to me that you know what you're doing?"

When I was hired at The Sharper Image to be the electronics buyer, I had to prove that I had a sense of what would sell. The VP of Merchandising simply handed me a copy of the catalog and asked me to look through it and guess what sold. He had the sales reports so he knew exactly, but all I had were my instincts. There was no bluffing here—either I had a feeling for it or I didn't. He was making an important hiring decision and couldn't afford to fool around. As it turned out, my guesses were very accurate and I even singled out the worst selling item in the catalog. I passed the test and got the job. If your prospective employee is for real, he or she won't have any trouble answering tough questions.

"Have you done this project somewhere else and been successful?"

"Who can I call as a reference for you?"

"What happens if you die?" (I ask this of contractors.)

That last one usually draws the response "Why are you asking me that?" Here's *my* reason: We were using an accounting software package and, while waiting for version 2.0 to be released, the programmer dropped dead of a brain aneurysm at his desk. No one else knew how to complete the project! Now I always ask, "What happens if you die?" We even include provisions for death in some of our contracts.

They may seem like questions you're asking because you don't trust the person, but you still need to ask these questions to fill in the background. Plus, you want to hear how someone else answers—so you're not specifying how you want something done.

If you have a problem or an interesting project, ask someone how he or she would handle it without your direction. Get a feeling for how the person would do things if you weren't there watching or giving direction. (Remember: The idea is to someday be at the beach while other people are managing your business the way you would, or better!)

If we're afraid to ask questions, we end up making assumptions. You know, to ASSUME means to make an ASS out of U and ME.

According to the *American Heritage Dictionary:*

as•sump•tion (a-sump'-shun) n.

1. The act of taking to or upon oneself.
2. The act of taking over.
3. The act of taking for granted.
4. Something taken for granted or accepted as true without proof; a supposition.
5. Presumption; arrogance.

I hate it when I make a deal with or hire someone only to find out that their work ethic or sense of quality isn't even close to mine. Now I ask beforehand, "What's your motivation on this project? What does a good job look like to you? What will this look like when it is complete?"

An assumption is a thought about the way something is or what someone thinks without any specific evidence. The trick is to recognize an assumption when you make one. Ask yourself if a fact has been specifically stated or specifically written somewhere. If not, you'll go off half-cocked thinking a certain way. This is dangerous, but you have a simple way out. When you find yourself making an assumption, stop and turn the assumption into a question. ("I'm assuming you will build this gizmo using 4130 Chromoly steel, is that right?") That way, you're not mistaking an assumption for something real.

> *If the assumptions are wrong, all that follows is wrong.*
> — Mark Affleck, author & business consultant

What do *you* mean by that?

My favorite question to ask is: "What do *you* mean by that?" We all use the same words with different meanings behind them especially when somebody uses a three-dollar word. The person sounds really intelligent, but I'm not really sure he or she even understands what the word means. Maybe the word stands for definition number one in *Webster's Dictionary,* and I'm thinking of definition number two or three. What does he or she mean by that word?

Take for example, the word cost. A friend of mine told me, "I bought this at cost." I wondered, whose cost? The manufacturer's cost? The distributor's cost? The retailer's cost? What does *cost* really mean here? There are many price points and middle parties in the product chain, so what price and cost are we talking about here?

In business, I think any question goes, except, of course, the illegal questions that you can't ask in interviews. But when talking about how you're going to do something with a contractor, partner, whoever, you need to ask a lot of questions.

You might want to ask someone, "How do you make your money on this?" It's amazing how people find ways to make money or make deals that will generate income in different ways for different parts of their business. In a business deal with someone, this question is very appropriate. You want to know what someone is going to do or how he or she will respond in a particular situation.

It all has to do with where your question is coming from. If you really want to know because you find it interesting or the knowledge would be useful, that's OK. Avoid asking questions just to make someone look bad or to embarrass them. Use that as your gauge to know if your question is appropriate or not. You can ask or say just about anything as long as your motive is clean.

Business Black Belt Notes

- If you need to know, you must ask the question.

- Use assumptions—yours and theirs—as the basis for your questions.

- If you've got a question, go ahead and ask it.

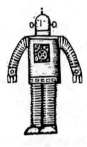

We're Full of Solutions Looking for Problems

A good answer evolves from many good questions.

☞ If I had two hours to solve a problem, I would spend the first hour and a half asking questions and questioning assumptions—mine and those of everyone involved. I've found that often the solution will reveal itself easily once the problem has been fully and properly identified.

Let's take the question thing a step further. When our grade school teacher asked a question, we were rewarded for being the first to answer. We knew that whoever was the fastest would get all the credit and look the smartest. Many of us are still racing to be the first with a solution so we can get all the credit for solving the problem. In doing that, however, we make many mistakes and overlook potential problems.

Most of us are too quick to come up with answers. We kick ourselves later for wasting time and money. We don't spend enough time and effort unfolding the whole problem. We're too busy trying to quickly find *any* solution.

In our haste to do it fast, we stop asking questions too soon. If you're really in a hurry for an answer, you're not going to explore all the angles of a problem. Take more time to ask more questions.

Remember the story about the five blind men and the
elephant? One leaned up against his leg and thought the
elephant was a tree. Another grabbed his trunk and
thought he was a snake. The third man held the elephant's
ear and thought he was a bird. The fourth one felt his huge
stomach and concluded it was a whale. Finally, the fifth man
caught the elephant's tail and thought it was a rope. They each
touched only one part of the elephant, and because they were
blind, they were unaware that the rest of the elephant existed. They argued
among themselves, each certain that the others were wrong, none of them
aware of the complete animal.

You can't just touch the trunk and blindly come away with a complete
understanding of an elephant. To get a good idea of the whole animal, you've
got to walk around it and touch it in many places. And don't just assume that
the elephant is gray. Ask someone who can see from a distance. Making assumptions and jumping to conclusions could land you in a heap of elephant dung.

Does this happen in business? All the time.

Most people stop asking questions too soon. "Let's get to the answer. Let's cut
to the chase." We have answers to all kinds of things, but we don't ask
enough questions. We don't spend enough time finding out what the problem really is. If you have an hour to solve a problem, take 45 minutes to figure out exactly what the problem is. If you ask enough questions, you'll get
a look at the whole situation. You're not just holding onto the elephant's
trunk, you'll have gotten a good feel for the whole animal. Given a clear
understanding of the problem, you'll be surprised how the answer appears
almost like magic in the last 15 minutes.

I find this to be true in devising our marketing strategies and developing
our products. We go through everything and really lay out the whole problem. Amazingly, the whole answer just develops itself and a consensus
evolves naturally so everyone can buy into the solution.

In the past, I would explain a problem to my family, friends, or business
associates, and they would immediately leap in with a solution. How could
they know the answer when they hadn't gotten all of the problem? As a

result, I learned a variety of techniques to get people to listen to me before they interrupt:

- "There are several facets to this problem. Please listen to all of them so you will understand."

- "I haven't explained this out loud yet. Please let me stumble through it completely so I don't lose my train of thought."

- "I need you to allow me to fully explain the situation before you consider the possibilities."

Clarifying questions are OK. In fact, they're encouraged. At least someone is trying to better understand the situation.

This process doesn't have to be time consuming. If you're bashful about asking tough, probing questions, you'll waste more time second-guessing yourself and your assumptions than you would take to just come straight out with your questions.

You wouldn't want your doctor to start operating before he or she was certain what was wrong with you and had considered the options. The doctor could diagnose many things but first must narrow the problem down precisely. The time it takes is worth it.

Business Black Belt Notes

- Spend 75% of your time asking questions and clarifying the problem.

- Explore all angles of a problem.

- Request that others allow you to complete your explanation before asking questions or making suggestions.

Why *Smart* People
Don't Learn So Well

At a certain age, people's minds close up;
they live on their intellectual fat.
— William Lyon Phelps

☞ Learned people often unconsciously use their existing knowledge
and data to block anything new coming in. This keeps them
stuck and makes them a challenge to communicate with. Here's
what to do.

Are you or anyone you know too smart to learn something new? Let's deal
with this subject right up front in case it applies to you. If you're reading this
book, you're obviously looking for some answers and good ideas you can use
and you're probably pretty bright. But you may have a problem.

Smart people gather information and remember it. And usually what we
are taught is based upon a particular premise or set of facts. As we learn and
master the information, the original premise for that information remains as
its foundation or *paradigm*.

Believe it or not, smart people are often afflicted with a severe learning
disorder. You've seen it before. I call it the learning disorder of the very intelligent. The existing knowledge on a given subject blocks the new knowledge
from coming in. And knowledge blocks are due to stuck paradigms.

For example, I have a degree in economics, the science of efficiently allocating scarce resources. The paradigm of economics is that resources are *scarce*. With that fundamental premise, how can someone talk to me about unlimited prosperity? I've been trained to believe that resources are scarce![1]

If you were to tell me, "You have plenty of resources," I filter it through what I already know about economics. The more I think I already know, based on my knowledge of economics, the less receptive I am. "Waddayamean? Resources are scarce!" I resist your point of view as well as any evidence to support it. I don't (won't) learn from you. Instead we argue. My existing knowledge has become the basis for my inability to learn—my learning disorder. I've built my knowledge on my paradigm of how I think things are or should be. That information clogs my filter and prevents new information from getting in.

There are a variety of ways to look at the same thing.

Imagine the starship Enterprise, in anticipation of an attack, with its deflector shields up. It takes a lot of energy to maintain the deflector shields. We often use our existing knowledge as our own deflector shield, defending our knowledge, paradigm or opinion. And that requires energy potentially useful for other things. It may be difficult to realize that the basis for your existing knowledge may have changed or may have been incomplete when you drew your original conclusions, but remember to consider it as a possibility when you see an argument brewing—and use that energy instead to enlighten yourself.

Look at it this way: Often, you'll have pieces A and B of a subject and someone else will have pieces C and D. You'll both argue the differences of A and B versus C and D instead of sharing each other's information to end up with A, B, C, and D. Instead of thinking "I already know that," think "How does that contribute to or update what I already know?" The idea is to expand each other's wealth of knowledge and experience, not to negate it.

---

[1] *Unlimited Wealth* is a great book by Paul Zane Pilzer, that clearly explains this exciting possibility and unravels the insanity of past economic theory. New York, Crown Publishers, 1990.

History is full of examples

In 1967 the Swiss actually invented the electronic watch. But the big watch-makers of the world (in Switzerland) at that time dismissed the mechanism because it had no hands, no main spring, no gears, or no winding. According to the watchmakers, it wasn't really a watch! Tragically for them, the Japanese, who had no ingrained paradigm for watch making, stole the market share for electronic watches.[2]

When it dawned on me to create a business plan template to enable people to use their computers to develop their business plans, a number of business planning professionals told me it would never work. No expert system software could really make the decisions to write a business plan for you. That was and still is true, because the previous software people were trying to use a computer program to write the business plan. Their paradigm involved complicated computer programming and they couldn't see how you could effectively create a business plan with it. My paradigm was different. Why not just give people a complete sample business plan already typed and formatted in word-processing and spreadsheet files? Our programming simply helps users select the section they want and prompts them through filling in all the information specific to their business. They could use any word processor or spreadsheet program to simply import my text files, and then edit them any way they want, but my method works in spite of the previous experts' warnings. And since they weren't originally my customers, it didn't really matter.

Show me

What people really want in order to write their business plans is an example to follow. Their biggest problem, they told me, is staring at a blank page not knowing where to start or what to say. My concept was almost too obvious. Having been in the computer business for many years, I almost missed it too. When I sold computers early in my career, many customers complained that they had just learned how to use their electronic calculators, which are not

Discovering the Future: the Business of Paradigms, an interesting book and accompanying videotape by Joel Barker illustrates and elaborates on the effect of paradigm paralysis. St. Paul, MN, 1985

much older than PCs. So I thought about what people were most familiar with now—word-processing and spreadsheet software. Most people had just learned how to use them and they were familiar applications. Why not give businesspeople something they could use that would take advantage of the software they already knew how to use? My product would work with any brand of word processor or spreadsheet. Earlier in my career, I constantly dealt with compatibility issues. "Is it Macintosh or PC compatible?" My templates had to work with both systems so the answer could always be "Yes, just tell me which one you want."

Business planning was a bitch

The next paradigm hurdle we needed to jump was that writing business plans usually involved reading many books on the subject, gathering a number of actual business plans, highlighting the best parts, taking notes, writing—just getting ready to *start* writing your business plan was a monumental task. No wonder nobody wanted to write them!

The concept of using a software package to write a business plan was a new idea. I had to convince people that finally it could be easy, even fun.

Thinking with a new paradigm might make something better or provide a solution to a problem. Perhaps you have a product or service that people can really use. Maybe you've identified a need and you can clearly see how to fill it. But it's possible that your potential customers are so caught up in their way of thinking and their way of problem solving, they can't see what you're offering them. People who invent or sell something new often face this sales challenge.

Today's fact becomes tomorrow's misinformation.
— Alvin Toffler, author

The learning disorder is a double-edged sword

You may be the person blocking new information. You may also deal with someone who's blocking information. To understand that you're blocking ideas is great—you're now aware of this "knowledge block" syndrome. But now you're dealing with 99.9 percent of the planet who are blocking information like crazy and you've got to get through to them. How do you do that? It's almost impossible, because they don't see things the way you do. I think I've have found a simple and effective solution.

If you say, "Let me shift your paradigm (or assumptions) for a moment." The listener may realize that you are coming from an entirely new angle. His or her defenses will temporarily stand aside. Your listener's shields can come down and he or she can be open to hearing you. If the person doesn't understand what a paradigm is, explain it. Now, your listener is prepared to look at things in a different way. He or she doesn't have knowledge built up in your paradigm, clogging receptivity to you, it's only built up in his or her own. So when you offer the opportunity to see things through a new lens, nothing will block the view. (Be sure you wait for the person to get with you. Listeners need a minute to disassemble their knowledge blocks when shifting paradigms. Then you can get through to them.)

Sometimes paradigm shifting means breaking the rules. Are these rules really hard and fast? Is this really a law of physics or nature we are limited by?

In BizPlan*Builder*, we followed the general layout for financial projections, but by using the power of spreadsheets, we could include many more useful percentages, ratios, and projections. Why not provide the analysis investors and bankers are looking for? Before the power of spreadsheets, this work seemed more trouble than it was worth, but now it's easy to do—so we pushed the envelope.

In many cases, paradigm shifting has turned out to be very profitable. A world of opportunities lies out there in other paradigms that most people will never allow themselves to see. After reading this chapter, you can make more of an effort to unblock new knowledge and free your mind to learn and absorb new ideas. And now you've got a tool to help you deal with the 99.9 percent of the planet who are using what little they know to deflect anything new.

Learning is not a zero-sum game.
You don't forget one thing for every new thing you learn.

You'd think that. . .

Paradigm paralysis and knowledge blocking are also responsible for our belief in lies. We can be so caught up in how we think things are or should be that we overlook obvious evidence to the contrary. Think about it. People could tell us anything as long as it went along with our preexisting notions and we would believe it. How many times have you asked a salesperson a question and they responded with a knee-jerk "Yes, it will do that." Did they even hear the question? Was it important that they respond accurately? Do they want to make the sale? Do they care about their credibility? What do you want to hear? Usually, I have something at stake when I ask a question and it's important to get a good, accurate answer. Don't be too quick to accept an answer just because it sounds right. You might ask, "Where does it say *that* in your literature?" Brochures have been carefully written and reviewed. If a product or service will do something, the brochure will most likely state this. (Incidentally, your own literature should keep your own salespeople honest. Also, contracts should contain everything you, as the customer, have been told verbally.)

Opportunities await you

Many outrageously successful businesses are founded simply on a paradigm shift. Likewise, many golden opportunities are missed simply because of a knowledge block. Look to understand the premise on which someone is presenting a concept to you. Just ask, "What paradigm is this based on?" or "Where are you coming from on this?" Then you'll have an idea for his or her basis of thinking and you can begin to understand the person's position.

To really be ahead in the marketing game, you need to know which paradigms your customers believe. You're not going to readily unstick them, but you can build perceivable bridges from your product to their needs. The tubeless tire, cordless phone, and business plan on diskette all created a bridge between a perception, a product, and a need.

Share this concept (and this book too) with your friends and associates. Remind each other of potential knowledge blocks when you don't openly accept and consider each other's ideas.

Shifting paradigms doesn't necessarily mean agreeing with or accepting something, but at least you'll be able to grasp its meaning. As you read on, you may need to shift your paradigms as we get into some other interesting subjects.

Business Black Belt Notes

- Knowledge blocking is the learning disorder of the very intelligent.

- The more people know, the less receptive they may be to new information.

- To get through to someone, say, "Let me shift your paradigm."

- How does new or different information contribute to or update what you already know?

- We believe lies because they are what we want to hear. Use your assumptions as the basis for pointed questions to find the real truth.

KARMA:
Your Cosmic Credit Report

It takes about 10 years to become an overnight sensation.

☞ What goes around, comes around. It starts with you—even if nobody else is looking.

A poor credit report stays with you for seven years no matter how good you've been lately. Eventually, you may catch up with your bills and develop the habit of paying everyone on time. Eventually, the old you and the evil things you did and said will wear off. However, each new infraction goes on your credit report and stays there for another seven years, so it's crucial to keep this thought in your consciousness at all times.

kar •ma (kär'mō) n.

1. (Hinduism & Buddhism) The total effect of a person's actions and conduct during the successive phases of the person's existence, regarded as determining the person's destiny.

2. Fate; destiny.

3. Informal. A distinctive aura, atmosphere, or feeling.

I use the first definition of karma, although much of the world probably uses the second—which seems like so much is out of your control. I think you have tremendous control over the quality of your destiny.

I think we are here on Earth to learn and to advance our spirits. I'm using my business as my primary learning ground, but learning is everywhere and in every situation. Learning is not better or more meaningful if it is painful or requires more effort. Pain and effort are merely side effects of avoiding your lesson. Do you need a quadruple bypass to change your eating habits or can you begin eating healthier foods and exercising right now? Must you go out of business to learn how to run a business? These messages and lessons just seem to get louder and harsher until we catch on. If you learn immediately (and that means apply the knowledge), there is no reason for increased pain.

In life, "shit" doesn't just happen. Shit happens when you're off the path and not looking at where you're going. Shit happens when you need to learn something. It's just a message that's gotten louder so that maybe this time, you'll get it and act upon it.

But could you get away with it?

I grew up watching the same kind of TV shows everyone else did. The good guys always catch the bad guys in the end. But I couldn't help thinking, "If the bad guys hadn't done [x], then they might have gotten away with it." For the longest time, I saw myself with some of the capabilities of the bad guys. Although I'd never done anything really bad (let alone worth a TV script), I was sure I could get away with a lot. As long as I didn't get caught, I thought it would be OK. But then I began to wonder *why* things would go wrong for me. I started to trace whatever it was that went wrong back to a time when I did something similar or was somehow responsible in some way—something I did or didn't do, something I said or should have said. Only then did I realize that I actually was responsible—was the source—for what happened to me. I realized that I'm always getting caught. No matter what, somehow Nature is always working to keep track of me and my actions.

Your integrity is really what you do when nobody is looking. "If I don't get caught, maybe I can get away with it" is not the point. It's up to you to monitor your own integrity because, if you don't, people may get a bad feeling about something you're doing even though they may not be able to put their finger on it or tell you they don't approve (especially if you're the boss). So it will seem (only to you) as if you're getting away with it, but eventually your evil deeds will reach critical mass and 'shit will happen.' You've seen this happen before. Some businesses go down the tubes because the people take too much advantage of their position (sexual harassment cases are simple examples). Actually, people are looking or will eventually discover the truth. Most people are onto these guys and eventually karma comes to bite them on the butt. Your choice is future respect or shame. And, once you are shamed, can you ever really get your integrity back?

Sometimes karma is all you've got against insurmountable odds

JIAN's had some big companies take a run at our products and even try to put us out of business. They failed. I think it's because we were doing the right thing and they weren't.

It's tempting to take shortcuts, such as making something cheaper, because they surface all the time. You think you can make a bigger profit by taking something out and people won't notice. Big mistake. People do notice. God is in the details. I want people to say about JIAN's products and service, "Oh, they put {x} in there—that's good. I like these guys."

Subtle and simple things are powerful. These are the very things that compel people to tell their friends to buy your product or use your service: The investment in quality will make your marketing efforts go 10 times farther. That experience of doing the right thing is underneath it all. I think the fact that I haven't been blown out of the water or had things go wrong is because possibly Nature is in support of that fact.

> *Contrary to the cliché,*
> *genuinely nice guys always finish first or very near it.*
> — Malcolm Forbes, publisher

You win and you win big when you play straight. There's always trepidation when someone buys a big ticket item like a car or a house. But if you're the salesperson with the good reputation, people are going to buy from you. In the past, it has seemed like only the bullies and liars got ahead, but now we're seeing that that's not true anymore.

As a buyer at The Sharper Image, I always went with the salesperson who was straight with me even though others had what looked like better deals.

When push comes to shove in a competitive field, people will go with the ones they can trust (or wish they had). There's too much at stake.

Venture vendors

In the early days at JIAN, we put our manufacturing out for bid with the up-front requirement that we got 90-day payment terms. We didn't have the luxury of a line of credit at the time, so our vendors were going to have to carry us. We figured they were motivated enough to get the business and that we could convince them to extend an outrageous credit line to us. It worked, and it turned out to be worthwhile to our vendors. In a sense, our vendors were our partners in our venture.

Two things are important about this arrangement. First, we were up front by saying that we couldn't pay for 90 days. Some people wouldn't be honest about their ability to pay, yet they would drag their payments out 90 days anyway. That's not fair to the vendor. The other important thing we did is that we knew we were going to be a good customer for our suppliers for a long time, not constantly shop around to chisel their prices. Both of these issues were driven and have been rewarded by karma.

Many people have developed a perception that business is evil; profit is evil. Someone gets rich at the expense of someone else. Given that thinking, when I become wealthy, a lot of people are going to think I ripped somebody off. You can become wealthy, feel good about what you've done and have other people feel good about you as well. An example: I agonized for quite a while about whether or not I should buy an airplane. I'd wanted one since I can remember, I had the money, and I could even legitimately use it in my business.

If I bought a plane, I thought everyone would think, "This guy's got no brains. We need to spend the money on practical things for the business. What's he doing buying an airplane?" But the actual response from people was, "We have the money, we can make more money, go buy an airplane." (One person told me, "You've been killing yourself for seven years—you deserve an airplane.")

I was the one thinking that I should be more practical. I was the one embarrassed that buying an airplane seemed decadent. The truth is that people want to associate with other successful businesspeople and they're happy that I have an airplane. The perception becomes "This guy worked his ass off so he bought himself an airplane. He must be successful."

So it's crucial that you live your life with integrity—day in and day out, moment by moment. As the years go by, you'll develop and maintain your reputation, so you might as well build a reputation for integrity. Down the road, when someone wants to make a deal and must decide who to do business with, you'll be the one likely to be chosen because that person trusts you. Wouldn't you rather be bitten in the butt by a future like that?

Business Black Belt Notes

- When 'shit's happening,' it's a loud message that you must take corrective action.

- Integrity is what you do, even when nobody else is looking.

- The universe eventually gives you what you deserve.

Focus on Your Goal,
Not on *How* You'll Get There

Don't tell me something's impossible.
Tell me what it would take to make it possible.

☞ After we figure out what we want, we immediately start to figure out how to get it. We can achieve the same result in many ways. Don't get too caught up in how you will succeed because you might miss the perfect opportunity for doing it—just a different way.

The phenomenon goes something like this: you establish what you want, then you set about the process of *how* to get it. Given your resources and knowledge, you develop a strategy, then a plan of action—as crude as it may be. All your energy shifts away from your goal to your action plan. The goal is almost lost in favor of all the things you plan to do.

How often has this happened to you? A salesperson is pitching their product and misses the part where you say, "Yeah, I'll take one." That was their goal, but the salesperson keeps on selling anyway. You want to buy. The sale just happened sooner than they thought it would. Have you ever been with a salesperson who thinks that the only way to make the sale is to give their complete pitch and do a series of certain things so *then* you'll buy. This salesperson is too focused on *how* the sale should happen versus being connected enough with you to realize that their goal was achieved without having to follow their predetermined plan.

If you're always looking for new ways to do things,
you'll never develop any bad habits.

Solutions to problems sometimes come very quickly—sometimes too quickly. And, they often come at you in a different way than you may have expected. You've already gone beyond the goal you want to how you're going to do it. All the freebies and easy solutions fly by you because you're so focused on how, not what.

We try to show how intelligent we are by saying, "Here's how we do this. This is the solution." If a better solution comes along that doesn't fit our plans, or it doesn't match our expectations of what we thought would or should happen, we may pass it by. We ignore it. We often lose sight of what we want—while our head is down working our scheme, we often miss the fact that we've achieved our goal, or that it may be at the end of a different path.

Go ahead and make something your goal and start to figure out how you'll get there. But always keep the result you want (allowing for its possible disguises) in the front of your mind, just in case a different way of reaching it comes out of nowhere.

Tune your mind for solutions

Try this: Think for a moment about the color red. Now look around right now for everything that is red. Notice how everything red jumps out at you. What do you see? Now try it again with the color green. See how easy it is to tune your mind for what you're looking for? Try this: Look at your life and focus for a moment on your problems. What's wrong? Now look at your life and selectively look for what works. What's working for you? Do you usually look for what works or what doesn't work? What if you were to consciously tune your mind to seek opportunities and solutions to your problems just like you look for colored objects? It's impossible to find solutions while your mind is tuned to your problems. It's also impossible to find solutions when you are looking for reasons why your problem is the problem it is. Instead, what are solutions that might work? I do this a lot and it's amazing how quickly ideas come to mind.

Anytime you're having a bad day, look to see what you are focused on. See what happens when you shift focus.

If you have invested a little time in analyzing the problem and clarifying any assumptions as you learned earlier, this process of finding a solution or achieving your goal becomes even easier.

Nature is constantly talking to you — with answers and directions

Ever wonder why you hear a certain song over and over again? Ever wonder why different people make similar comments to you? Ever wonder why particular situations repeat themselves? Try asking questions without being in a hurry for the answer—and be open to the messages and answers whenever they might appear—they're everywhere.

The idea is that you are looking for a new action to take, a new way of looking at your situation—you must do something different to change the results you've been getting when you do what you are already doing.

Business Black Belt Notes

• Set your goal and remember that you want to reach your goal even if you get there by a different method than you planned.

• It doesn't always take cash to get what you need.

• Tune your mind to look for solutions to get what you want.

• Answers will come, maybe not right away nor in a form you expect—stay open.

Gold Belt

Getting Out of Your Own Way

OK, some basics are looking good now. Earning a black belt evolves through many stages. It consists of developing basic skills and practicing basic techniques, then combinations of those skills and techniques. Plus, you must stretch and develop your mind and body constantly throughout your training.

Get Your Life *Off* the Roller Coaster...and into a Steady *Climb*

Should you quit while you're ahead?

☞ What if you did everything you need do to turn your life around—when it's at the bottom—and then continued these efforts when everything is good? You would continue on an upward trend.

The Roller Coaster

Whoever said "You should quit while you're ahead" probably never made it very far in business. Thinking like this might be useful in gambling, but hopefully you aren't gambling with your business. Maybe you are taking risks, but consciously building your business involves a different set of behaviors. Still, unconsciously quitting while ahead is the reason why so many people reach the brink of success only to blow it.

Life can be like a roller coaster—it's great, then it sucks, then it's great again. The speed may vary, but it seems to cycle like this. Here's how to get your life into a steady climb. Remember the last time things really sucked. Look at your situation when you're at the bottom of the roller coaster. You reach a certain low point beyond which you won't go any lower. You think, "The house is a mess, there are one too many socks on the floor," and you suddenly develop a cleaning craze. If you've gained 10 pounds, after 11 pounds, forget it. You're going to lose weight! Whatever your set point is, whether too many socks are on the floor, or the house has gone too many days without being cleaned, or you've gotten fat, look at what you do at that point. You pick up your socks, straighten the house, or stop eating. Things start going back to where you want them.

Now, at the top of the roller coaster, what happens? The house is spotless, the plants look good. You feel good. Next, you come home, take your socks off, throw them on the floor, and start eating. You think you can relax. You stop doing all the things that improved your life. You slack off and revert to bad habits, and the cycle starts to go back down again—the roller coaster.

Let's look at your business

If your business is at a low point in sales, maybe in Chapter 11 or in the middle of a lawsuit, maybe collections aren't there—you start selling, cutting costs, negotiating, and collecting. When money is coming in and profits improve, you're back on top—watch out for the roller coaster.

You see this pattern also with consultants and salespeople. They'll have lots of business going, so they don't promote themselves. Why should they? They're busy and they've got lots of clients. But slowly, the projects and deals start winding down. They reach the bottom, and all of a sudden, they don't have any clients or sales. Then they start selling again and they find clients. When they're at the top again, they stop selling—the roller coaster.

> *The trick now is to take the things you do*
> *at your low set point*
> *and do them at your high set point.*

So at the high set point, you've got lots of clients and you keep selling. For the consultants, the idea is to promote your services constantly. You can always tell prospective clients that you won't be available to help them for a couple of months. "Wow, you must be busy. . . you must be really good. . . we definitely want to work with you," they'll think. When you are ready for a new assignment, the client is likely to jump at the chance to hire you.

Let's look at how you operate:

When things are great, I. . .
sleep in
take lots of time off
eat whatever I want
can be abrasive to people
spend money on silly things

To get things going again, I...
get up early; work out
start calling customers
start eating healthy
am really nice to everyone
am conscious of my spending

_____   _____

_____   _____

_____   _____

_____   _____

_____   _____

_____   _____

_____   _____

_____   _____

_____   _____

On the left, make a list of the things you know to do when you hit rock bottom. What do you have to do in order to get yourself back on top? When you decide to make some changes, what do you know (in the back of your mind) that you must do? Do you go to an aerobics class three times a week or practice karate again three times a week? Pick some simple thing you can complete in one immediate action: Balance your check book or take out the trash.

Now, imagine yourself at the top. What would you do? Take a break? Slack off? Eat something really fattening? Think for a moment about what got you to the top. What kinds of things are going on in your life right now? Everything's going great, but what things have to happen before you start slacking off again? Knowing that you will probably be tempted to slack off, take all the things you listed that would get you going again and keep these things going. Life will continue to go up rather than roll back down on the roller coaster ride. When you've lost a lot of weight, keep working out. When you have a market leadership position, keep marketing. You want it to keep going. When you're ahead in a game, keep playing to win it. In a fight, keep fighting until the bad guy won't get up. (This reminds me of the horror films where the monster seems to be dead and our hero triumphantly turns his or her back, only to have the beast rear up.)

You might have a set point for growth. You must apply these principles if you want to get past, "Oh, my God! I've never made more than $50,000/ year in my life. How do I get to be a $500,000/year person? How do I sell 50 houses a year, when the most I've ever sold was 10? How do I go beyond that?"

Gravity does not apply to business.
What goes up must not necessarily come down.

If you take the things you do at your low set point and keep focusing on those activities, you'll go past your high set point (which, by the way, is imaginary) and not even know it. Forget the fact you've never made more than $50,000 in your life.

Let's say you haven't sold a house in a month. You'd better make some phone calls. When you've got houses selling every week, you still say, "OK, I've got to make some phone calls." You develop the habit of doing these things all the time.

When you've got that momentum going, you don't have to make as many phone calls as you do when you're in the pit. When you're down and you haven't sold a house in three months, you make 100 calls. Once you're at the top again, you'll only need to make about a half dozen. As long as you're consistent, you just keep making it happen. As you do, your success will accumulate and grow exponentially. You don't have to go back down. You'll pass your previous high set point and keep going.

> *If you always do what you've always done,*
> *you'll always get what you've always got.*
> – Unknown

Be prepared for success to feel weird

You might get to the point where I did and say, "This is weird. I'm making a lot of money." You'll have to get used to making a lot of money. Especially when you're used to having things go wrong all the time and cycling up and down. I remember having money and being able to buy a relatively expensive car or take $50,000 from my business and put it down on my house was really weird. Just having the money to do that was a new and unusual experience for me because I had spent so many years working hard but earning little. Now, everyday things are working. Every day I continue to be productive and more money comes in. I even had to get past my thought that one day, all this is going to turn to crap. My own rhythm of success and failure, up and down, changed as things kept growing. I would say, "Oh my God! It's supposed to go down." But I kept going because I kept doing the things I would do when I was down. And it continues to work.

Be prepared to feel weird. You may reach an altitude and experience the fear of falling. Don't look down or you'll cycle down. Keep looking up ahead. And, just because you stop sometimes doesn't mean you're a loser.

> *Success is the quality of the journey—have fun along the way.*
> – Unknown

Some days you won't feel like doing anything. Sometimes I feel like I don't want to do anything. I don't want to make calls or go to meetings. I don't feel like it. But I find stuff to do anyway. I've got to remember what I'm saying here. "OK, do I want to nose over now? Do I want to go down the roller coaster now?" That possibility is more uncomfortable for me than anything else I could imagine and it's very motivating. I know exactly what I do to make me start to go down again.

You know exactly what to do to start going down too. Write down what these things are and then you'll know where you're going when you give in to this pull. It will be easier to replace those activities with healthier ones. Once you get used to success, those things become natural.

Business Black Belt Notes

• Make a list of the actions you take after you've hit rock bottom.

• When you're at the top, notice the things you do when you start slacking off.

• Take all the things you do at the bottom and keep applying them— even when you're at the top.

• Even the thought of slacking off should make you more uncomfortable than the things you know you must do to build your success.

• Get used to the possibly weird feeling of not going back down the roller coaster again—of being successful.

One Day You'll Get Lucky. . .

(Or, you can just flip the switch now)

I want to be different. . . Like everyone else.

☞ **What's it like to spar with a Black Belt? You have to do it to know how much practice you'll need. There's really only so much preparing you can do before you go for it. It's important to get a little experience before further planning and training.**

For the longest time, I kept thinking I was going to get lucky and be in the right place at the right time. I thought business would happen and sales would just take off. The company I worked for would suddenly skyrocket and I'd go with it. I'd be recognized by management as the young star and be promoted to the position I deserved in place of those idiots who always seemed to occupy a position well above their abilities. And I'd be rich.

So, there I was at 29 years old. Somehow I wasn't in the right place at the right time doing the right thing and my ship wasn't coming in. I also realized that I wasn't going to inherit enough money to be happy. I reached a low point and realized I had to do something different.

From what I've seen of successful people and from my experience building my own business, success isn't something you slowly accumulate. You don't just carefully walk your way in and slowly work up your courage.

At some point you just get sick of your situation. You realize things aren't working and you know something has to change. Your knowledge and experience reaches a critical mass in your mind. You've seen successful people, you've learned a lot, and you've been putting off projects. One day you say, "I've got to do it." Instead of flipping out, you just flip the switch. It's as if something snaps inside and you decide to go for it—no matter what. I flipped my switch the day my grandfather's TubeSales truck passed me on Highway 101. That's when I knew I had to get realistic and get going.

You don't just dip your toe in the water and gradually wade in. Flipping the switch is more like taking a leap of faith. You have to plunge right in. One day you're off, the next day you're on. Your mind makes this paradigm shift. When it does, amazing things start happening.

> **Until one is committed, there is hesitancy,**
> **the chance to draw back, always ineffectiveness.**
> **Concerning all acts of initiative (and creation)**
> **there is one elementary truth, the ignorance of which kills**
> **countless ideas and splendid plans—that the moment one**
> **definitely commits oneself, divine Providence moves too.**
>
> **All sorts of things occur to help one**
> **that would never otherwise have occurred.**
> **A whole stream of events issues from the decision raising in**
> **one's favor all manner of unforeseen incidents**
> **and meetings and material assistance which no man**
> **could have dreamed would have come his way.**
> —W. H. Murray

I've found this to be consistently true in business as well as in a number of other activities.

Have you ever noticed when you decide to do something and you've paid your money, it starts to work for you? Many personal development and educational companies say that their workshops start the minute you sign up for them. Do you start losing weight when you sign up for a health club? To begin with, your food consciousness goes way up, then you lose weight when you start working out. (Fortunately, you now know how to get off the roller coaster.)

If you haven't got something in mind that you've always wanted to do, take a moment and come up with one, or several. You are going to have to stop doing certain things from the past because they don't contribute to what you're doing now. You know what they are, and there is no better time, place, or circumstance to improve your ability to put an end to them.

I assert that people know what to do, they just don't know when to do it and they don't do it soon enough. You know exactly what you've got to do—stop bitching, complaining, whining, and making excuses. *Flipping the switch is making the decision to do something different.* You're in the same place that you were 10 years ago, because you've been doing the same things for 10 years. You can't keep doing the same things over and over again and expect to have different results. You've got to do something different to get different results.

It's time to step into the ring

OK, so by now the signpost in your brain flashes "I'm going to do this." You feel it at a gut level. It's not like New Year's resolutions because those are too wimpy. You must assess where you've been, and where you're going. Realize that you've got to make some changes—do something different. Signing up for yet another workshop or seminar or reading another book won't work. Going out and buying new clothes or getting something to eat is not going to do it. Buying a new car or a new house won't work either. This is not about something to buy, it's about facing yourself. Asking for more advice or gathering more information is not going to work either. This next step comes from you internally. You have to say, "I am going to do this." *You* have to keep it going.

> *Teachers open the door, but you must enter by yourself.*
> — Chinese proverb

This is the part where you just make the decision. You don't have to wait to get permission from anybody. No one is going to give you permission to be successful. There is no note forthcoming from your mother or father.

But if you need to hear it anyway, you have my permission to go ahead and do this now. You have your parents' and friends' permission to do this now. You have the permission of the people who envy you and those who hate you.

This part is your decision to do. You must do this. There is no safety net. There's no more advice. There's no one else to talk to. There's nothing more to read or do. This is on *you*. This is the part where you do it.

This means change. If what you've been doing isn't working, throw it out the window and consider a new way. Usually, part of what you are doing is working and my bet is that you know exactly what has to change for things to be different. You just have to say to yourself (with feeling), "Stop, I'm going in a new direction." I did this at 29, but it happens for people at 20, 30, 40, or 50+ years old. I realized I had to work harder and smarter. I had to apply all the information I'd acquired over the years. I had to actually start doing all the things I knew I should do.

My problem was that I was holding back. I wasn't really going for it. I thought it was just going to come, and I don't have to invest all of myself. I thought I could hold back a little bit. I could do it 9 to 5. I didn't have to be fully present for it. I could just be on the sideline a bit.

In sales, I wasn't asking for the order! I had to learn to ask for the order and say, "So, are we going to do this business?" It didn't ever matter how smooth I was. I just had to do *something* and work on the technique later. I didn't care if I was stumbling over the hurdles. I didn't care if I was running into walls or tripping over myself along the way. I had to be willing to go the distance, start the business, and make the thing go no matter what. And then along the way, I'd learn how to work smarter and jump the hurdles. I'd learn how not to stumble, I'd learn how not to get tripped up. I would fine-tune my technique after I was moving along the path.

Circle the block until you're warmed up enough to make a cold call

When I first worked at Texas Instruments as a field sales engineer, I had no customers. I didn't even know who the right customers were to call. I took hand-me-downs from other reps, looked in the phone book, and scoured trade shows to find leads. A known potential customer was easy to approach, but the unknown were not. On the way back from these appointments, I invariably drove by a building that could house a potential customer. Instead of immediately pulling into the driveway, parking, going in the door and up to the receptionist with a good sales intro line, I'd circle the block and think to myself, "OK, what are you going to say? Who are you going to talk to? What if they're not interested? What's going to happen? Are they the right customer? Would they buy from me? Are they buying from someone else?

Maybe they're going to throw me out." After all this chatter, I would finally go in and introduce myself. Either they didn't use my stuff at all or they would say, "Yeah, we're looking for something like that. You're from T.I.? Come right this way."

I found that you can think about things, and plan, go around the block, worry, get ready, take seminars, read books, and wait for just the right time. Or you can go right in and talk to people. I learned that the quickest thing for me to do was to drive right in and go in the door. I wouldn't even think about it. I'd say, "Hi, I'm Burke Franklin, I'm from Texas Instruments, and I sell electronic components." It could be as blunt as that, which was actually disarming in itself because I didn't use some tricky sales ploy. The results I got were dramatic. I saved a tremendous amount of time and was generally welcomed everywhere I went. This seems to hold true for just about any subject I've gotten into. After landing and actually working with a number of customers, I then realized what I had to learn from books and seminars.

Just break the ice

Before I started my martial arts training, I had driven by the school for probably six months. Then one day, after realizing that I wasn't ever going to do anything about it, I stopped in, introduced myself to the instructor, and expressed my interest in taking Tae Kwon Do. He said, "Great! Come back tomorrow night. Classes are Tuesdays and Thursdays at 7:30. I'll see you then." That's how and when I started, and I stayed with it for five years to get my black belt. But I started. Six months thinking about it didn't count. Five years were going to go by no matter what. If I worked at it just a little bit a few nights a week, I would have my black belt at the end of those five years. What can you practice a little each day or week to accomplish a major goal over the next five years?

The more I practice, the luckier I get.

— Gary Player, professional golfer

Nothing happens until you go in, meet the people, fill out the paperwork, pay them, and schedule your first appointment. Thinking about it, planning, and thinking about it some more produces nothing. You can look at it a couple of ways:

The time isn't right and you don't have the money, or. . .
The time is always right and you'll get the money.

Think about this. What difference would it make today whether or not you spent $100 five years ago? None! Project yourself into the future. What difference would it make five years from now if you spent $100 or $1,000 per month right now? Money-wise, none, but in terms of experience, a lot! You might say, "But, Burke, you just don't understand!" Oh, but I do understand. Your mental, physical, emotional, and spiritual state must align with a simple statement:

I'm going to do this, no matter what.

"I'm going to do (x), no matter what" is a good mantra to use when your goal seems really challenging and you may not yet know how you'll do it. Start by doing everything you know how to do. Even if you don't know what to charge for your service, you've got to go ahead and do it anyway. You can't sit back and say, "Well I can't really proceed because I don't know how to charge for this" or "I don't have a computer" or "I can't really get going because I've got kids."

Take all the reasons why things can't work and say, "Forget it. I have all my reasons for why things can't work. But I'm going to proceed anyway. As I proceed, I will deal with all these things along the way. I will figure out how to either put them aside or make them a non-issue." If you don't have a computer, you could figure, "I've got to do this business, so where am I going to get a computer?" If you must, take a credit card and buy one. It's cheaper than waiting or spending what it would ultimately cost you if you didn't go ahead. I borrowed one from my friends. No matter what, there's got to be a way to solve the problem.

I accomplish more by doing something
than by writing it on my To Do list.

Just gather up all your reasons and excuses for not going ahead and say, "So what, I'm doing it anyway." Unless you're sick of your reasons or you consciously drive yourself to it, you're never going to do what it takes to get the results you want. There is no other way around it. You'll always have reasons. It will never be the right time. You'll never have the money. Other people will always want you to do other things. You'll always need other skills and abilities. There are other things you should be doing. You have to put all that aside or make them non-issues. At some point you realize you are flipping a switch.

What if you went ahead and did what you really wanted to do anyway? What would you do to address each one of those deterrents so they were no longer in your way?

Try this

In the left column, write down your reasons and problems that keep you from doing or having what you want. List them all first. Then, as if you *could* deal with these things, list what you would need to do or what would need to happen for each of these things to become non-issues in the right column.

I can't because. . .   In that case, I'll. . .

I already work 9-6   Spend just 1 hour per night,
                                    I could
                                    find one more client per day

I can't afford to run that ad   I could try a smaller ad to
                                    test the results. If it pays
                                    off, it's worth investing in
                                    more, larger ads

_____   _____

_____   _____

_____   _____

_____   _____

If you need to, take out another sheet of paper and continue this process for everything that is on your mind. Do you see that you really do know how to handle these things? Go back and read your Reasons and Problems List. Listen to yourself internally as you read them. When did you first hear them? Where did you hear them? When you hear these reasons, who's telling them to you? Whose voice do you hear? Notice that you heard these reasons from someone else. It's not even your voice, is it? They're not even your ideas!

If you can realize that these determining thoughts did not originate with you, then it will be easier to let them go in favor of some new ideas that are yours.

Making the steep curve

When I used to want to do something, I'd run out and buy all the equipment and magazines for it. As a kid, I was really into fishing. I bought a fishing pole and as much fishing tackle as I could afford. (The lures that they sell in tackle shops probably catch more people than fish.) I got all the equipment. Then I lost interest, because going fishing wasn't actually interesting after a while. I got into other sports, and started doing a lot of different things just because I thought they were fun and cool to do. Then I'd get to a point when I'd say to myself, "I'm bored, I'm not really interested in this anymore," and I'd quit. I know a lot of people who do that. Consequently, they dabble in many different things. They're dilettantes, not good at anything. They use boredom as an excuse to quit.

As you take on a subject, whether it's a sport, a hobby, or a business, the learning curve just gets steeper. The demands for getting good become a little more intense. If you're going to continue with the activity, you've got to buy good equipment (although I'd hold off until the glamour wears off and you know you really do enjoy what you're doing), invest in some lessons, spend time practicing. In the martial arts, you begin by learning some basic moves. After a month or two, there's not much more to learn. A front kick is a front kick, a side kick is a side kick, you know the punches and blocks. For a year or so, you don't seem to be really learning a new technique that makes it profound and interesting. What you're doing is perfecting the techniques you learned last year so you can combine them to be more advanced.[2] Here we tend to give up because we don't see any movement or improvement. We don't get a sense that we're advancing or getting any better. We realize that we don't want to make the effort to become an expert, and the sport or business really does become boring. That's why it's so important to find out what you really like doing, because only then will you do everything it takes to master the subject.

Now I don't even approach a sport without thinking first about what it would take to master it. I know the time, the effort, and the energy it takes to become a Black Belt, build a business, and get a pilot's license. They all followed the same pattern of starting out, learning something new, practicing a lot, spending a lot of time, studying, doing some background work, getting some theory behind it. I now have a feeling for how steep the curve is going to be, I know where the curve is going to get steeper, and how long something's going to take. I really don't want to start something new now until I'm sure I want to master it or that it's okay with me to just dabble.

Fast forward to your future

I said before that it's a little weird getting used to making money, especially if you're used to screwing up. When you're successful, you also have to get used to saying thank you to people who acknowledge you for your good work. Get used to the phone ringing and people wanting to buy your products or services. Get used to making and having money. Get used to yahoos and losers wanting to get a piece of your action because they can't make it for themselves (you'll learn how to deal with them.) Get used to dressing a little better. Get used to keeping going no matter what.

Remember, it doesn't matter how smoothly you do it at first, as long as you're doing it. In the interest of action, stumble over some of the hurdles. Be willing to make it happen, even if you run into some walls or trip over yourself along the way. You'll learn to make the jumps. You've got to go for it anyway.

---

[2]   Leonard, George. *Mastery*. New York, New York, Penguin Books USA, 1991.
When we get on the plateau where it requires repetitive practice, we're really etching a groove in our mind.

Business Black Belt Notes

- Flip the switch from "I'm not ready" to "I'm doing it anyway."

- Once you've made the decision, things will happen.

- Use this as your mantra: "I'm going to do this, no matter what."

- Do something different—no more excuses.

- Get used to being successful.

- Don't hold back—go for it all the way

Doing What You *Really* Want

I write because I'm personally amused by what I do,
and if other people are amused by it, then that's fine.
If they're not, then that's fine also.

— Frank Zappa, musician and composer

☞ Sooner or later you'll get up the nerve to pursue your true calling.
And let go of what pulls you into whatever rut you got stuck in.
(I let go of my get-rich-quick addiction.)

I assert that deep inside we really do know what we want to do in life.
Unfortunately, we're too scared to go and do exactly that. Perhaps it's too
far to go from wherever we are. What would people say? There are too
many hurdles in the way to get there. The reigning star in that business or
sport (or whatever) is just too good and too far ahead for us to compete with
them. Bullshit.

For years I was in sales. I hated sales. I hated being a salesman. I could
cover it up by saying I was a "marketing representative," but still people saw
me coming. I was definitely a salesman. And since I didn't like what I did, I
held back much of my energy from it. You can't really give a job everything
you've got when its very nature embarrasses you. So consequently, I wasn't
really good at sales. But that was OK. You see, I was really a *marketing* person at heart. I wanted to write advertisements, design brochures, and mail
literature to customers. I would still be selling but allowing the customers
to make up their own minds in private with no pressure. Besides, I could

reach many more people that way. It was OK that I wasn't a successful sales-man because that really wasn't *my* thing! It was deceptively close to applying my *real* talents, but failure didn't hurt my feelings. My real talents weren't under the spotlight and at risk of criticism. What if I failed at the very thing I thought *was* my true calling, in my case, marketing? This fear kept me from pursuing what I really wanted to do.

We must maintain our escape route

I kept finding sales jobs because I (unconsciously) needed to have an out just in case. I knew I would quit because sales wasn't the marketing job I really wanted. It's like driving down the street and not consciously acknowledging the "Not a Through Street" sign, hoping that maybe we'll get through any-way, somehow. But when we don't, we can say it really wasn't going to work out anyway. If you do this, take a moment to sort out the truth in the priva-cy of your own mind. It's time to get into something that really excites you or change your job responsibilities and hire someone else to do what you're doing now.

Learn from your mistakes?

I suspect that no one ever told you that you learn from your successes. So, consequently, you could do 100 things in a day and have 99 of them go right. And, what do you focus on? The one thing that went wrong. You hash out in your mind what could have been done to make that one thing better. How could you have not made that one mistake? How could you improve your-self? You almost completely ignore the 99 things that went right.

Direct marketing people take the exact opposite approach. In fact, they make a science of understanding what it is that is successful. All the testing used by direct marketers is to see what works. Which advertisements pulled the best, which mailing list pulled the best, which headline made the most people call, which offer did people buy the most?

Yet in our personal lives, we're always looking at the weak areas that need work and we overlook our strengths. In martial arts, you learn to focus on what you have the capability to do, not things you don't. For example, if you have long legs, you might emphasize kicking. If you have short legs, you don't emphasize jump kicking just because you think you should. You want to emphasize an attribute you have that gives you a strength you can win with.

Our path of learning looks like a pattern of mistakes

If we pursued the career we really wanted, we would have no excuses. No excuses. But we've failed at so many attempts in the past, made up excuses, and tried something else. What if we look at this pattern from a different perspective? The mistakes of the past were honest mistakes made while in a *learning* mode. Yet, mistake-making and excuse-making developed into a habit we are now stuck with. This is not *learning!* We're so used to screwing up, embarrassing ourselves, and ducking out that we take less and less risks with everything we do. Yet now, when we have learned quite a lot from all of our past disasters, we're actually highly qualified to successfully handle opportunities that used to loom as big risks. We are probably more qualified than ever to succeed at whatever we want. From here, we need not be afraid to apply our knowledge and experience to really go for what interests us. If we were to apply everything we've ever learned through our mistakes (as well as our successes), we would in all likelihood become more successful the next time. This not only applies to our careers, but to everyday decisions we make for or against building our businesses. Think about it. Where can you convert a previously hobbling memory of a mistake to forward some action you must take now?

How can you have any fun?

A seminar leader asked me, "Why are you here?" I responded, "I want to have fun." I'd been working my butt off for a long time and wanted to finally enjoy myself. The leader responded, "What are you good at?" I said, "You don't understand, I just want to have fun." They said, "No, *you* don't understand. What are you good at?" (What does being good at anything have to do with having fun? I wondered then.) As I heard myself, it occurred to me that they had a point. If only I mastered something, then I could really enjoy myself. Hmmm.

Growing up, I was never really encouraged to be good at just one thing. I needed to become 'well-rounded'—I needed to be good at a lot of things. Like a jack-of-all-trades but master of none. Anytime I wasn't good at something I had to practice at becoming better in an area where I was weak. (I'm sure you'll agree that practicing to improve a weakness is not always fun.) That was a good start at first, but when the learning curve got steep—the part where mastery of many different areas of an activity became necessary, I would get "bored." (Yeah, that was it. Bored. Or was it lazy?) Avoiding the work it took to really master something, I would go off looking elsewhere for something that came easy to me. Unfortunately, things that seem to come easy initially are often rarely valuable to develop if you want to build yourself into a wealthy and world famous expert. It seems in our society, that we're not taught to emphasize what we can be good at and continually build on it. Too many people learn to become 'good enough' to get by at what seems to come easy. Besides, you shouldn't have to *work* at something that you're good at. Staying with what you're 'good enough' at can be a fatal distraction that keeps you from mastering what you really want to do, and doing the real work to become who you want to be.

How to turn this around to work for you

As we're exposed to many things, we learn to do many things, and we become half-baked at many things. When you hire someone for a project, you want an expert. You look for the person who's the best in that area. If you are the one being hired for this job and you are a jack-of-all-trades (and a master of none), you are not going to stand out or command the big bucks. I advocate the value of developing expertise. Yet it takes a lot of time and practice to develop expertise. If we have a few upsets or can't get immediate gratification, we often give up. Why? A couple of things are working against us. Our society promotes the fantasy that if you drink the right beer, drive the right car, wear the right clothes, etc., you're going to have anything you want. I don't often see anywhere in our society where we're taught to master something to achieve a similar result except in the books written by people who've done exactly that and became very successful as a result. On the other hand, we occasionally see people who seem to enjoy extraordinary circumstances from birth. Many Olympic athletes can thank their parents for dragging them to practice every day since they were six. (We don't often see this part—the 10-15 years of torturous practice—we're just amazed to watch the masters perform.)

So, if the right acquisitions and the right circumstances haven't given you the right stuff, you're really on your own to figure out what it is you want to do and then work hard enough to get really good at it. It seems like you're working against all the odds. But when you overcome them, you will enjoy your accomplishments, your job, and the money that comes from being in demand.

Is there a workable shortcut?

I found one that worked for me. It starts with looking at things that you're naturally inclined to do and that you're interested in. Perhaps you already have been training like an Olympic athlete. Before all this came to me, I had been berating myself that I was 29 and still not rich. I used to wonder why I hadn't gotten lucky yet. I knew I probably wasn't going to win the lottery. But why wasn't my ship coming in? Why wasn't I at the top of some big corporation? Then I learned something very enlightening from a workshop. Part of my reason for taking the workshop was to unlock the reason why I hadn't found the job I was looking for. It also unhooked my addiction to get-rich-quick schemes.

We were asked to list all the jobs we had ever had. I even included the time I cleaned the house for my mom and got paid for it. I included odd jobs in high school, in college, and during summers. I just brainstormed every job I ever had. I'd had a lot of jobs. What I didn't realize was that there was a pattern.

Before I continue with my results as the example to make my point, quickly do this process for yourself. I promise you it will be worth it.

Grab a pen or pencil and do this brief exercise

In the first column on the next page, list all the jobs you've had. In the second column, look at each job and consider why you took it. In the third column, did you get enough of whatever you put in the second column? It's much easier if you complete each column before going on. For example, list all the jobs you can think of first, then the purpose of each one.

Job	Purpose for job	Achieve purpose?	How did you feel? What did you learn?
Mowing the lawn	*Money*	*No*	*Not enough money for the work*

For myself, I looked at the first job and said, "Well, I really wanted the money." I looked at job number two and realized it was for the money. Going through the whole list, the reason I had taken every single job was money.

In column C, the question was "Looking at column B, did you get enough of whatever you put in column B?" Did I get enough money? No, never. I had never made enough money at any job I ever had. I was amazed to see this all together in one place on one page, like what I might expect to see from a survey of the demographics of my customers. I could see a certain pattern. I had never done a mental database report on myself and my behavior.

Column D asked, "How did you feel about it?" I assure you that I felt lousy about each of those. What's wrong with this picture? I had never made enough money and I didn't have any fun. I didn't like what I saw. I at least wanted to start enjoying my life. I thought, "Well, I'm not making enough money doing what I'm doing right now anyway. What if I just start doing a job that I really like?" I enjoyed writing sales letters and brochures. As a salesman, I felt I could write great brochures that would help me in my own sales. I was always putting together mailing pieces and I really felt it would be a lot of fun. It's something I could do with a vengeance. I could really be an evangelist for that kind of thing. So, I started my business developing sales materials: Tools For Sales.

I didn't know where the money was going to come from. I didn't know who my clients were going to be. First, I made myself some business cards. Second, I called everyone I knew and asked them if they knew someone who needed new sales literature or had some ugly brochures that needed fixing. I took anything. It's amazing how, when you are really into it, you can create and find projects. I could see a lot of places where I could help and offered to do the work. Pretty soon, I had projects coming out of my ears! And guess what? For the first time in my life, I was making more money than I ever had.

What are you good at?

The following simple exercise will assist you to develop a personal mission statement. It works best if you follow your stream of consciousness and write down whatever comes to mind. Some things may seem embarrassing to write down, but writing them down will get them out of the way for your next thought, which may be the one you're looking for. Read each question carefully and write down whatever comes to mind. So, here goes:

What do you love about yourself?	What are you good at?	What would you do with people if all was right with the world?
Sense of humor	*interior design*	*throw parties*
attractiveness to others	*cooking*	*design houses*
my ears	*brushing my teeth*	

Now, circle the two most important items in each list. Using those six items, make a sentence that describes what you are all about. It might go something like this:[3]

With my sense of humor and attractiveness to others, I use my interior design skills and cooking talents to design homes where people can throw wild parties.

In my case:

With my ability to see what's needed to make something or a situation successful and using my understanding of technology, I apply combinations of technology and modern thinking into useful tools people can profit from.

Try it for yourself!

With my _____ and _____,

I use my_____and_____ skills

to_____

_____

_____

> *It's easier to make money doing something you like,*
> *than figuring out how to like something you do for money.*
> — unknown

Marsha Sinetar wrote a book called *Do What You Love, The Money Will Follow.*[4] It's true, but when you're so tangled up in needing to make money, it's really hard to allow yourself to do what you love so the money can follow.

---

[3] I first did this process with Michael and Christina Naumer of the Relationships Research Institute in Santa Rosa, California. They're a wonderful, very personable, and realistic couple who lead workshops and seminars on relationships. For information, call them at 707-354-3444.

[4] Sinetar, Marsha. *Do What You Love, The Money Will Follow.* New York, Paulist Press, 1986.

You might need to hear this a thousand times for it to be fully absorbed in your mind. Then you can go ahead, believe it, and take action. If this is the 433rd time you've heard this, so be it. You're one step closer.

I think Nike has the answer: "Just do it." If you don't, you'll never know. So what if you blow it? Who's watching anyway? You can always make an excuse and move on. Incorporate what you learned and try something again in the future. Sooner or later the balance will tip. Doing things right will outweigh doing things wrong and you'll become successful. (In fact, many companies are successful because they simply make fewer mistakes than their competitors!)

What do you really want to do anyway? Try this eye-opening experiment: Tell people what you'd really like to do and ask them for suggestions. "Who does _____ [what you're thinking of] and how can I talk to them?" Ask questions based upon your assumptions. How can you apply everything you've learned elsewhere to doing what you really want to do now? Adding your own experience would make your version of a career unique and more valuable.

Besides helping you clearly define your career perhaps you'll also better understand and appreciate the kind of people you'll need to hire to do the things you aren't good at, hate, or won't do... but need doing anyway. This makes it much easier to let them do what they do best while positioning yourself to do what you do best.

Business Black Belt Notes

- You know what you really want to do.

- Figure out what you love to do, then figure out how to make money doing it.

- Combine what you love about yourself, what you are good at, and what you would do for people into a comprehensive statement of purpose, a personal mission statement.

Ya Gotta Get
Your Hands Dirty

Success comes before work only in the dictionary.
— Vidal Sassoon, hair designer

☞ **We're led to believe that most businesses were built with less effort than they really were.**

Someone has got to do the actual *work* of your business. I remember when I was a little kid, my grandfather took me for a walk down the street. He showed me this fabulous home. It belonged to a garbage collector. He explained to me how this man started out by offering to take out the neighbors' garbage. Soon he was doing the whole neighborhood and charging for it. He ended up owning the largest garbage company in Los Angeles. He was wealthy for sure, but his fortune did not come without a lot of dirty work—literally.

By the time I came along, my grandfather had already made his money in the tubing distribution business. He had already done the dirty work and all I saw was the wealth. I saw the ease, the affluence, and the nice things but I didn't see what it took to make them. I would hear stories about how he built his company, how he'd been there until late at night cleaning tubing, how he borrowed money from his family and risked everything by taking chances.

Don't believe what you read

You'll see a cover story in a magazine claiming Joe Blow has built a successful company from scratch, with no education or experience, coming from a poor family, and overcoming all odds to become successful. We read two pages about his success, get all excited, and think, "If he can do it, I sure can do it!" But many articles are misleading, because we think it takes less time than it really takes. Many of us never really see what it takes day to day to build a business. Perhaps in their effort to inspire you, some writers lead us to believe that this person either got really lucky or they were very smart and made things happen in an incredibly (meaning not believable) short time. What makes matters worse is that the person being interviewed—and I've been guilty of this myself—makes the process sound easier than it really was because the easier it sounds, the smarter he or she looks. It's wrong to set your expectations for the kind of business success you should enjoy on a minimal effort you might be willing to put in. The successful person you read about appears to have worked less than they did, invested less money than they did, and had fewer problems than they really did.[5]

You've got to be prepared and willing to do more work and solve more problems than you could ever imagine. Magazines are full of stories of how people handled problems—you will face most of those problems combined. That's why you must absolutely positively love what you are doing and what your business is about.

> *Never mistake a clear view for a short distance.*
> — Paul Saffo, Institute for the Future

Ideas and advice are worthless without implementation

People who want to come along just for the ride aren't very helpful. They've got to be willing to help drive. Standing back in a safe place "advising" is not very helpful. In fact, when someone comes along and offers a suggestion as to how to solve a problem (a consultant, employee, or prospective employee),

---

[5] Sigafoos, Robert Allen. *Absolutely, Positively Overnight.* Memphis, St. Luke's Press, 1983. Read the real story behind Fred Smith's experience founding Federal Express and you'll see a harrowing story of building FedEx that would scare off most business people.

I think, "Great!" Now someone has got to go make it happen. "Make it so" as Jean Luc Piccard of *Star Trek: The Next Generation* says. That's where this employee or consultant can be of real value, by actually implementing their solution and taking full responsibility for the results. These are the people who get paid the big bucks, the ones who can actually implement their innovations. Standing back and saying "I told you so" is worthless. Enough said.

Chop wood. Carry water.
— Zen saying

Business Black Belt Notes

* We don't usually see what it took to make a business successful.

* Those who make the big money are the implementers.

* When you build a business to a certain level, you'll start to attract everyone who has a product or service to sell to businesses. And things to do, problems to solve, and projects will multiply.

* Because it takes more work than you can imagine to be successful, it's crucial that you love what you do and what your business is about.

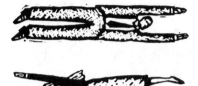

The *Process* of Achieving Results

An achievement is much like a process, but you miss a lot along the way.

☞ Building a business or enjoying a relationship is a process that provides the learning in life, which is more important than its value as an accomplishment.

To build a successful company, you need to approach it with enthusiasm for the *process* of building it, rather than just what you're ultimately going to buy with the money you'll make. Answering telephones, making sales calls, talking with lawyers and accountants, perfecting your designs—enjoying those tasks day in and day out is what actually makes you successful. The person you become as a result is what gives you satisfaction, along with money to spend.

In an earlier chapter, I recommended keeping your eye on your goal and worrying less about how you will achieve it just in case the opportunity to achieve it leaps out at you in an entirely different form than you may have planned or expected. The idea is to maintain your goal in sight, but don't lock onto a particular method for achieving it—remain open to the process that unfolds along the way to achieving your goal. Appreciate the process for what it teaches you as well the satisfaction that achieving your goal will bring.

Goal oriented versus process oriented

Why do we lose sight of the process being more important than the goal?

You figure out what you want, lock onto the method for how you're going to get it, compute what it's going to take, and then start to focus on all the necessary details. By this time, it can be easy to lose sight of what it is you want. All you know is that somehow the day-to-day activities will ultimately get you whatever it was you want. Doing them becomes a chore to be completed. You may not see them as a process.

Writing this book is a process for me. It brings out many stories and makes the difficulties of my business more interesting because I have a story to tell that might help someone else. So now the process of my business is more interesting. And processes can be improved. I'm not suggesting that you learn to enjoy breaking rocks all day. But when you do appreciate the process you are going through, it's almost miraculous how you can see ways for improving the process.

For example: In my TaeKwonDo training, it took me a long time to learn how to throw a "wheel-kick." (Stand facing your opponent, left-foot forward. Spin your head and body around to the right and kick him in the head with the heel of your right foot.) I resisted the process of practicing. I was awkward, what I was doing wasn't working, and I wanted to move on to something else. When I fully accepted that I would just do it (I mean feeling the "OK, I'll do *all* of it"—in my mind, heart, body and soul—doing each component over and over as well as implementing the coaching), my practicing became interesting, even amusing, and I progressed so quickly that I got to the point where I started teaching others how to do a wheel kick.

In the dictionary, the word practice means *applying your knowledge*. It doesn't just mean doing something until you do it perfectly.

As we build JIAN, we take our business processes, painful as some of them are to deal with as well as automate, and build them into our products so other businesspeople like you can use them for their benefit. It's the *practice*, and getting better and better at it, that is success.

If you can go with the concept that we're here on Earth in life to learn and develop, then everything we do from moment to moment is an important and interesting part of that process.

People are most happy when they are moving toward their goal,
not necessarily after they reach it.

— Steven Snyder, Creative Accelerated Learning Methods

That's not to say you don't want to reach your goal. You do. I want to finish this book. But I'm very happy working on it because I know it's progressing. When the book is done, it may be fairly anti-climactic. So what I need to do is reload and have something else to do next. After writing the book, what I'll look forward to is promoting it, having it out there, and hopefully, talking to audiences full of entrepreneurs about building your businesses.

I'd rather screw up than stand still.

A guided missile is off course most of the time

When I say I'd rather screw up than stand still, I think of taking small steps, seeing what works, putting in a course correction, and keeping going. I don't learn much by not taking a step in the direction I want to go.

Is more better?

We're not taught process, we're taught goals. We're taught to achieve, to go get, get, get. How much is enough? You'll have to answer that for yourself. I'm finding that my learning experience is compounding daily and it's something no one can steal from me. If I remain constantly conscious throughout this process, my ability to generate revenue, ideas, and products, as well as attract quality people becomes more powerful every day. I go into situations, eyes open, looking to learn. Sometimes it's expensive, usually it's profitable—you don't have to be right all the time, just most of the time to be successful.

When a person with experience meets a person with money,
the person with experience will get the money.
And the person with money will get the experience.

— Leonard Lauder, chairman, Estee Lauder

In the book *Jitterbug Perfume* by Tom Robbins, one of the characters, Dr. Wiggs Dannyboy, explains that our hurry in life to do all the things we want to do is caused by the ever present, although not always conscious, knowledge that we will die. We must get everything in before we die. If we didn't die, we'd have plenty of time to do everything we wanted to do and perhaps we could relax.

I've been in a hurry for a long time to do many things and buy many things. Only after accomplishing my major goals (make several million by starting my own company, buy a house, and especially own and fly an airplane) did I realize that I still had to make myself happy. Working at The Sharper Image gave me the first-hand experience of having lots of stuff and the addiction to buying more. I learned that the 'stuff' made me happy temporarily, but my ongoing *process* of life is what drives me, interests me, and motivates me now. And, I can feel a sense of satisfaction deep down inside as if it is a sensation of completion and balance as well as motivation to keep learning and sharing what I learn.

Business Black Belt Notes

- Keep you eye on your goal, but keep flexible as to the methods for achieving it.

- Appreciate the process of achieving your goals.

- You don't have to be right all the time, just most of the time, to be successful.

- Practice means applying your knowledge.

No Excuses, No Blame. . . No Kidding

When the smoke clears and the dust settles,
you have either a success or an excuse.

☞ The people who accept the final responsibility become the ones in charge—it doesn't seem to work the other way around.

In a world of lawsuits where someone can sue a company because its coffee is too hot, you might wonder how you would get ahead by taking total responsibility for everything and everyone around you.

One of the things I like about martial arts is that you can't BS your way through it. If you miss blocking a punch, you can't say, "Well, gee, I blocked that punch," while you're lying on the floor. Either you blocked it or you didn't. You can't BS your way to a black belt and you can't really BS your way through business either. (At least, not for long.)

Some people brag about how they BSed their way through school. Only now they are faced with BSing other BSers. Trust me, these people are easy to spot. It's remarkably refreshing to meet someone who can really deliver. In fact, to be really unique or unusual today, try shooting it totally straight with people.

I met recently with a product expert, Bill, who felt that he was getting a raw deal on his contract. I sat down at the meeting and immediately said, "We're screwing you on this deal, aren't we?" (The contract was at a stage where we had it stacked completely in our favor and it needed work.) He said yes, relieved that he didn't have to fight me to prove that it was a bad deal, a deal I myself wouldn't have taken if I were him. Then we could get to the details that needed fixing and not waste time being defensive and making excuses. Why not just call it like it is and move forward?

> **Genius does what it must, and talent does what it can.**
> — Edward Robert Bulwer, Earl of Lytton, author

Your business is hot because you are there

Arrogance aside, this book is hot because I wrote it. Given that bold intention, I did everything I could to make it interesting and useful. I must take responsibility for my excellence all the time—you must too. Your business is where it is because of the fact that *you* are there.

If I hold that thought, "It's going to be great because I'm here," then because I'm working on this, *I must therefore make it great.*

Many people don't take enough responsibility for the fact that they are there. The fact that they're there means that the product, service, and business needs to be really great.

I had trouble with one employee. He told me, "My sales territory's got no history, no sales." I pointed out to him, "Hey, the very fact that you are there is going to make this happen." He couldn't (wouldn't) get it. He wanted the territory to be already producing, to see that he was already going to make money. He couldn't see the opportunities in his territory and that he could have made it go. He could have sold a lot of software, built quite an empire for the company, and taken a lot of credit for doing it. But he would not take responsibility for what he was doing, for his own presence in the situation, and for the fact that with his energy, he could create something out of nothing. As you study men's and women's successes throughout history, you'll see how people who can make something out of nothing are huge successes, and this ability is consistent among great business successes.

> **Guilt: The difference between what you are doing
> and what you think you should be doing.**

I'm only human. . . .

Let's say I'm your dentist. How many mistakes will you allow me to make while drilling in your mouth? How many mistakes do you allow the airline pilot flying the plane you're in? Likewise, customers expect a certain degree of perfection in the products and services they buy from you.

OK, you've got to experiment sometimes to see what works, but restrict that to an appropriate environment that can't be used as an excuse for sloppiness. The point I'm making is that you should have no room for error in what you do if you want to build a reputation for quality. Saying you're only human leaves room for inattentiveness to what you are doing. You may think it relieves you of responsibility. It does not. It didn't help MacDonald's when they were sued for a hot coffee spill. Sure mistakes happen, but you cannot let yourself off the hook with such an excuse like *you're only human*.

> *It does not do to leave a dragon out of your calculations,*
> *if you live near him.*
> — J.R.R. Tolkein, author

Either you make life easier for your customers by providing them with a lot of good stuff or they'll find someone else who will. I'm sick of hearing why something didn't work or whose fault it was. If you're responsible for managing a project or other people who are managing a project, you need to be sure of what they're going to do so that there's no *excuse* to tell about what they did or didn't do. In other words, while you're talking to them, you're looking way upstream for where the excuse is going to start. Make sure what they do does not become an excuse.

The best excuses that you'll believe are the very ones you use yourself. This concept is the converse of my story of balancing my checkbook to have customers ready to buy from me. It usually works like this: We ask someone to do something or buy something and sure enough the reason for not being able to do it is something we totally empathize with. I could have kept beating my head against the wall calling customers only to hear the trend grow about how everyone hadn't completed their budgets because subconsciously I didn't have mine completed (and I was procrastinating doing anything about it). Therefore, I would believe the excuse wholeheartedly because it fit conveniently into my blind spot. Either you let the situation go on as hopeless or use their reasons as your insight into your own blind spot and do something about it. If your reason for not buying something is, "I don't have the money" or, "I don't have the time," it's likely you'll hear that frequently from other people, much to your frustration. Like your customers, you aren't looking deeper into how you can have the money (structure the deal) or have the time (commit to a date). When you do, you'll find it easier to get past those objections and your business will skyrocket.

ONE person is accountable for the overall outcome of a project

Until I learned this and put it into practice, I often heard, "I didn't know who was accountable for __." This happens when a team is working on a project without a team leader who is ultimately responsible for the whole enchilada. When one of them knows his or her ass is on the line for a project or service, then that person will make sure that it works.

Either you have the results or you don't. When you blame others, you've given them the power. Your power. When you look to see what you contributed to a situation that went wrong and learn from that experience in order to do something different next time—to assert yourself to assure that things work out to your satisfaction—then you will have the power. I wrote this book to empower you. Your power is in what you can do, what you can change and what you can improve.

Be careful of your compulsion to appeal to the lowest common denominator

I don't recommend changing your entire company policy just because one customer in a hundred complains. That's not to say that you don't want to please your customers. Sometimes 1 out of 100 customers is not happy with the way you've done something, and yet the other 99 like the way you've done it. Time and again, I've been tempted to change my company policy just to appeal to one angry customer or one unhappy employee. You can jump through a tremendous number of hoops to make changes just because that one vocal person wants the product one way. This may sound like heresy, but think twice before you leap to appease them. Maybe you're better off losing that one customer or employee. Remember where your bread is buttered and who is buying from you. We often overlook our silent, but satisfied customers just to quiet a loud complainer. Look a little deeper into situations like these before you do anything drastic. This isn't to say you shouldn't try to please the unhappy customer in the moment—you must do everything to send them away with a good impression—you just don't have to necessarily change your entire company as a result.

Business Black Belt Notes

• In the end, you enjoy success or an excuse for failure.

• No mistakes are OK.

• Before making changes to please one loud customer, consider any adverse effects on the rest of your customers.

• Anticipate the future excuses others may give and do whatever it takes to assure you get what you want and not an excuse about something else that happened.

The Way of Transformation

The man who, being really on the Way, falls upon hard times in the world will not, as a consequence, turn to that friend who offers him refuge and comfort and encourages his old self to survive. Rather, he will seek out someone who will faithfully and inexorably help him to risk himself, so that he may endure the suffering and pass courageously through it, thus making of it a 'raft that leads to the far shore.'

Only to the extent that man exposes himself over and over again to annihilation, can that which is indestructible arise within him. In this lies the dignity of daring.

Thus, the aim of practice is not to develop an attitude which allows a man to acquire a state of harmony and peace wherein nothing can ever trouble him. On the contrary, practice should teach him to let himself be assaulted, perturbed, moved, insulted, broken and battered—that is to say it should enable him to dare to let go his futile hankering after harmony, surcease from pain, and a comfortable life in order that he may discover, in doing battle with the forces that oppose him, that which awaits him beyond the world of opposites.

The first necessity is that we should have the courage to face life, and to encounter all that is most perilous in the world.

Only if we venture repeatedly through zones of annihilation can our contact with Divine Being, which is beyond annihilation, become firm and stable.

— Karlfried Graf von Dürckheim

Green Belt

Using What You Have

Things are coming together. By now you develop a sense for what is working and what needs more work. Keep going…

Become Your Own Coach

He who stops being better stops being good.
— Oliver Cromwell, English general and statesman

☞ **What you say to yourself in the privacy of your mind can either help you or mess you up. Here's what to think to keep improving your performance.**

One of the best places this forward-thinking process comes in handy is in practicing sports. Notice when you flub a golf swing, you tell yourself, "Darn, I hit a bad shot," or "Oops, I sliced it. I hate it when that happens!" That's not productive thinking. What does that do for you? Nothing. Does it help you improve your swing? No, you just get mad at yourself. You're frustrated with the game. And, your game cannot improve with this attitude.

A more productive thought would be "OK, I sliced the ball. How can I hit it straight?" You already know what you're supposed to do to hit it straight. Think, "What do I need to do to hit it straight? I know, I'll _____ to hit it straight." Then, every single stroke you take becomes a learning experience.

The same thing occurs in tennis. You hit the ball late and it goes out of the court. You think, "Darnn, I hit the ball late again." What would your instructor say? "Hey stupid, you hit the ball late again. You sure are lame, you're never gonna get good at this game!" I don't think so. Only you might say that. But that's the thinking we will eliminate here. Your instructor actually says, "Let's try that again. This time get to the ball and hit it sooner." (My instructor is from Argentina and he says, "Move more your feet.") That's a more productive thought—something you can use—and when you get to the ball sooner the next time, you'll hit a better shot.

When you're playing by yourself (and even when playing *with* an instructor), you tend to use this negative self-talk—the conversation with yourself in the back of your mind—about how you're playing the game. It's unconscious, but you do it. When an instructor is present, at least someone is giving you positive or productive comments.

Let them know that you know that you stink

Speak the internal verbal abuse aloud. When you miss a shot, you say to your opponent, "Gawd, I'm soooo bad at this," as if they were thinking it too and wondering why they were playing with you. Perhaps if we can beat our opponent or instructor to the negative thought about our performance, we can prove that we really are good enough to recognize a bad shot. Then we can still psychologically maintain an upper hand. Is it better to maintain that upper hand at the expense of improving your game? If you're into maintaining your psychological upper hand, the upper hand becomes more important than improving your skill. Consequently, you remain at one level, making excuses, berating yourself, and going nowhere.

The point here is to comment internally only with productive messages and you will effectively become your own coach. At least, between lessons you'd be practicing what you learned and not grinding bad habits further into a rut. Look at what coaches actually do. The coach gives positive direction about what to do to improve your next shot or swing. They acknowledge you for really doing something well. They push you to do more, do it better, harder, and faster. If you were to tell yourself what it would take to improve your previous action and acknowledge yourself for what you did *right* in the previous action, you could productively coach yourself.

You need coaches to gather positive commentary

Now you might be thinking that you can do everything yourself. Not so fast—you still need another qualified person to observe you, be your coach, and recommend corrections. (Remember what you learned in the chapter "Qualify Your Advice" and use that to find a good coach.) Also, paying a professional for advice is far different from receiving coaching from friends and family, especially when the coaching is unsolicited. A coach knows certain things about the subject that you still might not yet have in your head. He or she will tell you what to do and this advice is what you use for self-talk when the coach isn't around. You need a coach to collect some good recordings of good advice you can play back to yourself later.

Now, instead of working against yourself and taking a long time to learn something, you can plug in these positive commands while practicing and teach yourself to do better. You won't undermine all the instructor has been teaching you. You get more out of the coaching and your performance improves.

Anger produces nothing except something else that you'll regret.

Conserve your energy—you need it to move forward

This concept carries over into everything you do: sales, management, relationships, parenting, working with people. You're going to make mistakes. When they shoot movies, they often shoot many takes—miss takes—to get a scene right. They know they have to do it again, and they just get on with it. You can too. Burning up precious emotional energy and time (yours and that of others as well) does nothing to get you closer to solving your problem, completing a project, or improving your score. Indulging in anger only raises your blood pressure, wastes time, and scares the hell out of everyone around you. They become defensive and tend to pass the blame to keep you from focusing your displeasure on them. This is the time when you most need everyone's participation and candid input. I've found that when I immediately shunt my energy away from screaming about something that went wrong to asking questions and taking steps toward making it right, I begin to feel better. And everyone else seizes the opportunity to quickly put whatever went wrong aside and put in place the corrections to assure that the same mistake is never made again. When we're doing something about the error, we're closer to achieving the results we want. This is productivity.

The amount of energy you have is a function of your resistance

I find if you just flow with the activities around you, you have a tremendous amount of energy and you get a lot done. If something goes wrong, you can resist it and try to get around it, "I don't want to do this or that.... Damn these interruptions." I don't dwell on problems being problems or avoid dealing with them. I just deal with stuff as best I can, delegate tasks to people, and just keep going rather than spend a lot of time grinding my mental and emotional gears. Mental friction wears you down. If you can let go of this stuff and know that you'll find solutions to the problems, you'll discover peace of mind. Otherwise, the energy drain is like having one foot on the brake while the other is on the gas.

Business Black Belt Notes

- Coach yourself by using positive commands to produce improvement.

- A coach pushes you to do better the next time—do that with yourself.

- Coaches provide good samples of what to say to yourself while you practice.

- Immediately channel anger and frustration to positively dealing with a problem.

- The energy you have left at the end of the day depends on going with the flow.

The Pain / Need Ratio
(The Discipline of a 14th Century Samurai)[6]

I have no parents ....I make heaven and earth my parents.

I have no home ....I make awareness my home.

I have no life or death....................I make breath tides my life and death.

I have no divine power...................I make integrity my divine power.

I have no means.............................I make understanding my means.

I have no body...............................I make endurance my body.

I have no eyes ....I make the lightning flash my eyes.

I have no ears................................I make sensibility my ears.

I have no limbs..............................I make promptness my limbs.

I have no strategy...........................I make unshadowed-by-thought
my strategy.

I have no designs ....I make opportunity my design.

I have no miracles..........................I make right action my miracles.

I have no principles ....I make adaptability my principle.

I have no tactics.............................I make emptiness/fullness my tactics.

I have no friends ....I make you, mind, my friend(s).

I have no enemy.............................I make carelessness my enemy.

I have no armor..............................I make compassion my armor.

I have no castle ....I make heaven/earth my castle.

I have no sword ....I make absence of self my sword.

---

6   Based on E. J. Harrison's *The Fighting Spirit of Japan: the esoteric study of the martial arts and way of life in Japan.* Woodstock, NY. Overlook Press, 1982.

When They Hit You on the Head, Say "Thank You"

*A practitioner must learn to perform at top speed all the time, not
to coast with the idea that he can 'open up' when the time comes.
The real competitor is the one who gives all he has, all the time.
The result is that he works close to his capacity at all times and,
in doing so, forms an attitude of giving all he has. In order to create
such an attitude, the practitioner must be driven longer, harder and
faster than would normally be required.*

— Bruce Lee, *The Tao of Jeet Kune Do*

☞ Learn to think of pain and setbacks as valuable learning experiences. Dwell not on the perceived pain, but on the improvements you will make as a result of them.

You learn to improve yourself when something painful happens. You learn fast from your mistakes when you've just been thrown on the ground. Instead of getting angry about it, take the pain as a lesson and appreciate that the lesson wasn't any more damaging. Likewise, embrace your problems because they are there for your development and growth.

I think to myself, "Hmm... what am I going to learn from this?" Anger produces nothing except something else I might regret. I now waste very little energy becoming angry. I find that the time and energy spent on anger would better be channeled toward solving the problem. Whatever it was that happened, I can do nothing else about, except to set about fixing it and learning something so I don't make that mistake again.

Once during line drills in karate class, our fourth degree black belt instructor started screaming at us, "Hit him in the head, wake him up!" (The drill worked like this: One line of students was supposed to throw punches and the others were supposed to block and counterattack.)

This was a practice session, so we weren't very serious. We were rather mechanically throwing easy punches. When the instructor yelled for us to really punch, he woke us up. Then, when one of us got tagged pretty well in the head, we learned pretty quickly that we needed to block better. It was more humiliating than painful since we were wearing helmets and gloves, but it made us learn to be quick and accurate. I thank that instructor because if I'm ever in a fight, I can block fast and that might just save me some severe pain.

I didn't dwell on the fact that I got hit in the head at practice. My attitude was "Hey, I'm glad I learned that here and not on the street." It was a painful lesson, but not nearly as painful as it could have been in a real-life situation.

The sooner you make mistakes, the less they cost.
— Rick Itzkowich, Productive Learning & Leisure

Learning doesn't have to be so painful if you're sensitive to what the lessons can teach you. As I write this, my car is in the shop. One of the sensors on the engine went bad so the engine stopped. Rather than swearing at my car for the inconvenience and cost, what if I were to consider that everything is connected in Nature—there are no accidents; this is not merely a coincidence. Is this a quiet message representative of something else possibly to come? Looking at my car metaphorically, I might interpret that I'm being insensitive to something going on or someone around me. If I continue being insensitive too long, my "machine" will quit. This "machine" could be my business, and I don't want that to quit. If I hadn't realized that my car's broken sensor might be a clue / parallel to my own insensitivity, I might be in for a more painful lesson if something or someone else quits as a result of my own failure to sense a problem.

This may seem like a quirky example, but take a look at where it can lead. While my car is in the shop, I'm making sure I'm more sensitive to the people I work with. I got the message that I've been driving along, building my company, and probably becoming insensitive to my staff. I appreciate this situation because it's a cheap message (especially since my car is still under warranty).

Looking further, I realized that my employees have actually been asking me for assistance and deeper listening for a while and I've ignored it. Nature finally came along and said, in a slightly louder manner, "You're not getting it, Burke. Let's give you a breakdown so you must stop." It's up to me to recognize and interpret the message. It's actually very simple; just think literally. What does a *sensor* failure mean? If whatever it was that failed were a representation of me doing my life, what would it mean? Usually, the breakdowns have a pattern—many problems can be traced back to a common cause. In other words, if the 'engine sensor' message wasn't obvious, other similar breakdowns (home thermostat, water level floats, people telling you that you're not listening, repeated songs that I hear on the radio, etc.) would occur indicating that I was out of touch. *I* wasn't *sensing*.

The stronger the messages get, the more expensive, time-consuming, and painful they become. If I hadn't acted on that message, what would Nature need to do next in order for me to understand?

Naturally, we want to avoid pain, but in our haste to do this we end up missing many of the messages coming in. We don't learn the lessons. If we attempt to dissipate our pain by blaming others or "circumstances" how can we learn how to improve ourselves? If we want to get on with it is soon as possible, put the painful experience behind us, and forget about it before looking deeply into our contribution to the situation, we are doomed to have Nature give us another chance to experience the pain at a higher level.

I could go on here with similar situations and their corresponding messages, but you'll see how they play out in future chapters. Without going crazy with analysis, you can use these messages as subtle guides for action that is important to take for 'things' to go more smoothly in your life. You will also feel less offended and that the world is out to get you. It's actually out to teach you. Learning (acting upon your knowledge) will indeed pay off.

Nature is a ruthless teacher.
The trick is to get the lesson when Nature whispers.
Not when it bangs you on the head.

Competition also teaches us about improvement. It's painful to hear a customer say, "Your competitor is killing you with [x]." But you need to know so you can take the appropriate action to improve your product or service. So, when a competitor lands one on your head, say "Thank you." You'll get better because you learned by responding to the message rather than getting angry at the messenger.

In martial arts, it's very clear when you get hurt and when you don't get hurt. When your opponent punches you, it hurts. If you block the punch, it doesn't hurt. Responding to the pain makes you better.

Some people think others are out to get them. If you think about it, no one really has the time to be out to get you. They're too busy being out for themselves. Maybe you just got in the way. The world is just out to be. Your job is to pay attention and learn.

Trade your pain for gain

One of the early techniques we learned in karate sparring—especially when you're first starting out or working against a superior opponent—was to always make them pay for attacking you. My opponent may get inside and score a point against me (a back-fist to the head. . . whatever), but rather than back off, telling myself I'll score next time, I would punch or kick them immediately. The lesson was: You may get me, but it will always cost you. The next time they attacked, a portion of their focus would be spent on defending my counterattack. Therefore, their offense would be weakened. You also see this in football. The receiver catches the ball only to be hit extra hard by a defensive player. The idea is to A) punish him for making a gain and B) distract his attention on future plays with the expectation of pain.

Similarly, in negotiations, you can ask for something in return every time someone requests a concession from you. They ask for [x] percent off and you agree if they'll take [y] units. If they ask for delivery in [x] days, you ask for immediate payment in [y] days. Always get something in return for everything they ask for. As a result, you'll end up with a better deal or they'll stop asking, because they'll learn that every request costs them something.[7]

Business Black Belt Notes

- Pain can be your gain when you consider the lesson it teaches.

- Be thankful that the experience wasn't any worse.

- Listen carefully to Nature's messages (literally) while they're still whispers and act accordingly.

- Shift your overall attitude to a learning mode rather than launching into anger or fear.

- Limit the advantage others take by making counteroffers in return.

---

[7] Dawson, Roger. *The Secrets of Power Negotiating*. Hawthorne, New Jersey, Career Press, 1995.

The general smiled. "He is a man who has all my respect.
He possesses a quality of. . . how to express it? . . of *shibumi*."

Nicholai knew the word, but only as it applied to gardens
or architecture, where it connoted an understated beauty.
"How are you using the term, sir?"

"Shibumi has to do with great refinement,
   underlying commonplace appearances.
A statement so correct that it need not be bold,
   so poignant it need not be pretty, so true it need
   not be real.
Shibumi is understanding, rather than knowledge.
   Eloquent silence.
In demeanor, it is modesty without prudence.
In art, it is elegant simplicity, articulate brevity.
In philosophy, it is spiritual tranquillity
   that is not passive; It is being without the angst
   of becoming.
And in the personality of a man,
it is. . . authority without domination."

"How does one achieve this shibumi, sir?"
"One does not achieve it, one. . . discovers it. . . .
One must pass through knowledge and arrive at simplicity."

— Trevanian, from *Shibumi*. New York. Crown Publishers,1979

We Are Reflections of
The People Around Us

Not he is great who can alter matter,
but he who can alter my state of mind.
— Ralph Waldo Emerson, essayist and poet

☞ Different people with their variety of baggage come before us in life to teach us something—you can resist them only to have their character return over and over again to your show or you can learn from them and move on.

The concept of seeing a part of ourselves in others—good or bad—is not new, yet it requires some in-depth interpretation to see its benefits. Using this truth to learn more about yourself and your behavior can produce amazing results forever.

My situation was their objection

I was making sales calls one morning and everyone I talked to was objecting with the same reason! These were different people in different companies, but on this day, they each told me that they weren't sure of the amount of money they had to spend, they hadn't completed closing the books for the month so they couldn't make any financial commitments right now, their budget wasn't complete, and other variations on this same theme. Their objections had nothing to do with the product, the season, or anything else you might expect. And, they were interested in buying. But why was I hearing the same theme? What could I do? I started to wonder what I had in common with these people beneath the surface. I realized that I hadn't balanced my checkbook or turned in my expense reports for a couple of months—I wasn't sure of my own financial position either! I could have kept on calling more customers, but my solution was to leave the office, go home, and take care of my personal finances immediately. (I was going crazy making calls and getting nowhere anyway.) Guess what? When I returned to the office early that afternoon, knowing my financial position, an order was on my desk that had just been called in!

> ### What we trip over is our gold mine.
> — Unknown

Give this seemingly paradoxical approach a try. Instead of lapsing into what may seem like a hopeless situation, look to see what it is within your customers' objection that applies to you. In other words, if *you* were making *their* excuses for not buying, what would you need to do to get yourself past the objection? Put yourself in their shoes and if you were to become a willing customer, how would you change your conditions to enable you to buy? This is easier than it may seem. The first step is to think in very literal terms. In my case, everyone didn't know what their budget was (they didn't say they didn't have enough money). I used their clues as direction for action I needed to take. I took that action (balanced my checkbook) and suddenly *they* were ready to buy.

> ### There's nobody else out there.
> — Paul Larson, Founder, The Summit Organization

What others say (especially if it seems to be a trend) reflects what you need to do. Do it and your customers (and others) will miraculously shift. Similarly, if you want to be listened to and understood, the quickest path is to listen to others and do everything you can to understand them.

What you may be angry about in other people's behavior is an indication of behavioral changes that you must make. Let's just say that you need to do something different; maybe it's the very thing they're doing that you yourself do. You only recognize it when someone else does it, or their behavior is compelling you to mature in a positive way to handle them. Perhaps you must establish that you no longer tolerate a certain behavior—set new, higher standards for yourself and others—and decisively remove it/them from your life. I would even go so far as to suggest that you already know that you need to take that step but have, until now, been unwilling to do so.

As I write this, I'm going through a transition in my management style at my own company. One manager always seems to have an excuse for why things didn't happen, couldn't be done, or why current projects should be delayed. I've been thinking that if I could get him to change, just see that he's got everything it takes to make all these projects work, he'd be a hero. I find myself making excuses that our projects don't get done because he keeps screwing up. If I had a boss, I think he or she would politely explain, "We need this job to get done and be managed with some leadership and attention. . . and Burke, I think we need to find someone else who can handle it. I think the best solution is to let you go."

I hate to fire people, but it's part of a management maturity step I must take. Avoiding it just makes my life miserable. Part of being an effective leader is the ability to choose and recruit talent, it also means removing unproductive people. In this example, the person's behavior compels me to take an action that actually forces me to grow as a person. If I had had the nerve to do this many months ago, the problem wouldn't have reached its current size. I knew what had to be done then, but was afraid to handle it. Now, as I take on a more powerful management attitude, these kinds of things will be dealt with more easily and swiftly. If you can avoid getting sucked in to these situations and instead use them as compelling growth experiences for yourself, you'll expand your repertoire of effectiveness.

Letting this executive go turned out to be the right thing to do. I really needed a stronger, more experienced person in that position. Plus, it let others know that I could and would fire someone.

You're wrong (and you're stupid)

I have this employee who is very intelligent and very argumentative. When he disagrees with you, you get the feeling that you're wrong, you've left something out, should do more homework, and that he thinks you're stupid for ever considering such a project. I, on the other hand, am totally delightful. So, what's wrong with this picture? What might I have to learn from this employee? OK, should I just go ahead and fire him because I find him annoying and don't need his crap?

After some serious soul-searching to figure out what about me he could possibly be reflecting and what I needed to see to expand my awareness of myself, perhaps perceive things differently and make some changes, I saw an obvious (to me) connection. (Keep in mind, the reason we need the "reflection" is because we don't see it ourselves—it's too close to the core of our being. It's the very filter we see everything and everyone else through.)

Maybe Jack reflects my inner contempt for people's stupidity and I'm now getting a physical manifestation of my own thoughts and feelings so that I can recognize their power and negativity. Jack has many redeeming features, but there are times when he (I) exude such a violent disdain for other people that seems so overwhelmingly repulsive that I actively want to get rid of him and not be around him. He shows me what my anger would look like if it were to manifest itself in physical reality. My vehement objection to his behavior and repulsion by it must be a reflection of what others perceive about me when I'm that way, although I've gone to great lengths to cover it up. In his form, it's loud enough for me to hear, see, and feel what it is that oozes out from my tightly shut container. It's not pretty. When I listen to Jack, I feel like I work very hard to grasp the value in what he's saying because there is so much to hear. But the anger, argumentation, and venom that's laced throughout his communications and intentions with me and others sometimes makes it unbearable to be around him long enough to complete an interaction. (People sometimes don't follow my direction or hear what I say because the surrounding cloud of negative energy accompanying it makes it next to impossible to pick out the gems from the flak.)

The interruptions, non-listening, rejection of ideas, single or narrow mindedness I perceive is only my own, amplified sufficiently to be visible to me.

Do I need to keep this person around to have his message rubbed in over and over again? Perhaps I have many of these people around, they just aren't as forthright as to be recognizable. I appreciate Jack for his volume and visibility. Even if I do let him go, I still must deal with myself.

"There is nobody else out there." We are all just reflections of each other at any given moment. This concept goes a long way toward providing an ongoing learning experience as we evolve.

> ### As I cultivate my own nature, all else follows.
> —Ralph H. Blum, *The Book of Runes*

I wrote this chapter on a plane after several weeks of extreme frustration with these two people. The process of asking the question "What is it about me?" and following my own advice has been tremendously insightful and freeing for me. I'd been grinding on what I should do, why they were around, what to do with them, and it was driving me crazy. I grind my teeth and want to eat a lot, and I want to go out and buy expensive things, thinking it would make me feel better. (I almost bought a new Porsche 911, but my dog couldn't fit in the back seat—you should have seen his face—I couldn't buy the car.) All along, I knew I needed to do something; there was a message I needed to get. Eating or buying something wouldn't solve my real problem. Going through the process of writing this chapter at least helped me understand. Also, I recommend writing by *hand* (there's something about writing long-hand versus writing by computer that's cathartic), in a stream of consciousness, in private, which will enable you to peel off your thoughts and get down to the core elements of your behavior that you must understand in order to grow, evolve, and move on.

I've worked out my differences with Jack—actually I let go of much of my anger and judgmentalness as a result of what I discovered about myself. My problem with Jack has vanished... as if Jack got it. Like I said, when you change where you're coming from, then others miraculously change in your perception of them. You cannot expect them to change first—that's what perpetuates your problem with them.

Become your own mental mechanic

How did I get to the bottom of what Jack's reflection of me showed me? First, I acknowledged that my perception of him had nothing to do with him. Therefore, trying to change him was futile. You see, Jack is not the first and only person to represent this behavior, and, unless I look deeper into the truth about what it means to me, I'm doomed to invite another Jack into my life until I get the message—the understanding of what his presence means to me. Second, what I was being shown about myself had not originated within me. It was something I had picked up along the way in life—perhaps I had misinterpreted a situation in my childhood (based on extremely limited knowledge, information and experience) and had drawn an inaccurate conclusion about someone or something on which I continued to base my assumptions about life. Or, trying to be cool, I had imitated an adult, not realizing that their behavior was inappropriate—either way, I needed to give that not-so-original idea/behavior up because it was working against me now.

Realizing that this behavior or attitude is not really part of who you really are makes it infinitely easier to let go of it. I think of it like editing my mind like I edit a word-processing document—just overwrite the old thinking like you overwrite a sentence then save the document back into your memory. Anyway, I looked back into my life for the first incident when I had behaved in Jack's way. That first time is important because it includes all the influential factors that started your point-of-view / thinking / attitude / behavior in this direction. Even though I had repeated this behavior for years, I knew there was a first time. I started by scrolling back through my memory from the most recent situation, looking for the time before that and the time before that until I reached the first.

Pondering that first time, I looked around at my circumstances, the people who were there, what they were doing and saying at the time. What was going on? How did that happen? What did I see? Where did I get my initial direction? What was I told? Then, how did I build on it and perpetuate it throughout my life until now? This will take some quiet time of reflection. When I back-tracked my Jack-like behavior and saw all of this, it hit me like a ton of bricks—it all became so clear. I remember what was going on, who they were talking about, the words, what I was told and how I used my intelligence and creativity to expand on this theme. It seemed like a good idea at the time and I felt intelligent and superior for grasping the concept and building on it. But it wasn't a healthy, loving way to be. Realizing that I merely recorded someone else's opinion way back when enabled me to quickly adjust my thinking to a more positive approach—a point of view that I knew would really work for me today given my additional 35 years of experience in life. I've gone through this process many times on a variety of subjects and it never ceases to amaze me that what I used to think can be so easily updated to more useful and productive thoughts and approaches to people and situations.

Business Black Belt Notes

- Behavior you see everywhere is an indication of your own current behavior.

- Your customers' objections are your objections—what can you do to overcome them?

- What can you learn about yourself from the people around you?

- Where did you get your original thought about how someone or some situation is?

Recommended reading

These two books will give you another point of view on life and living. The first one removed my fear of death and dying, the second made many things become crystal clear. I highly recommend them:

Weiss, Brian, M.D. *Many Lives, Many Masters*. New York, New York, Simon & Shuster, 1988.
Redfield, James. *The Celestine Prophecy*. New York, New York, Warner Books, 1993.

More Than Five Senses You Can Use

Only in quiet waters things mirror themselves undistorted.
Only in a quiet mind is adequate perception of the world.
— Hans Margolius

☞   In addition to your five senses, many other "senses" provide quality direction—beyond the limited scope of your intellect.

I was taught that we have five senses: sight, smell, sound, feel, and taste. Is that it? On a physical level maybe, but I contend there's more to it than that. What about our subjective senses, our gut feel or intuition? We must look beyond our physical senses and their limitations to include our emotional, intellectual, and spiritual senses as well. Do you use all of your senses? Can you improve them with exercise and training?

I've heard that we only use about 5% of our brain. . . . So, what's the other 95% doing? I suspect that much of the brain operates these other senses that we don't acknowledge or give much credit to. If you don't recognize something, how can you know to use it? No wonder we feel like limited beings. There's so much more to us that can make us very powerful, yet because something is not so easy to see, we disregard its validity.

The more I learn and experience the more power I think people really have. I respect nature, the supreme being for sure, but let's use what we've got and do what we can.

Why didn't I follow my gut instinct?

I submit that these extra senses make up our gut feel, our intuition. According to the dictionary, intuition means the act or faculty of knowing or sensing without the use of rational processes; immediate cognition, or an impression. Our inner voice speaks through our intuition. We know we should listen to this voice, but often we ignore it because there is no rational reason for paying attention.

Since we don't often acknowledge our intuitive senses, how can we put them to use—let alone trust ourselves with these powerful tools? If you bring them all to bear in what you're doing, you have so much more power. Let's take a look at some of these overlooked and seldom acknowledged senses.

Sense of Appropriateness

What is the right thing to do? What's the right thing to do between people? What's the fair thing to do?

Murphy's Law says that if something can go wrong, it will go wrong. The corollary to that is when you least want people to see you, that's when you run into the most important people. If you go out in curlers thinking, "I hope there is nobody there that I know." Of course there's going to be somebody there that you know. That's Murphy's Law. So, you always need to look good and act appropriately.

What people need to see in you is consistency and credibility. And you must always be *on*. That means that you cannot allow your mood or feelings from a previous encounter to affect your interaction with the next person, or your continued demonstration of integrity.

Sense of Balance

This can mean many things. You have a physical sense of balance on a bicycle. You also have a sense of balance in life in terms of time spent on something, between things, how you feel about yourself, and you balance your success among business, family and other things.

Sense of Being

Sometimes we feel as though we are invisible. For instance, if we don't show up at a certain party, it wouldn't make any difference anyway. When one person is missing from a meeting, there can be a tremendous difference in the ability to discuss an issue. Imagine yourself sitting in a meeting, and consider for a moment the energy of your presence and the contribution you make. You can contribute your energy wisely wherever you are and make a difference, or you can poison your environment with negativity. Given that you *do* make a difference everywhere you are, what responsibility do you take for what you contribute to every situation?

Sense of Belonging

When things aren't going right (i.e., my way), I feel as though I should be somewhere else where things *are* going my way. I don't belong here—wherever I am at the moment. For a long time, I felt as if I wanted to get out of wherever I was, be somewhere else, doing something different, with different people. What got me into this mess, I discovered, was just *going with the flow*. Sometimes this is a good thing, but I had allowed circumstances to dictate my life even though I could have made different choices. This left me in situations where I was unhappy, where, consequently, I felt I didn't belong. I then resisted everything that was happening—which is not exactly going with the flow. A sense of *not* belonging can be a good indication of not being true to your goals and feelings.

Only when I took charge of where I was going, who I was with, and what I was doing did I feel like I belonged. Even if I made horrible choices, at least I made choices. I learned from the results and made better choices next time. I belonged to my situation and made the best of it.

Sense of Direction

This can be a real problem if at least one person traveling with you doesn't have a good sense of direction. We men seem to think we were born with a very strong sense of direction and to prove it, we often won't use maps or ask for directions. But, part of having a healthy sense of direction is recognizing the need to check and recheck your bearings (ask for directions). (Remember to focus on the goal of getting there and stay flexible on the process.)

Common Sense

> *It's amazing how uncommon common sense is.*
> —Mark Twain, author

The dictionary defines common sense as the native ability to make sound judgments. In a later chapter, I discuss *doing the math*. This helps a lot when applying common sense to business deals. Common sense is also your ability to do the right thing in spite of direction or procedures dictating action that may not be appropriate to a particular situation. (Common sense dictates that hot coffee is usually very hot whether or not there is an official warning notice, and pulling the lid off a cup while driving is not a very smart move.)

Sense of Commitment

Are you going to go the distance or not? Are you going to come through, no matter what? Do you have a sense of what that's going to take? Are you being popular in the moment with the person who has just made a request or demand of you by agreeing to do something with the intention of making an excuse for bailing out later? Or do you acknowledge your agreement to do what you said you would do, write it into your schedule, then do whatever is necessary to follow through?

Sense of Humor

Just because you are a professional doesn't mean you have to be boring. I bring my dog to the office. He howls a lot, especially when we're on the phone, but it's fun to have him there and everyone who visits our office loves him. It's one more thing that makes JIAN different and a fun company to work with.

Think about this: The entertainment industry is one of the most lucrative businesses to be in. Do you entertain people? How can you make your business interesting and even amusing? My childhood dentist glued a mop and a face to his X-ray machine. I wish my current dentist did that too. I often choose to do business with certain people simply because they are more fun than others.

Sense of Rejection

I won't dwell on this one. You know what it is. But are others really rejecting you or is it what you represent? You might remind a person of someone who was mean to them as a child, and for no apparent reason, they hate you. It's not your fault.

Rejection works both ways, and the opposite may happen with you. A person may remind you of a jerk from your past. You have to work harder to give this person a break—because this person is not the person from your past. Although your mind is stewing in the past memory, you must consciously override the memory and be aware that you are with a different person.

Sense of Rhythm

There's rhythm in the universe. We're talking about business here, so I am referring to how rhythm applies to business. Patterns repeat in economic activity. Real estate prices go up and down. Stock prices go up and down. Certain factors go into these things, but there is a rhythm in it all.

Sense of Space

There are several things to look at here. First, how much space do you need to work in? How big should your office be? Also, how close or far away do we sit together? Many people have studied the "territorial imperative," the appropriate distance you feel is right to keep between you and another person. For example, the distance acceptable between you and someone else can be much closer in an elevator than it would be if you were standing out in the desert.

You can also look at space in a business sense. How much *space* do you have in the market? Your company may have a competitor who competes with one of your products, while another competitor competes with a different product. Your other products may go totally unchallenged. I think in terms of the chessboard as a spatial representation of my business. That way

I can see where I need to do more building, more improvement, or more expansion.

I see many people locked into their business models. They could take many opportunities that would appeal to their customers. But they say, "That's not our business. We can't do it." They become very myopic.

The classic example of this was the railroad companies. They saw themselves only in the railroad business versus being in the *transportation* business. Their view was limited to trains and tracks, but the other view includes all modes of transportation. If the company heads had expanded their thinking, they could have seen sooner that their business had room to expand.

In your own business, you must imagine or visualize how you can increase your space in your market.

A Sense of Style

Notice how you react to a slob. What image of yourself do you portray? What is appropriate for you or for your business? I know I feel more comfortable when our accountants come in wearing suits and ties, although I rarely wear a tie myself. I might be concerned if they wore jeans and had ponytails. I also like the fact that my flying instructor wears a leather flying jacket. It goes with the territory.

Style also applies to how you do things, how your office is decorated, and how you approach your staff. Look around. Some people have style and others don't. What is your sense of style? Is it appropriate?

A Sense of Timing

Just as in music, timing has much to do with rhythm as well as the notes that come before and after. Some things must be done before others. Customers must be in a certain state of mind before being ready to buy. Sometimes you must wait for the right opportunity before you leap. Will you wait for a harmonic convergence before acting or is now the right time? We can ANAL-ize too much and miss an opportunity or we can make our move.

A brilliant executive is one who can spot a pattern
with the fewest possible facts.

— Fred Adler, Investor

Also, how long is something going to take? I find myself showing up 10 minutes late, often because of my bad sense of how long I need to get ready, out the door, and travel somewhere. (I seem to think that I can just "beam" over to my appointment.) It's one sense I'm trying to improve.

A Sense of Urgency

Some things can wait, others cannot. Successful business people all seem to possess a strong sense of urgency—some things need to be done now... because if they're not, an opportunity will be lost. Forever. To a business owner, instilling a sense of urgency into your people is crucial. However, I've found that it's easier to hire people who are inherently motivated and already possess a strong sense of urgency than to train those who don't get it. When you interview prospective employees, ask them to prioritize a list of your current action items to test their sense of urgency.

A Sense of Value

How much is something worth? Don't you hate it when you pass on an opportunity to buy something because you didn't have a sense of the right price to pay for it, only to find out later that it was a bargain?

Value = Wow! / Price
— Christine Sofranko, Southwestern Publishing

Often, you don't have much time to respond to a good deal when you come across it. How can you know how much something is worth? If you develop your sense of value, you'll know. You'll know what you'd pay for it or what someone else might pay if you were to resell it to them. I look at catalogs and at the prices on all kinds of things, so that I'll know a good deal when I see one.

When he looked at a potential item for his catalog, Richard Thalheimer of The Sharper Image knew what he would pay for something. He knew what his margins were, when he had to pay for it, and how much space and copy it would take to sell a product adequately. As a result, he's been tremendously successful.

As the creator of BizPlan*Builder*, I have a sense of the value of a business plan and the effort it takes to write one. I know that consultants charge

$1,500 to $7,000 or more to write one. I also know that you'll take a great deal of time explaining your business to them in order for them to write it for you. I also know how much time and effort it takes to write a good plan from scratch. I understand the value of my product to my customers. So I know how to market my product. I can sell it at a profit to me, yet at a reasonable price for someone who needs a business plan.

Team up with others to combine sense strength

Other people may have a more refined sense in any of these areas. This is how to make the best use of your management team, your employees and strategic partners. (And it's where your competitors can gain an advantage.) If you're travelling somewhere, you might want to hook up with someone who's got a better sense of direction than you.

Acknowledge you have these senses and you'll already be using more of your brain. You will become more conscious because you'll be aware of other thoughts and feelings that you've got to work with. Using these additional senses will dramatically improve your ability to do business.

Business Black Belt Notes

- You have more than five senses. Develop and use all of them.

- Our additional senses are like gut feelings.

- Our additional senses are in the 95% of the brain we don't use.

- Exercise and train your senses to improve them.

- You improve your ability to do business when you become conscious of these other senses.

A Trick to Remember

I'm interested only in God's thoughts, the rest are details.
— Albert Einstein, physicist

☞   What if you could naturally trigger your memory at a future date or time so you would remember to do something?

This is a little trick I discovered. I call it a *situational reminder*, a useful tool the next time you need to remember to do or get something, especially if you don't have a pen and paper handy.

I first used it once when I was driving down the freeway, listening to the radio. I thought, "I've got to remember this song because I really want to buy the CD, but I have nothing to write with." With all the distractions between then and the next time I would make it into a music store (whenever that would be), the title would probably slip my mind completely. So, I thought I would try something.

I pictured myself standing in the music store. I was looking around, actually seeing the CDs and tapes. (It's tough to do while you're driving, but it still works.) I experienced myself in the store. And as I did that, I thought, "OK, the next time I'm in this place, I remember the title of this tune and the name of the band who plays it." I etched in my mind a mental note about this situation.

Sure enough, I just happened to walk into a music store with some friends about three weeks later, having completely lost conscious memory of the CD title—and it struck me. The visual cue of standing in the store and seeing the CDs triggered my memory of the song and the artist's name. I remembered to buy the CD.

Create a visual association

It's like having a mental file folder of things to do triggered by an external stimulus—a particular situation where it is relevant to remember. These external stimuli are sure to happen sooner or later (like whenever I would walk into a music store). The action you want to take is generally only necessary in the presence of that stimuli, otherwise it's unimportant. In other words, the action is only something you would need to remember when the situation was right. The only time I needed to remember a band and a CD was when I was in a music store. Any other time, the memory was useless. So I attached my situational reminder to a situation when I wanted to retrieve the memory.

This trick also works when you need to remember to call someone. I visualize myself looking at my telephone. As I'm looking at my phone, I say to myself, "Remember to call So-and-so." I visualize the phone and imagine making the call and sometimes even talking to the person. Further, to make it really sink in, I'll imagine the person's face and imagine part of our conversation.

It works even if you aren't consciously trying. I landed at the Dallas/Fort Worth airport recently and suddenly remembered a golf shop there. On a previous trip, our sales VP and I had discovered the golf shop and talked about how bizarre it was to have a golf shop in an airport and the memory stuck. I hadn't been there in six months and had completely forgotten about the golf shop there. But it came to mind the moment I walked into the airport terminal. I thought, "Hey, I want to get that Callaway putter."

Easier than programming your VCR

In fact, what you're doing with this technique is simply programming your subconscious mind. You can naturally do this with anything you need to remember. How do you remember where you parked your car? You naturally look around to get a feel for the parking lot and the position of the car. Your mind will automatically direct you to it when you come back out of the shopping center. You face the parking lot and think, "OK, the car is over *there*." If you altogether forget where your car is, you probably weren't conscious in the first place and didn't do this process.

Here's another example: I'm standing in the shower and I realize that I need to remember to bring a diskette from home to the office. I see myself walking into my home office. I picture where the diskette is. There's the desk, next to the window, the top drawer, and to the right are the blank diskettes in the blue box. I imagine myself grabbing the diskette and taking it with me to the car. I visualize enough surrounding things so that I imagine a complete action. Otherwise, I might remember to pick up the diskette only to set it down on the kitchen table and leave it there.

Put things with your car keys

When I need to remember to take something with me, I'll simply put my car keys with it. I'll pile everything that I need to take in one place along with my car keys so there's no way I'll forget them when I leave (which is often in a hurry—or when I'm preoccupied with a new thought).

Other suggestions offered in this book can easily be remembered by using this same situational reminder technique. When you get more ideas, remember to incorporate this technique so you'll apply the ideas when the right situation occurs.

Business Black Belt Notes

- When you think of something you need to remember, visualize yourself being in the place when and where you'll need to remember it.

- While seeing certain key things, say to yourself, "Remember ___." *"The next time I look at the telephone, I'll remember to call John."*

- Include as much detail as possible and imagine a completed action.

- Imagine for a moment that you need to remember something and apply this technique.

The Pain and Pleasure of *Constant* Consciousness

Accidents happen
when you are thinking about something else.

☞ You must pay attention to everything all the time. The world is moving too fast and mistakes are too expensive for you to allow yourself to "space out."

You must always be conscious. You can't just put yourself on automatic pilot and do whatever—unless your instincts are sufficiently trained to respond immediately to sudden events. Since you experience a broad spectrum of sudden events from everyday problems, from oncoming cars to fortuitous business opportunities, you can't possibly react fast enough if you haven't been paying attention. By remaining conscious, you are aware of things, people, opportunities, and problems coming up. You can take appropriate actions before anything becomes an emergency. Emergencies are usually expensive and painful, but many can be foreseen.

In my workshops, people would often say, "You mean I gotta be conscious of what I say, things that I do, the expression on my face, how people respond to me, how I drive. . . all the time?!" The answer is yes. I fly airplanes and every time I'm not conscious of everything going on, something happens. These are the moments of sheer terror. If I don't pay close attention to flying the airplane, I could descend 500 feet and hit something.

The next time you're on the freeway, take a look at the people driving next to you. Are they driving their car or are they somewhere else? What if you or they drifted five feet? "Oh, it was an *accident*, I didn't see you coming," they'll say. What were they doing while they weren't seeing you coming? If they were conscious of their driving, they would be looking around, they would have seen you coming, and they wouldn't have accidents. Neither would you.

Traffic accidents. . . more on messages. . . I digress

(From time to time throughout this book I'll talk about the messages from nature that are constantly coming to us.) While we are on the subject of accidents, let me suggest that each kind of accident has some meaning to your life. Certainly you are not numb to what is going on around you, but you may not be picking up the hints Nature gives you about the action you must take if your life is to work the way you'd like it to. Nature provides many coincidences. This may seem way out there, but if you will accept and absorb this point of view, you'll join a rare number of people who put this awareness to very productive use. The good news is that Nature is very straightforward—everything is literal.

> *When the student is ready, the teacher will appear.*
> — Zen saying

Traffic accidents, for example, are an extremely loud wake-up call for those of us who just aren't with the program.

- Getting rear-ended means that you stop in front of people with little or no warning. Perhaps you are holding back other people in your life.

- Rear-ending someone else means you are not aware of the person in front of you, which is not a good idea if you follow too close or if you go while they are stopped. Perhaps you are pushing too hard.

- A broadside (T-bone) accident means that you didn't see the other car coming and pulled out in front. Perhaps you're not looking around enough to see what others are doing, what projects they are working on, and are just moving ahead on your own.

You can interpret other types of accidents for yourself. It's actually kind of fun to figure why things go wrong and what meaning they might have for you in all areas of your life. You'll discover that handling the issue that can be "sourced" from you will almost miraculously change the *coincidental* events occurring in your daily life.

Much has been written and many writers seem to agree that we are on this Earth in this lifetime to learn. If you look, I think you'll see that the signs are all around you. And if you don't get it, Nature just turns up the volume. Unfortunately, car accidents are part of the learning, if you are not conscious of the messages that come in more softly.

> **Consciousness does not occur unconsciously.**
> —Michael Naumer, Relationships Research Institute

It matters every day

When you are conscious of what you eat, you won't stick just anything in your mouth and one day wonder why you're fat. When you make phone calls or work on projects, you're conscious of your time. You get a lot of things done because you didn't let time go by and say, "Oh, I didn't get anything done today."

Someone once said, "God is in the details." (Others say, "The devil is in the details.") Using all of your senses (described in the previous chapter) helps being conscious all the time. Attention to detail makes a difference. When you compare a higher quality product and a lower quality product, you can tell which is well made. The conscious combination of appropriateness, balance, belonging, common sense, direction, rhythm, space, style, timing, value and, most importantly, attention all adds up to quality—what a customer is going to appreciate and buy from you. Someone will purchase your product or pay for your services over someone else's.

Business Black Belt Notes

- Practice constant consciousness.

- Nature is a ruthless teacher; the messages are literal. The idea is to get the message while it is just a whisper.

- Are you conscious of the expression on your face right now? (You should become aware of this because it affects others and their feelings toward you.)

- Look for the lessons in the things that happen to you and others. Use each situation to observe how and what you are doing.

A Black Belt in Business?

Live your life in a way that you would recommend it to anybody.
— Anonymous

☞   Here is my pitch for studying martial arts—it provides a wonderful metaphor for life as well as a few practical tools to get you by.

One night while I was in Tae Kwon Do class, I was sparring very poorly. I was holding back, being defensive, and not responding. After being clobbered a few times, I absently wondered whether I was managing my company the same way. While I had a minute left in the round, I decided to get in there and aggressively kick some ass. Guess what? I turned my sparring around and started winning. Indeed, my business was also being run sloppily and I needed to wake up and put some energy back into it. My karate training, in parallel with my business, graphically illustrated how I was getting lazy managing my company.

I recommend participating in a sport to observe your behavior from a different perspective. The next time you're playing your favorite sport or doing your favorite thing, look for ways that you similarly run your business. After all, your behavior is consistent from activity to activity—it all comes from the same brain, with the same mind and the same consciousness.

Put your foot in someone else's mouth

After watching some Bruce Lee movies and participating in my own karate training, I saw that Japanese management emphasized corporate karate. Like the big guy in the movie who gets pounded so fast he doesn't know what hit him, most American and European automakers had been punched out and left in a daze by the Japanese. While American managers were talking in terms of "home runs" and "touchdowns," Japanese managers were strategizing, maneuvering, and striking. Perhaps it was because, instead of baseball and football, they grew up with martial arts.

Martial arts began as training for survival, while the purpose of most American sports is...(selling cars and beer?) If American management had seen the feet and fists coming, then it could have blocked, counterattacked, and won the fight. Today, we are more aware of the strategy, and can deal with the assault.

I wonder if more of us learned and practiced the martial arts, we would pay more attention to detail, practice with more intention for mastery, and develop an intense personal as well as company-wide preparation and conditioning for success. "Action" under these conditions comes with incredible force, very efficient use of energy, and precise targeting. That's what it looks like to me four nights a week when I practice Tae Kwon Do. It's far more than the punching and kicking, it's the physical application of a philosophy. It seems to have direct applications in business. When your body and mind are so tuned, then your nerves are in excellent condition—something any well-prepared businessperson can use as much of as possible.

Application

When we were negotiating with the purchasing and marketing managers of a large software retailer, one of their tactics was to ask us to increase our advertising allowance to $100,000—an amount they thought would generate sales of $1 million through their stores. This was great leverage of our advertising investment with this reseller. I felt like I was on the hot seat. When I'm sparring in Tae Kwon Do, I flow with an attack—it works for me—it worked for me here too. The merchandising manager was shocked when I responded with "OK, what if we committed to $200,000 in ad co-op, would you commit to $2 million in sales?" I was serious. I didn't have the money at the time, but I had all year to get it. If they were so sure of the marketing programs they were pushing, this shouldn't have been a problem. Now they were on the hot seat. We passed the test as a player in the business and they took us seriously as a vendor who would play ball. (We actually invested about $125,000 that year.) We continue to allocate 10% of our retail sales to retail marketing co-op programs. Sales have been skyrocketing ever since.

Why we sponsor karate for our employees

Why not Jazzercise, horseback riding and other sports or activities? Here's why: I'm interested in eliminating fear. The first step I've found is that by eliminating physical fear, it makes it much easier to eliminate other fears. Fear of what?

- Trying new things
- Failure
- Making phone calls
- Approaching people
- Taking charge
- Speaking your mind
- Asking for an order

We need to move fast to take advantage of opportunities to build this business and these are crucial things that must be done every day with no unconscious hesitation. As an entrepreneur, this may seem obvious and painless to you, but the people you hire are not likely to be entrepreneurs and need a little assistance. I owe it to my vision to hire the right people who will support my vision. I will support education for any employee who wants to develop their skills in the direction of furthering the vision. I have a big vision and I need people with the skill and the nerve to accomplish it.

In your head and insecure

There are those who accuse me of being out of my mind. In fact, by being in your mind (in your head), you miss much of the reality that is happening around you. I just don't buy into most of the fears of others. So, if I don't act afraid of the same things they are, I seem out of touch—with *their* reality. I'm just not afraid of many potential problems, because I've never seen most of these imaginary problems ever really happen. That doesn't mean I've never thought about them, or that they actually couldn't happen, but I know that in my moment-to-moment existence in the here and now there is plenty of time and resources to deal with just about anything that does happen.

So, if you go into what seems to be an unknown with your eyes open and your senses tuned, you can handle any situation that arises. In my experience, this ability has provided far more security and peace of mind than anything else I've done or know of. Generally, what I've found is that I actually have lots of time—especially when I'm not wasting it by being in my head imagining all the evil possibilities that could befall me. Solutions are available. Look for them. This is a wonderful and productive distraction from panic.

In India, they tie a baby elephant to a small log that it cannot move. By the time the elephant matures it has given up on ever moving that log although it could easily drag it away. The Indians count on the fact that the elephant never continues to try and has given up—so they can get away with securing a large elephant to a small log. *My theory:* Most of us at some point (especially if you go back to childhood) endured some physical harm—or the threat of it—and have been left with a lingering subconscious fear of others. Our first experience of fear was usually in the presence of a large looming character (an angry parent, a tormenting older sibling, an unfamiliar stranger, maybe even a pet). Although we grew up, got older, wiser and bigger, like the Indian elephant, this subconscious fear of physical threat (learning that he can't move the log) remains. When I reached black belt, I had a revelation that I was no longer afraid of this potential physical harm.

I was sparring one evening with a seven-year-old named Nathan. Although I outweighed him by 160 pounds, I wanted to see what a seven-year-old Black Belt was made of. I took a swing at him, he stepped in, blocked it, and kicked me really hard in the stomach. This kid had no fear! He had obviously handled his fear of larger people. I suspect that his karate training had much to do with it. In martial arts training, you learn that you can take on just about anyone, and if you learn that when you are seven—the same time when just about everyone on earth is bigger than you—the fear of larger people is offset.

Translate this experience to a business situation: Take away the fear of a larger competitor or an imposing deal and you are actually dealing with individual people. You can handle people. Without fear of them, it's easier to be patient and hear what they say, get closer to them to understand what they want, dance with their conversation to interpret what will drive a deal with them plus you'll step in to address potential problems before they become real problems. This is how a business black belt flows with a partner or an opponent.

In summary: By practicing the martial arts, you eliminate a primal fear. With this fear gone you have freedom, security and time to think—to be out of your head (out of your mind) in situations where others often panic. You enjoy the time and ability to actually see solutions and opportunities. In fact, you'll often see problems coming way down the road and never end up in a in bad situation in the first place.

Business Black Belt Notes

- Everything you do comes from the same mind—you are the same person no matter what you do or where you are.

- Physical fear is your first fear—the foundation of all your fears. Practicing a martial art to eliminate this fear, go a long way toward freeing you fear from allowing fear to dominate your every move.

- Overcoming subconscious fear of harm will unleash a powerful way of being.

- Choose a martial art to practice and improve your business skills.

$$+ \times = ?$$

Do the Math

Play for more than you can afford to lose,
and you will learn the game.
—Sir Winston Churchill, English statesman

☞ Sometimes an obvious no-brainer good deal falls apart when you
add up its components.

I recently received a very clever phone pitch. A telesalesperson called to con-
gratulate me for being such a good magazine customer. She offered me 5
magazines free of charge for 60 months. I thought this was outrageously
good. She explained that the magazines wanted to increase their circulation
for their advertisers. I had been subscribing to a number of magazines so I
deserved to get this offer. I was going to receive several different magazines
to review and then I could receive them for 60 months.

I thought about it for a moment—and did the math—60 months is 5
years. That's a long time to be receiving a free magazine. My first alert.

Then she told me, "All you have to do is. . . please help us out with a service charge of only $2.99 per week." At first, I thought $2.99 a week isn't
too bad. Then I thought, "Wait a minute!" Multiply about $3.00 a week by
52 weeks. That's $156 a year. $156 per year divided by five magazines equals
$31.20 each! Yikes! That's a lot for just a "service charge."

This special offer was a total rip-off, especially when you consider what it
costs to subscribe to most magazines. Most magazines offer a year's subscrip-
tion for anywhere from $10 to $20. So just by doing the math and translat-

ing weekly, monthly, and annual amounts puts the whole thing into perspective. Five magazines should weigh in annually at about $70 tops!

Look at the line items

My company got a quote on our new packaging that included a reference book, several diskettes, labels, box, assembly, and so on. In large quantities, the overall price of $300,000 seemed in line. But when I looked at individual purchase orders for each component of our order and thought about how much each book should cost at a quantity of 32,000 units, the price per book seemed too high.

If I subtracted even 15 percent and took 35 cents off a $2.35 book, the cost came down to $2.00 each—which is what I asked our materials manager to negotiate. After going through most of our order, I demanded better pricing on many items. Overall, we saved over $35,000 on that one purchase. That's a significant amount of money. Just adding up the numbers and considering the financial impact of each of the components of every deal can make a huge difference. It took less than 15 minutes.

You need to get into the habit of doing the math. When you get a bill from a restaurant, especially if it's done by hand and not by computer, recalculate it. I'll bet that two times out of ten, it's wrong. There may be extra charges for things you didn't order or didn't get. The totals could be wrong, sometimes significantly wrong. (By the way, some waitpersons add the gratuity but still don't total the bill in the likely event that you'll add an additional tip as a knee-jerk action in the rush to get out of there.)

Once I was scanning my hotel bill line item by line item. I happened to see "2 movies" at the bottom of the bill. I said, "Wait a minute! There is a seven-dollar charge in that bill that isn't mine. I only watched one movie." Without hesitation, I pointed it out to the clerk who immediately removed the charge. The minute that took would be worth about $420 and hour.

Cheapskate or not, practice and develop the habit

Although you may seem tight, the *habit* of checking needs to be developed. If you're willing to accept a $7 error on a $700 bill, I'll bet you'd give up $5,000 on a $50,000 print order. It's significant and it all adds up.

You've got to develop this discipline across the board to catch those things. Over the years, you could easily overspend $30,000 - $50,000 on mathematical errors alone. It's frightening to consider how much money you can waste without even realizing it.

Now look at *how* you buy

Let's go beyond how much things cost to *how* you acquire them. Many people go out, buy something, then go to their accountant to see if and how they can get a tax deduction on it.

If there's something expensive you want to buy—a house, boat, plane, or equipment—I recommend that you talk to your accountant ahead of time and ask, "What's the best way to acquire or pay for this item?"

Recently, I bought an airplane, a 1980 Beechcraft V35B. I could have rented airplanes from my flying club for much less than I could buy one. But I went to my accountant and asked, "What's the cheapest way for me to acquire this plane and deduct it from my taxes? I could do it through my business, but what are the ground rules? How can I justify it?" I didn't want to go out and buy the plane first and then ask my accountant, "How can I write this off?"

Now I see how the IRS views the justification and deductibility of business aircraft. If your tax bracket is between 30 and 40 percent, making sure that you follow the IRS rules means your savings could be significant, enough to actually afford an airplane.

Save and wait, or buy now and make payments?

I was brought up with the idea that I should save my money until I had enough to buy something I really wanted. I find that I am unable to save. I don't have enough discipline or patience to religiously save up for something I want. I end up spending it on smaller things and never get to the bigger things. Having a financial institution I owe money to is very serious so I know I must make the payments. In fact, to me it's more motivating to make my payments every month than it is to save. I've discovered that this self-induced stress of creating the situation where I *must* make payments is a greater incentive for me. I keep going because I have to, otherwise I might become complacent and stop growing. Upping the ante also keeps me out of "scarcity" thinking. When I really want something or it makes good business sense, I go out and buy it now on credit knowing that I can handle the monthly cashflow to pay off the debt.

Saving the money for an airplane was just never going to happen. Instead, I went to the bank and said, "I want to buy this airplane," and got the loan. Now I have to make payments. I do what I must to make the payments. I certainly use the airplane a lot because I enjoy flying. I go see customers and product developers with it. I also hustle a little more because I want to keep it.

Interest is the premium you pay for immediate gratification

Is what you want worth having now, enough to pay the debt? If I use a credit card with 15 percent interest, I look at the price of something, tack on 15 percent, and I see if that is worth it to me. If I could buy something at half price by getting it now, adding only 15 percent might be worth it.

Don't necessarily shy away from paying interest on something. In a way, I am for putting things on credit cards. If the value of the thing will pay off more for you to have the item, service, or the seminar right now, charge it. If the return on investment is greater than the price plus the credit card charges, it can still be a good deal.

The economics of shopping around

When I first started my brochure and sales promotional business, Tools For Sales, I knew I needed a computer. I also knew, being in the computer business, that I could probably get a good deal. I shopped at all the stores for the best prices, but still I thought I could get a better deal if I waited a little longer or found a friend in the business who could get me a discount. In the meantime, I borrowed a Macintosh from friends at Apple Computer and drove several miles into town to print documents at a cost of 50 cents per page. (Laser printers sold for $4,500 in those days.) This went on for about a year! Finally, I got a deal on a new Mac with a laser printer and some software. It was amazing how much more productive I was by having all the right tools to work with.

It would have been far better for me to have used a credit card, paid full retail at the beginning of that year, and purchased everything I needed—old technology or not—enabling me to productively build my business.

You must adjust your focus to the bigger picture—go for the big money and sometimes overlook the small premium you might pay because you didn't shop for the best deal. The fine line to be drawn here is the value of your time. This is important for you to absorb for two reasons:

- You, the busy businessperson, have more important things to do than spend your time shopping around for minimal savings.

- You, the person selling your product or service, must promote the value, convenience, and immediate benefit of buying and using your product or service today and prevent your customers or clients from wasting their time.

Although I suggested using your credit card to buy what you need, be careful. Too much debt too soon sinks many a beginner. I made my purchase decisions based on one criteria:

Does it generate immediate cash or not?

Could and would I use whatever I bought as a tool to make money? I was careful not to get sucked in to buying a quantity of something just because the per-unit price made it a bargain. Buying a quantity of something, although it would save money in the long term, would cost valuable cash that I needed for other important things. Do the math: immediate cash or long-term bargain?

Business Black Belt Notes

- Add up the numbers and study the financial breakdown of every deal.

- Translating costs into the weekly, monthly, and annual amounts can put the whole thing into perspective.

- Mathematical errors alone can cost you thousands of dollars over the years.

- It's not so much how much things cost but how you acquire them.

- Interest is the premium you pay for immediate gratification.

Money

You'll never get rich by just saving your money.

☞ You can make a profit from doing the right things, understanding people with the money, and applying a few simple principles.

Do you really think you're going to join the ranks of the rich and famous by saving a few hundred or even a few thousand dollars every month (compound interest notwithstanding)? Wealth is not about saving some money and eventually getting rich. It's about making a big, gutsy move, generally starting with just one. You see an opening and you take it. Believe me, it can be very frightening—you're betting the farm.

Do as the big boys do

Look at the people who've got the big money—they did something like that, they bet the farm. Steve Jobs and Bill Gates may have started out doing smaller things, but they obviously eventually put some kind of big deal together. These super-successful people are ones like Conrad Hilton, Henry Ford, and Ross Perot. You can learn a lot from their stories and the stories of others—read them.

In my own experience, I had many clients and was developing marketing and promotional materials when I had this flash of an idea that became BizPlan*Builder*. Writing business plans was slightly out of the norm of what I was doing, but this idea turned into a product I could create and sell.

When I first thought about it, I got this feeling, a tightening in my chest. No, it wasn't a heart attack—it was excitement. I thought, "Wow, I've got to do this." That is probably the single best indicator for knowing you're doing the right thing. Whether you leave your job, develop a product, or start your own business, you have an overwhelming sense of "This is it!"

Be careful here

If your excitement comes from how much money you will make, you may be in for an ugly surprise. (At the end of this chapter, I'll give you an experiment you can try to practice a new form of building success.) I recommend not doing anything just for the money. Let the feeling of how much you want to do something guide you. When I started my business, I made a big move, a concentrated effort to put the original version of BizPlan*Builder* together. I easily worked until 3 A.M. writing and editing. I spent all the money I had on advertising. It was a one-shot deal. I didn't go out and start a whole company at first. I just made the product, ran the ads, took the orders, and started going. No one had produced a similar product yet, at least I hadn't seen it before. I knew I just had to do it, and not really for the money. I just thought I had a product that people could really use—it's amazing how many poorly written business plans are out there.

The *art* of business

What if you were to look at your business, product, or service as an art and think about what would make it a better work of art? The industrial design that goes into most of the products around you is an obvious form of art. Look a little deeper for the human touches that make things a little nicer, a little more attractive. It isn't all science as some people might have you believe. More and more I see products and services that incorporate *human* touches.

More than thinking about what would make you more money, keep in mind that the overriding factor is how you can improve your product, service or business to be more artful, more human. And at the same time you're making your product better, you can figure out a way to market it that would make money. To rewrite the famous line from the movie *Field of Dreams*, "If you make it, they will buy it." (Of course you have to promote it too! More on that later.)

Sometimes you might do something that doesn't look like it's making money at all. But the perception of this improvement may make it worthwhile. For example, The Sharper Image catalog is known for all of its gadgets, toys, and cool things to have. At one point while I was working there, we were selling a suit of armor in the catalog. This $1,500 suit of armor took a page and a half to describe. I remember looking at a sales report with CEO Richard Thalhiemer and noticing that we had only sold three of those things. Because the armor was unusual and fairly expensive, it did not sell very well. But Mr. Thalheimer, who had one in his office, liked the idea of a suit of armor. He really got off on the fact that he could even offer them for sale. Many other people did too. "Wow, you can actually buy a suit of armor? That's amazing."

What the suit of armor did for the company was not bring in direct money, but it helped build an image. The word on the street about The Sharper Image catalog was "Oh yeah, that's the catalog with the suit of armor in it." The suit of armor attracted attention. Even though the product seemed very costly in the catalog, it generated a lot of business indirectly.

I think Nieman Marcus did the same thing when they offered "His and Hers" Lear Jets on the inside cover of their catalog some years ago. I've never worked there, but I can only imagine it was done for high-impact image making. They also probably knew their customers would really get a kick out of it, even though they knew few people would actually buy. The product was certainly memorable and generated a lot of talk. (Recently, Victoria's Secret updated this concept with their offer of a diamond-studded Wonder Bra™ offered for a million dollars. It made headlines and, I'm sure, many catalog requests!)

In my business, the good news is that we too can build much refined art into our software products. In the software business, we make that effort and investment up front. Software is very inexpensive for us to duplicate. For a very reasonable price, many people can benefit from the refined information and layout that would ordinarily cost a fortune to develop for themselves. What can you do or promote in your business that will achieve a similar result?

How to make money at something

Doing what you love tends to be the kind of thing you would do for free. Even doing a job you dislike may be worthwhile for a while when you know you're getting paid for it. But when work is fun, it seems like you shouldn't really get paid for it. If this is true for you, you must get past that thinking and figure out how you're going to make money doing what you love.

To add the business component to what you love doing, you've got to figure out a way to get paid for it. Every time you do something in business, you've got to give value to your customer in some form that can be purchased. Ideas by themselves are difficult to sell so they must be converted into a tangible product or service a customers can understand and buy.

When I looked at using my sales skills to help others more effectively promote their businesses, I determined that the tangible product I would offer would be in the form of brochures and other sales tools my clients could use to increase their sales. My next problem was to figure out what I was going to charge for my services. When I first started, I looked around to see what was a reasonable hourly rate. In 1986, I started at $40 per hour.

To make money this way, set a goal of how many billable hours you need to generate the amount of money you want. Think of it as doing more of what you love, so that you can afford to continue doing what you love.

Many clients are uncomfortable with an open-ended deal, or paying an hourly rate for a project that could take forever to complete or get right. So, you could track or project how much time certain projects take and price them accordingly. Then figure out ways to be much more efficient at completing them, such as investing in better equipment. But most importantly, focus on the value the completed project provides for your customer and price it according to the value they receive. The money you make will be the difference in the value you provide and your cost for providing it. The scary/exciting part comes when you see how much money you're making while having fun doing it. Also, just because a skill or ability comes naturally to you doesn't mean that others have or enjoy the same skill or interest.

Successful people have a keen sense for what they're good at and for what their time is worth. You've heard that time is money. How much *time* does it take to make money? Now let's look at how much money could you make if you applied your time to the most profitable activities.

How much is your time worth?

Assumptions:	8-hour day; 244 workdays / year				An extra	15 Minutes Utilized Each Day for 1 Year is Worth:	1 Hour Utilized Each Day for 1 Month is Worth:	1 Hour Utilized Each Day for 1 Year is Worth:
If Your Annual Salary is:	Each Month is Worth:	Each Week is Worth:	Each Day is Worth:	Each Hour is Worth:	Each Minute is Worth:			
$8,000	$667	$154	$33	$4.10	$0.07	$250	$83	$1,000
$10,000	$833	$192	$41	$5.12	$0.09	$313	$104	$1,250
$12,000	$1,000	$231	$49	$6.15	$0.10	$375	$125	$1,500
$14,000	$1,167	$269	$57	$7.17	$0.12	$438	$146	$1,750
$18,000	$1,500	$346	$74	$9.22	$0.15	$563	$188	$2,250
$20,000	$1,667	$385	$82	$10.25	$0.17	$625	$208	$2,500
$25,000	$2,083	$481	$102	$12.81	$0.21	$781	$260	$3,125
$30,000	$2,500	$577	$123	$15.37	$0.26	$938	$313	$3,750
$35,000	$2,917	$673	$143	$17.93	$0.30	$1,094	$365	$4,375
$40,000	$3,333	$769	$164	$20.49	$0.34	$1,250	$417	$5,000
$45,000	$3,750	$865	$184	$23.05	$0.38	$1,406	$469	$5,625
$50,000	$4,167	$962	$205	$25.61	$0.43	$1,563	$521	$6,250
$60,000	$5,000	$1,154	$246	$30.74	$0.51	$1,875	$625	$7,500
$75,000	$6,250	$1,442	$307	$38.42	$0.64	$2,344	$781	$9,375
$100,000	$8,333	$1,923	$410	$51.23	$0.85	$3,125	$1,042	$12,500
$125,000	$10,417	$2,404	$512	$64.04	$1.07	$3,906	$1,302	$15,625
$150,000	$12,500	$2,885	$615	$76.84	$1.28	$4,688	$1,563	$18,750
$200,000	$16,667	$3,846	$820	$102.46	$1.71	$6,250	$2,083	$25,000
$300,000	$25,000	$5,769	$1,230	$153.69	$2.56	$9,375	$3,125	$37,500
$500,000	$41,667	$9,615	$2,049	$256.15	$4.27	$15,625	$5,208	$62,500
$750,000	$62,500	$14,423	$3,074	$384.22	$6.40	$23,438	$7,813	$93,750
$1,000,000	$83,333	$19,231	$4,098	$512.30	$8.54	$31,250	$10,417	$125,000
$5,000,000	$416,667	$96,154	$20,492	$2,561.48	$42.69	$156,250	$52,083	$625,000
$10,000,000	$833,333	$192,308	$40,984	$5,122.95	$85.38	$312,500	$104,167	$1,250,000

Treat your time as if you were making the money you'd like to make. Always ask yourself, "What's the best use of my time right now?"

Leverage yourself

Let's look at what you know about making money (I presume you intend to make money legally). Perhaps these will be familiar:

- Work really hard and the money will come because you deserve it.
- Go with a good get-rich-quick scheme that that seems easy and you'll get rich.
- Corner and hoard valuable resources and charge high prices as long as you can.
- Invent something, get a patent on it and sell it. (One of the better ones.)
- Marry someone rich. (Probably the easiest, but there's a catch.)

However, I believe that the secret to wealth is to:

Leverage your ability to help a lot of people.

Go beyond the financial leveraging that you learn about in the get-rich books and seminars, where you borrow a lot of money against the investment you're buying. If you can help a lot of people with the same amount of effort that you put into helping one person, that's where real wealth is created. Look at it from the karma perspective of "What goes around, comes around." If I help one person, I can make X amount of money, but if I help ten people enjoy the same benefit as the one I could make perhaps ten X the money.

You must find out where *you* are most effective. For example, I was out selling my marketing services to one client at a time. However, I knew how to sell to thousands at a time because of my marketing and advertising experience. The point here is that you must learn how to leverage yourself.

The very wealthy have figured out a way to leverage what they do to help a lot of people without much additional effort. The magnitude of their wealth is in direct proportion to their ability to help more people. (I don't think this was their conscious intent. Nevertheless, they efficiently provided a valuable service that generated the reward.)

Look at Bill Gates of Microsoft. He's got one primary software product, but everybody is using his operating system in their computers. He's managed to help a lot of people. And the beauty of the software business is that he can inexpensively duplicate the software while selling it for the full value that it provides. That's why he's the richest guy in the United States in 1996.

Henry Ford mass-produced cars. He learned how to leverage mass production so many people could drive inexpensively.

The paradigm of working harder and making more money doesn't work anymore. A lot of people have had heart attacks doing that. They don't end up making that much more money either. The paradigm of playing dirty, holding others back, keeping resources scarce so people have to pay more for things works sometimes. But today, the greatest wealth truly comes from leveraging your ability to add quality to many people's lives. How can you build this leverage into your business?

About people with money

Over the years, I've heard many people refer to a wealthy person by saying, "He's got so much money, he could care less about the price. . . ." That's a big mistake. Guess what? The more money people have, the more value conscious many of them become. How do you think they got wealthy in the first place? They are extremely aware of their spending habits, cash flow, and return on investments—any investment—including social and philanthropic ventures.

It's smart to want to do business with wealthy people, but don't assume that they don't care about the price or have money to throw away. You'll insult them and send them to a competitor. Contrary to popular belief, most wealthy people have worked very hard for what they own, and they're not about to watch it slip away.

The real difference between the wealthy and those who aren't is that wealthy people place a high value on lasting quality as a good investment, convenience and on having things exactly to their liking. Wealthy people also know that they can generate more money, so they're not afraid of investing in the best. To them, life is not static. You're not stuck where you are, you can generate more money. (Like Jay Leno says for Doritos, "We'll make more.") That means they'll more readily pay for such things as custom designs and valet parking.

Others think themselves limited—on a fixed income. There's nothing they can do to make more money. While they focus on that thought, opportunities are whizzing right by.

I made the transition from a struggling small-business person to a successful company president with the ability to buy just about anything I want. I'm now more careful about what I spend my money on. Things I've wanted or have wanted to do for a long time, I choose very carefully. I spend my money on things that are functional, to my liking, and of lasting quality. Why jump into your car every day and think that it's a piece of junk? For a few dollars more per day (a few hundred dollars per month), you could jump in your car every day and think, "This is great!" How long are you going to live? How long are you going to wait to do and have what you really want?

What do you call people who lose things? Losers

I tend to keep and maintain things for a long time. Since I know that about myself, I'm confident enough to invest in the best. It took a while for me to give up trying to save money by buying the cheap stuff because I hate throwing away something in good condition, albeit cheap. The longer I kept it the more it reminded me of my dissatisfaction.

> *Quality lasts long after the price is forgotten.*
> — Sir Henry Royce, co-founder Rolls Royce Motorcar Company

What difference would it make today if you had spent an additional $100 on something five years ago? Don't you squander enough cash on silly things as it is? Why not surround yourself with quality items you can use today, will serve you well, and hold their value and utility in the future?

Try this experiment the next time you play Monopoly

As an experiment, the idea is to help the other players win at Monopoly. That's right. You want to help them make money. Since this is just a game, you can afford to try this at least once. Most of us play Monopoly by trying to buy all the real estate and gloating over the rent we'll get when someone lands on our property. What if you made deals with the other players for joint partnerships? For example, rental on all four railroads is $200 but only $25 each. If you became partners with another player who owned two rail-roads ($50 rent) and combined them with your two railroads, split the com-bined rental, you would both have four chances to earn $100 each, not just two chances to earn $50! What if you applied this way of thinking and oper-ating in your business?

We handle our business affairs much the same as we play the game of Monopoly. Why wouldn't we? Our thoughts, attitudes, and knowledge of business all come from the same brain. Why would we do anything differ-ently? We talk a lot about win-win situations. But when we get caught up in the heat of a business deal and a lot of money is on the table, our primal instincts take over and we get ugly, unless we've had a direct personal expe-rience otherwise. I did this experiment myself with the fear that if I wasn't my evil, slumlord, aggressive business self, I would get clobbered. As it turned out, I made a ton of money and won the game! I recommend creat-ing this direct personal experience within the safety of this simple game.

I think you'll find that good, profitable business is not just about making a lot of money, it's about assisting people and making people's lives better. I'm proving this to be so at JIAN. What if everyone on the planet did that? We'd have a pretty nice place to live.

Business Black Belt Notes

- Wealthy people do watch where their money goes.

- If you want to make money, you've got to make gutsy moves.

- Make improvements more for your customers than for the money.

- Cash that you can earn right now is more important and valuable than a long-term bargain.

- Leverage yourself and your resources to help more people with the same effort.

Purple Belt:

Managing Yourself

Your training up to this point has been mostly centered around just yourself. Now you must begin to include others in your practice. Develop your footwork to move and flow effectively in relation to them. You begin to experience what the effects of what you've been learning have on other people.

Connect with the Inner Adult

I'm very easy to work with. . .
just give me what I want.

☞ If you're interested and are a little patient, you can communicate with just about anyone.

Just like we must appeal to another's inner child, we must also address their inner adult. In fact, you must be prepared to appeal to people in whatever state of mind they're in at the moment. Someone could be distracted, angry, sad, thrilled—you need to be able to reach the spirit within. No matter what state of mind a person is in when they encounter you, you can usually appeal to their good side.

A few years ago, our customer service person asked me to handle a customer on the phone who was "really pissed off at us." He'd said a number of rude things to her and wasn't going to go away. Before I picked up the line, I thought for a moment about what to do. It wasn't as simple as putting myself in his shoes. I had no idea what his problem was. All I knew was that I could listen to understand who he was, what he was doing and where he was coming from. And, no matter what, he was going to be happy when I was done talking with him. I picked up the line and said, "Hi. This is Burke Franklin. I'm the guy who wrote BizPlan*Builder*. Is it not working for you?" It turned out that he couldn't get his word processor to number the pages properly. That pisses me off too. I told him, "I hate it when that happens...," and we worked through how to fix it. He apologized for his initial outburst and we said good-bye. A happy camper.

As you know, people often need to blow off some steam. I recommend letting their steam blow by and not taking it as if it were directed personally at you. How could you have done enough to someone for them to be that angry with you? Obviously, their anger has built up from other reasons, so why should you absorb it? What would a karate master do? I wouldn't engage the anger. I'd let it go by me as if it were coming from my TV, then step back in as the person who is part of their solution and not part of their problem.

You're going to have to get out of your own head and determine what to say, think and do and how to be authentic to reach and communicate with them in their most favorable frame of mind.

On the other hand, I could appeal to the person in you that would be pissed off. I could appeal to the person in you that's frustrated. Regardless of whether you're distracted, angry, or whatever, I can either fuel your current state of mind or I can allow for it to be there but reach you inside and connect with another part of you. It's a matter of intention.

Underneath it all, I believe we are all fundamentally the same, and we want the same things:

- We want to love and be loved.
- We want to be taken seriously.
- We want to have fun.
- We want something worthwhile to do with our life.
- We want to have enough money to do the things we want to do.
- We want to express ourselves authentically.

If you can set your distractions aside for a moment and accept their distractions, you can reach through the facade of their mood and talk to the person inside. This is not a technique like learning the perfect script. "Gee, I see you're angry, can you set that aside for a moment?" It's something you have to feel. Connect your humanness with theirs.

Realize that they aren't frustrated with you, even if they are—even if you are the focal point of their anger. By knowing you can, by expecting that you can, always be able to appeal to the good side in every person. Appeal to the essence of the person in everyone you come into contact with and you will usually connect with the being who wants what we all want.

Business Black Belt Notes

- Fundamentally, as humans, we want the same things.

- Our mechanism works the same, our experiences make us different.

- There is a part of me that can connect to a part of you.

- Set your distractions aside, focus on the other person, look past their distraction to the person inside.

Emergency Response

Experience your greatness, not your self-doubt.
— Ron Bynum, Essence Partners

☞ There are a variety of situations that take me by surprise. My inability to effectively respond has allowed me to either miss a wonderful opportunity or agree to something I'd later regret.

What compelled me to write this section was a chance encounter with a beautiful woman when I acted like a deer frozen in the headlights. This has happened to me a number of times before and until now, it never occurred to me to develop a response that I could practice and use in emergencies. (Being a single male looking for the ideal woman—this situation seemed like an emergency.) [8]

To give another example, I recently hired a consultant, only to realize soon thereafter that he was incapable of doing the work and that we really didn't need it or him anyway. Like most entrepreneurs and successful business managers, I have a bias for action. Every project is critical and I want to do them immediately. Combining that need with a good sales pitch by someone who seems capable of giving me what I want adds up to a potential problem, if not a disaster.

---

[8] I owe the emergency response concept to Darshan Mayginnes, who helped me develop several great responses to salespeople and employees.

In both of these situations, I am susceptible to trying to wing it. They seem like great ideas at the time but since I haven't thought them through or been able to plan for them, I take the easiest route. In the case of the woman, I did nothing. In the case of the consultant, I said OK. I never realized that there are situations where my brain runs off down the street and I should have a practiced response that I can immediately use to ensure the appropriate action without having to think about it. It's almost like a fire drill. You don't expect to have a fire, and you know it will happen unexpectedly. You'll probably panic when it does but if you're prepared in advance, you'll know exactly what to do automatically.

I do have an emergency response for pushy salespeople promoting deals that are too good to be true, etc. "I don't make decisions like these impulsively. I'm going to think about this and get back to you. And here are a few things I need answered. . . . Here are a few things I need to do. . . . Here are a few things I need to know. . . ." This response keeps me from making mistakes, inadvertently shuffling priorities, spending money where I shouldn't, and distracting my employees from other projects that are equally or more important. It also helps to take the salesperson out of the "pitch" mode and put them into an "engineering" mode. I tell them that I'm sold on the concept, but I need help integrating their product or service into my business (or whatever). If they persist with a pitch—more convincing and less listening to understand and help with my situation—then I see red flags. Their deal will last a few days or a few weeks so I can take my time.

When to be prepared

(Here's a short list I prepared for myself)
- When introducing yourself to a room full of people and telling them who you are and what you do—in thirty seconds.
- Introducing yourself to potential business contacts at a party.
- When your airplane engine quits at 7,500 feet.
- When a maître'd seats you at a poor choice of tables.
- If someone grabs your girlfriend's purse.

Obviously, this list can be a long one, but think of a situation that you should be prepared for and plan a simple, no-brainer response.

Here is an example of my thirty-second introduction:

Hi, my name is Burke Franklin. I'm the president of JIAN software. We develop and publish a line of powerful software to help you build your business. Our key product is BizPlanBuilder, which is a complete software package to help you write a compelling business plan for investors, bankers, senior management, or even your employees. It takes advantage of your word processing and spreadsheet programs on both Windows and Macintosh and sells for about $99.

Rare opportunities from rare situations

The point here is to understand that there are situations where you have blind spots and are susceptible to stupidity. If you honestly reflect on past situations, you should be able to recognize yours. Take a moment to *write* down a description of a situation and then list what the parameters of a good response would include or look like. From there you can create a statement you can readily use while your brain and common sense are down the street. It's a lot like writing and rehearsing a script for a special scene in a movie. At this point you will have disengaged yourself from acting like a deer frozen in the headlights. The mild panic state will be sidestepped and you can think creatively enough to take the next step.

The key is recognizing you have a problem, developing a method to deal with it, and then practicing it so you can deliver it without thinking. Ask people you trust to give you honest feedback.

It's showtime

The first step in the process is to center yourself. If this is an emergency, you don't have time to meditate for an hour, but you can prepare an instant meditation that will work. Take a moment to search your memory banks for a place and time in life where you were completely happy. No worries, no criticisms, and everything is great. There I am, five years old, swinging in an old tire hanging from an apple tree at my grandparents farm in Northern California in the summer. Where are you, what are you doing, what is around you, who is there, when is it, how old are you? Build a complete scene. This is your "happy place." Keep this as a handy film clip in your head that you can refer to anytime you want. Go to your happy place. When I go to my happy place before I hit a golf ball, I'm amazed at my results. Going to your happy place does wonders for your state of mind and your capacity to think under pressure. Also, the energy you exude in this process will be clean, free of any fear, anger, anxiety, and other things that might put people off. Now you are ready to implement the response you've developed. If you're worried about potentially dangerous situations on the street, most martial arts or self-defense training will prepare to you respond with a good move without thinking.

The flip side—Just Say No

The reasons you give for why you can't do something only offer a handle for someone else to use to coerce you to do what they want. They can use your reasons against you—argue their value judgments to discount your reasons— as if the reasons you give are less important than the favor they are asking of you. You run the risk of getting into a debate about the value of your reasons instead of how you might creatively solve their problem. In the privacy of your own mind, make your decision: yes or no. If it's no, say no. The more reasons you give, the more you expose yourself to being dragged into something you don't want to do.

Business Black Belt Notes

- Identify the emergency, compulsion, or fatal attraction.

- Establish the parameters for your emergency response.

- Plan and practice your response so you can do it without thinking.

- When the situation occurs, go to your "happy place" and follow your script.

- Make decisions without necessarily giving your reasons.

Lead, Follow, or Get Out of the Way

And when we think we lead, we are most led.
— Lord Byron, poet

☞ Much is said about leadership and leaders, and about the value of being a good follower or student. In martial arts, much attention is paid to getting out of the way. This concept has value in business as well as everyday life.

I was reading an article in *Fortune* magazine and saw a picture of Ted Turner in his office. In about three places he had a plaque that read "Lead, follow, or get out of the way." If you don't know what to do—maybe you're just starting—the best thing to do is just get out of the way of others who *are* moving. This chapter is not about leading or following, but about getting out of the way.

Think of driving on the highway. You see some guy who is in a hurry and you're not. Get out of people's way. When I'm in a hurry or making a business go, I want non-contributing people to just get out of the way. Let me get done what I need to get done. If you're living by the rule of "What goes around, comes around" and people are still slowing you down, you'd better take a second look at how you might be slowing others down.

You're probably going too fast and if you continue, you'll get into an accident and die, perhaps taking a couple of other people with you. If you're in a hurry to drive somewhere and all the lanes are crowded with slowpokes and you're stuck, go with the flow. Chances are everybody is slowing you down for a reason. Whenever I'm in traffic and all lanes are slowing me down, I think, "There must be a cop around here somewhere." And nine times out of ten, sure enough, these slow drivers I was pissed at have just saved me from a speeding ticket.

It's important for all of us to respect those who are in a hurry. It's a necessity of consciousness even if you're not focusing or in a hurry, but you recognize those who are. Get out of their way, knowing that it'll come back to you sometime in the future. I believe you can consciously generate positive karma. You can build the karma flowing in your direction so when you want to go, everybody will be out of your way.

I see it happen on the road. I see a guy come zipping up behind me flashing his lights. I think, "Boy, that guy must be in a hurry to go to the airport." I'm just going out to the store, so I get out of his way rather than be a jerk and impose my so-called right to hog the lane. I know there are times when I need to get somewhere in a hurry and want other people to get out of my way and let me through. It never ceases to amaze me how well this works and I remember to practice this principle.

In business, someone may want my assistance or permission for something they want. It may not be strategically relevant to me at the time, but I know it's important to them so I give it to them. I know that sometimes I'm going to need some strategic assistance, that it may not help someone else's business interests, but at least they'll help me by getting out of my way. The opportunity for this seems to happen in every management meeting. Somebody wants to do something—I say, "OK." It's part of letting go— what every entrepreneur is asked to do to allow his or her staff to contribute to build the business. I'm not talking about making a big effort. It's just recognizing someone else is in a hurry or on a mission. I don't need to get involved in everything.

I could make a product that another company sells because it seems like it would go with my business. But I'm not going to do that just because I'm envious that they have a product and I don't. For example, I could make accounting software. I know my customers are business owners and would probably buy it from me since they buy other software from me. But I'm not going to gum up the market with yet another accounting product to confuse customers or impede another company. I'm not going to make accounting companies have to compete with me, unless I know I could really make a difference and sell something much better to my customers. Why should I screw up the market for others just to be there?

Some companies do that. People buy trademarks in other countries just to sell it to you, when you get there. These are the jerks who won't let you pass them on the freeway. It's OK though, they're creating bad karma for themselves. It'll just come back to nip them in the butt. If you get in other people's way, you're going to find people in your way too. (Sometimes, I just wish I could see them get theirs!)

In martial arts, getting out of someone's way is a useful tactic. If somebody big is coming at you head-on, step aside, and they'll go right by. There is an art to getting out of the way. The idea is to do it with minimum effort and motion—even guide them past you. You don't want to get run over. Nature respects this art. So get out of the way and you won't get run over either.

Business Black Belt Notes

- When someone is in a hurry, get out of their way. Think of it as a karmic investment.

- If "things" are slowing you down, there must be a good reason— perhaps you're going in the wrong direction and need to look around, so take it easy.

- If you want others to get into your market and injure your sales, do the same to them.

- Choose your engagements carefully. Many things you can let go by.

Leadership?

*You better know where you're going
because sooner or later, you could be out in front.*

☞ How will you lead your business and how will your business lead
your industry?

I've heard that there are more than 500 books on leadership—and none of
them agree on what leadership is! I used to think leadership was leading a
group of marines over the hill by saying, "Come on, men. Let's go!" I was
afraid to be a leader. What if they said, "No, we don't want to follow you"?
How would I feel? Like a lousy leader.

Real leaders, I thought, are people like General Norman Schwarzkopf or
Billy Graham who have thousands of devout followers. However, at the same
time, I have been skeptical of leaders and had thoughts about their ineptness.
Like one CEO of a computer company, who at the dawn of the computer rev-
olution, refused to make his computers DOS-compatible and with that single decision, murdered a $200 million company. Which kind of leader would
I be? And what would others think about me? How could I become a
successful and respected leader? Let's talk about first preparing yourself for
leadership.

Let's say your company is a market leader or wants to be. The problem
many leaders experience when they're in this position is "What do I do
next?" Most people can follow a market leader by copying them, knocking

them off or by focusing on a competitive niche. But once in front, will they know how to carry the torch?

The following story illustrates the uncomfortable situation you could find yourself in if you're not prepared for leadership.

My friends and I were in a sailboat race in the San Francisco Bay. We had to follow a race course marked by buoys in a pre-defined sequence that was only disclosed at the start of the race. This was done by raising a series of nautical flags. Since my friends and I were not great sailors, we weren't taking winning this race too seriously. Consequently, we missed the nautical flags that spelled out the race course, but we decided not to worry about it, just to have fun, and follow the other boats.

The race started, we were sailing along, actually doing very well. Lo and behold, by about the second buoy, we passed the lead boat in our class! Now, without knowing the race course, we didn't know where we were going. There was some finger-pointing and heated conversation, because now we actually had a chance to win this race. We took a guess and sailed off into the distance. When we looked behind us and saw the number two boat turn left and make for the finish line we realized we'd made a wrong turn. By the time we corrected our course and crossed the finish line, we were dead last.

Leadership is knowing where to go when there is no one else to follow.

This experience hit me like a ton of bricks. I believe this also happens often in business. One way of doing business is to go into a marketplace and compete. You establish your market position with whatever competitive advantages you have and race against your competitors. With hard work you may find yourself a market leader.

Another way of establishing a successful business is simply to create a market, which is what JIAN did. When you create a market, there are no leaders. You've got a new product. You've got no one to compare to and no one to follow.

We rarely think we might be in a leadership position when we start something. We think surely others are there ahead of us and that it's been done before.

Although many things have been done before, what are you going to do when you're in the lead position? It takes foresight. Pay attention and definitely plan your course. You could start in an industry where you are the 1,000th-ranked company. Eventually you might work up to the top. Now what would you do? Prepare yourself to be in the lead, because it just might happen.

What takes you over the top and inspires people to support you

Most people are looking for direction, and they just want you to give it to them. Where does this come from?

I find that we must first have an overwhelmingly inspirational reason for being in business in the first place. I occasionally demoralize, insult, and disempower my employees on my way to learning how to be a brilliant and inspirational leader. But what keeps them around is that, overall, what we are doing has significant meaning to the world. And I'm intent on improving myself constantly as well offering them opportunities to grow. The experts who help us develop our software are very helpful. We enroll employees in seminars. We even sponsor karate lessons. But we do more than just sell business software, we're convinced that we are improving the way business is done everywhere in the world.

> *My vision is to facilitate compatible business*
> *practices throughout the world,*
> *enabling us all to easily do business together.*

Just because I think I am doing good is no excuse to be ruthless. I must correct my mistakes and learn. If you have a worthy purpose or create one for your business, something greater than just making money, you'll enjoy a sense of direction in which to lead that will unite many people in support of your vision. This isn't something you can fake—people can tell.

Tell your customers, too

You have a progression of experiences that have led you to where you are today. These experiences contain the elements of what drives you. We've found that briefly telling our story to our customers is a compelling and powerful emotional message that provides solid credibility about what we're doing. It's important for people to know about the origins of our business so they can make an informed buying decision. A survey of our ads a couple of years ago revealed that customers responded with "Interesting products. . . never heard of the company. . . I like the products, but I don't know much about the people who make them. . . . Looks good, where did the company come from?" When we included a brief paragraph describing our background, sales increased dramatically. People can relate to your motivations. Your customers likely share your frustrations and will appreciate the solutions you're selling. In the book, *The Soul of a Business* by Tom Chapell about Tom's of Maine®, the company that makes the natural soaps, deodorants, and toothpaste, Tom confirms this through his own focus group research. Their customers state that they buy from Tom's of Maine because they share Tom and his wife's interest in natural products. The Tom's of Maine story is a crucial element in all of their marketing and packaging materials. Your reason for being in business is a strong motivator for people and will keep you on track as you move forward on your way to business success.

If you read my brief story in the front of this book, you understand why I'm in business, and why I wrote this book. Let me take it a step further by stating our "big hairy audacious goal," a concept from the book, *Built to Last* by James C. Collins and Jerry I. Porras.

By the year 2000, we will have contributed to the success of one million customers.

We developed this goal as a group and everyone is behind it. At the time of writing this book, 2000 is three years away and we have 150,000 customers in our database. For the goal to be met, we need confirmation of our contribution to each customer's success! Also, recognizing the importance of such a goal, we added the following core values to build a foundation from which all of us are inspired to come to work every day:

- *Integrity*: Honest, committed internal and external relationships. Feel your feelings. Do what's right for ourselves and our customers. Tell the truth. It's amazing when people can express their feelings about things or ideas without fear that they may cause harm in some way or get in trouble.

- *Full Self-Expression*: Respectful communication of creativity, ideas, concerns. Freedom to express ideas, concerns, and possibilities.

- *Constant Improvement*: Ensure quality and productivity across all areas in the company. Seek knowledge and apply it to ourselves, our customers, processes, and products. Some people like to keep things the way they are. Others see ways to improve them. This core value enables anyone in the company to make suggestions to anyone else. And they do.

- *Discipline*: Define, refine, execute, measure and complete all activities in support of agreed-upon goals and objectives. It's easy to lose focus and do whatever is interesting today. Or embark on a half-baked project only to be distracted by the next half-baked project. This core value empowers everyone to say, "Hey, wait a minute...!"

- *Sound Decision Making*: We make decisions we L.I.K.E. Our decisions are based on Logic, Instinct, Knowledge and Experience.

- Acknowledgment and Appreciation: We regularly acknowledge and appreciate ourselves, fellow employees, customers, vendors, and partners for the contribution made in support of JIAN's vision.

These core values define who we are and how we will behave as we progress toward our "big hairy audacious goal." You can establish these for your business by yourself, but as you add employees, it is much more powerful to start with a blank sheet and co-create them together. This also helps establish why you and your products are worth higher prices and a higher profit in your market.

Business Black Belt Notes

- Know where you're going because sooner or later you could be out in front.

- Leadership is knowing what to do when you have no one to follow.

- Learn as much as possible about the course before competing in any race.

- Have or develop a higher purpose for your business that you and others can really get behind.

- Tell your company story in your ads and on your packaging—share your passion.

- Develop your goals and core values with your employees—have them create them.

Management by Centrifugal Force

"Come to the edge,"
he said.
"We are afraid,"
they said.
"Come to the edge,"
he said.
They came. . .
He pushed them
. . . and they flew.

☞ Here's how to think of your business structure, regardless of the structure you actually have, and have what you want done the way you want it while still empowering your employees to be creative.

This has been my most difficult chapter to write. I've read a variety of books on management, listened to a lot of advice, and learned quite a bit in seminars. As a manager of others in a large corporation, I saw myself as an intermediary between my employees and upper management. Policies came down from up high. These weren't my ideas—I just had to facilitate their implementation. When money had to be spent, it wasn't my money, it belonged to a ubiquitous corporate owner. *Talking* about management is easy (Theory X, Y, and Z). But managing your own company seems to be something else entirely.

Having no upper management to blame from time to time for "stupid policies" removes the safety net. Being emotionally involved as the head of your own company makes it difficult to simply be a textbook manager. As the boss, you are in charge and as such, you are the *source* of these policies and ultimately responsible for developing good ones as well as enforcing them. Let's start here: in the March 18, 1996 issue of *Fortune* magazine (I recommend grabbing a copy or getting one via the Internet at http://pathfinder.com/@@3V*oPgUApjg8 Usul/fortune/), Hubert Saint Onge says it best when he identifies nine dilemmas leaders face (I added my own experience beneath his headings):

1) Broad–based leadership vs. high-visibility leaders

Should top executives lead with their own charisma or should they foster leadership throughout the company with middle managers, team members, and others?

2) Independence vs. interdependence

How do you promote entrepreneurship, a sense of ownership, and P&L responsibility while at the same time encouraging managers to give up some of their turf in order to work together?

3) Long term vs. short term

We have both a five-year vision and a sales goal for this month. Quarterly numbers mean little to me—how much did we sell today, this week, this month? By the way, how are we coming on those projects that will build our business to $100 million?

4) Creativity vs. discipline

My employees encourage me to empower them to do things their way. I ask them to measure everything they do and analyze the results, so we follow-up and expand on what's working and stop doing what doesn't work.

5) Trust vs. change

I feel it's my job to maintain the vision and watch the landscape for opportunities to build our business. Just when people get settled in, we often see a need to shuffle people around and change our priorities. It causes problems and the explanations aren't always clear, but I feel I'm doing the right things.

6) Bureaucracy busting vs. economies of scale

Our CFO needs to know who's buying what so she can allocate cash and make sure we pay our vendors on time—this begets a process of budgeting and POs that slows things down. However, someone can walk a PO through the system to get something they need right away.

7) People vs. productivity

How many people do we really need? What can we outsource and will the contractors do a better job for less (less headaches too)? Do we hire a great manager and a bunch of doers or do we look for player-coach types?

8) Leadership vs. capability

At what point do we stop discussing strategy and go do something? As a visionary and strategist myself, I have a hard time staying put long enough to get any one thing done. I have capable people, but their projects need to be prioritized and coordinated with each other to move in the direction I want to go.

9) Revenue growth vs. cost containment

How much money must you spend to make money? How much energy goes into saving a marginal expense when that same creativity and effort could generate ten times the sales?

There seems to be a profound difference between managing a company and leading one. As I write this chapter, I have 26 employees, with a management team of 6. Here are some practical things you can do as your company's leader that will help you get done what you want to get done and preserve your sanity, as well as make your employees happy. The first step is in how you conceptualize your organization.

Management: The Concentric Circles Model

Look around you at Nature. The universe is organized in circles. Round planets orbit stars, and stars orbit in our galaxy.

Management should flow with the universe. The physical translation of circular management works for people in a nicer way. Employees can feel buried under a pyramid structure; information flows (or trickles) down, and the physical perception of gravity can have a negative effect on the employees' thinking. "It's a long way to the top. I've got to work my way up." Gravity is heavy, serious, and no fun.

What happens as a company grows? I've seen communication deteriorate the further it travels from the source (top management), and I've seen it accelerate. The employees who greet the customers can actually be more intense than the company president! In a top-down, pyramid structure, gravity fights against information flowing back up. If it's circular and flat, things go out, but things can also come back in.

The concentric structure has a low center of gravity allowing it to move and respond to the marketplace with greater agility. Information is managed at a central location (like a file server), marketing goals emanate from one place (where consistency and quality can be maintained), and communication can flow in and out easily. In this way, energy is conserved. The goals and direction of the company are set by the central leadership while perimeter employees meeting the public have more flexibility to adapt to their individual markets. Most companies can be viewed this way, but this point of view must be genuinely endorsed if not originated by central leadership for it to be widely adopted throughout your organization. When everyone—employees and management—shares the picture of this new structure (a right-brain spatial perception), everyone can enjoy a new level comfort in communicating throughout the organization.

Communication by centrifugal force

Let's say I have an idea and I give it to my VP of R&D who adds his thoughts. My VP of Sales is there and he has some ideas to add. The original idea has picked up speed and mass and is swirling around me. As these VPs leave the meeting, they begin to discuss it with others—the idea picks up

more speed, is further refined, and is carried along with even
more intensity.

I visualize how my company is set up, and I don't see a
pyramid or a matrix. I see people around me in a circle with
others beyond them. There is no rigid hierarchy. Many are at
the same level and we can all relate to each other as human beings. We are
all in the middle of our own circles with each other orbiting around.

This seems to emulate more how the universe works instead of the ineffective way humans have concocted things.

At JIAN, we think in terms of people around us. We don't have people
below us. We've shifted our thinking to look out and see people more equally because we're on the same plane. I look at my salespeople, at people in
their universe, at the people in my controller's universe. My salespeople and
my controller are certainly in my universe, their planets circle around the sun
(me) and we all have our own little moons.

I think we create a healthier perspective when we do business from this
point of view. It's a more humane style of management. We're all at the center of our own universe, so this way of thinking can work for everyone.

At first, in my own organization, I felt uncomfortable behaving in an
"I'm from a higher level and therefore better at what you do than you." If you
see yourself in a hierarchy looking down, then you must be better than everyone else. From there, how can you hire people who can do their job better
than you? In a concentric style, you can handle looking out and seeing people who are at your same level but are experts in their own field.

I'm able to see and respect others for who they are and what they can do.
I don't have to worry about how I'm going to convince them to work *under*
me. That's always a tall order. It's also another reason many people avoid
leadership positions. They don't want to be "up on a pedestal" because it
seems to make them a target.

It took me a while to complete this book because I needed to include a
section on management. I sucked as a manager. A visionary, yes, an entrepreneur, yes. But as a manager, I wasn't accomplished at anything and my
employees weren't doing what I wanted them to do the way I wanted it done.
Allow yourself to be an explorer. If you're a know-it-all, everything must go
through you. If you lead the expedition into the unknown, point out the pos-

sibilities, and let people respond to the opportunities, they will feel compelled to jump on the opportunities and solve the problems.

The method behind the madness

I wrongly expect people to see things immediately the way I see them. After I quickly explain what we're doing and where we're going, I expect people to grab the ball and run with it. That doesn't always happen.

You need to figure out how to communicate your vision and paint the picture. The problem with entrepreneurs and visionaries is that often they are so far ahead of everyone else. They're not leading just one step ahead, they're leading ten steps ahead. They've already gone over the horizon and everyone is left wondering where to go.

Show them what it all means

My CFO recently sent me an e-mail suggesting that I'd lost my marbles. I wrote back a two-page e-mail explaining my whole strategy behind our program to have a database on our Web site where our customers could look up professional business advisors in their area at the push of a button. I realized that her note was also a little message to me that I needed to explain my vision. And when I did that, she and everyone else could understand what I wanted to do. What she and everyone else needed to understand, perhaps, was the method behind my madness. I needed to invest some time in explaining my logic. In the process, my logic became clearer to me as well.

I've spelled out in writing the long-term vision of the company, where we're going, the big picture, and where each person's job fits into that picture. They need to see their jobs in the context of everything else. This process works well when you include your key management people and guide them to come up with the words to articulate the vision, strategies and priorities they will be responsible for.

> *Everyone has a right to understand the purpose of his actions*
> Russ Varian, Varian Associates

Often, a visionary entrepreneur will think he or she is doing this grandiose thing with tremendous importance for everyone on our planet, but they gloss over it very fast. They expect everyone around them to immediately grasp the importance of their dream. In the visionary's mind, the picture is in color and perfectly clear. It's so obvious, and such a no-brainer because they see how it fits into the big picture. But those around them must also fully understand their vision and see it as well as the visionary does. You cannot over communicate your vision. With the big picture in place, you can get on with the details.

If you ever want to take a vacation, work on different projects, or simply enable yourself to grow your business, you must have some smart people around to take on the business. For the longest time, I thought I was the smartest person on earth. "If you want it done right, then you have to do it yourself," I always heard. Then I realized that I had nothing to do with building a bridge, designing the Boeing 747, or any advances in medicine. Other people on the planet must be smart or even smarter than me!

> *It's better to get something done their way*
> *than nothing done your way.*

The limits and components of doing it my way

Usually I want everything done the way I would do it. It's sometimes disturbing to watch someone do something in a way that I would never do it. Their way isn't going to work. Or is it? I have talked about spelling out the big picture. Now, the employees are supposed to grab the ball and run with it. And, in the interest of getting results without doing all the work myself, and trying to reconcile doing things my way or allowing them to do it their way, I've discovered there's some latitude as to how things can be done.

First, give the outside *boundaries* that the person cannot go beyond. For example, you can discount the product, but you cannot go more than 10%. This discount is your limit. Period. The salesperson has some flexibility; because they're being paid a commission, it's up to them how flexible they are.

Next, there are some specific *ingredients*: Your parameter is no more than 10% off, but you must always mention the fact that our software works with any Windows and Macintosh word-processing and spreadsheet applications. You must always mention that we have a 60-day money-back guarantee. However you pitch it beyond that, go for it, but you must mention those two things, and you can't go more than 10% off. With those key ingredients, the sales person can go pitch it, and I know my key ingredients have been met.

What we found out early on is that our customers really wanted to customize our software to fit their business using the word-processing and spreadsheet software they already had. Therefore, our salespeople must include those concepts, among others, in their presentation.

> *Things that go without saying,*
> *often go without doing.*

I can't afford to let employees learn from their mistakes

My style has been to see a problem and immediately begin throwing potential solutions at it. What about this? What if we did that? I pride myself on my creativity, my ability to solve problems. As the company president, I also enjoy a vantage point where I can see all the areas of the business. As a visionary (i.e., I can see how the company might do things in the future and what it might look like), I think I see the problem differently. I see more facets to the problem even after asking people to more fully explain their perspective, therefore I must come up with the solution or therefore I come up with the best solution. . . . And since I don't think my people have the full perspective, how can I let them figure it out on their own? You're probably wondering how long I can do this. How big can the company get if I have to be in on every problem? I'm wondering too.

The management books say to let the employees figure it out, let them make mistakes, let them learn. At whose expense?! This is a problem, especially when you think you have the answers. And your employees [will] resent you for always jumping in. You may think your behavior teaches them to solve problems. . . why can't/don't they learn from you? Actually, you're training them to wait. Wait for you to solve the problem because you always do. Why should they even try? By shotgunning solutions, you also confuse them. Which one are you going to go with? What are you really thinking? Rather than solving the problems, I've created chaos.

Here's my new method that has been working: Using my perceptions and perspective of a problem, I restrict my input to asking questions. I guide the problem-solving session by asking employees how certain criteria can be met. By asking questions, I guide them around or toward problems that must be addressed and I ask them for the solutions. My premise is that if they fully understand the problem like I feel I do, then they will come up with a better answer. And it's their answer.

An example:

We were discussing "advertising specialties," promotional giveaways for trade shows and for the salespeople in the retail stores. Items included hats, T-shirts, luggage tags, business card holders, chocolate, plastic shopping/literature bags, etc. We all had a lot of good ideas, but certain criteria needed to be met. I could exercise my authority as president to dictate what we should do, but I wanted the team to come up with something they all felt good about. Rather than throw out a few ideas of my own that I knew would address some issues I was concerned about, I explained the issue and asked that they come up with ideas which addressed my concerns. Our T-shirts needed to say something our customers wanted to express (not what we wanted to promote). Our giveaways had to be things our customers would keep and use, as well as prefer over other similar items given away by other companies. The group eliminated the chocolate and the cheap plastic shopping bags.

Leading by asking questions and setting certain parameters has them thinking about more things. They understand what concerns me and can make better decisions on their own in the future. Do not make suggestions— use your knowledge and experience to ask questions to lead your employees to solutions.

Stay loose

You probably come up with solutions to problems fairly quickly. You've got your answer, why keep talking about it? Depending on the magnitude of your problem, you may need to engage your management team in further discussion. Besides, you pay them to manage certain parts of your business and their input is valuable. Sitting through a meeting when you think you've already made up your mind is difficult. The trick is allowing others to arrive at the answer so they feel the credit for it and will drive it through to completion. Equally tricky is allowing someone else to come up with a better solution. If you present your solution and make your stand, to accept a better solution requires backing down and possibly losing face. Of course to avoid backing down will require considerable debate, which only digs your hole deeper. Not taking a stand too quickly or too soon enables you to objectively evaluate the possibilities first, develop consensus and then take a stand as a team. No egos get engaged and the process flows smoothly. And you won't be the only one driving the project forward.

Opinion vs. point of view

I've discovered a semantic phenomenon. I ask for a lot of input before I make a decision. I ask, "What do you think about X?" And I often get a wide range of answers with an equally wide range of emotional attachment to those answers. When my decision goes contrary to someone's input, they naturally get upset. "You didn't listen to me," they say. The problem I've found is that I've asked for their *opinion* rather than positioned my questions as asking for their *point of view*. Opinions carry more emotional baggage than do points of view. Asking for a person's point–of–view leaves open the possibility of asking for more points of view. Opinions can be argued. Points of view can't. If you enjoy lengthy debates that can never be resolved, engage people's opinions. And the battle will still rage after a decision has been made. I don't have time for that. I ask, "What's your point of view? And what else should I consider?" People know their issues have been included and they understand that you will be soliciting others as well. A decision can be made without a raging debate, especially when I use the issues as guidelines to let the team come up with the course of action. I step in to break a deadlock or when it's clearly my call.

Include your team from the beginning

We formed a team to develop an entirely new system to take and fulfill orders, provide product support and customer service, and generate reports. We held several meetings to lay the foundation and discuss a few of the parameters. Our next meeting couldn't be scheduled for several weeks due to business trips, but in the meantime I met with an old friend, who I knew was an excellent systems guy. In my mind, I was having him over to take a look at what we were up to, have our internal Information Systems Manager size up his technical skills for the project, and generally see what a few of our options were. I had the meeting without the team, thinking that I would give him the big picture and get some facts and figures before our next team meeting. I got so excited that I went ahead and hired him to do an initial study and develop a preliminary system plan. When the other team members heard about what I had done, they went ballistic. What was the point of having a team if I was going to go ahead and do whatever I wanted without consulting them? To them, it looked as if I was proceeding without their input. To me, my buddy wasn't ready for their input—he had homework to do so when we did meet, we would have fleshed out our options and could proceed with the details. What I should have done is inform the team that I found an outside expert whom I wanted them to meet. He was coming in to see what we were up to and we were going to interview him as to what he could provide. As I look back on this, this quick impromptu meeting may have enabled the other team members to allow the outside expert to handle some of their homework due for the next meeting as well. Even if you insist that it's your company and you can do whatever the hell you want, if you want to grow past your capacity to do everything, you'll need to allow your people to be involved. Let them contribute even if you perceive that it delays the process. In the long run, it's a good investment in time and sanity.

What if we moved the company to Hawaii?

For the longest time, I wanted people to take me seriously, take my advice, do what I wanted them to do, and give me what I wanted. Maybe this has never been a problem for you before, but as a CEO, business owner, or successful businessperson, you must be careful of what you say more than ever.

I sometimes forget that I am in a position of authority. I want to run my ideas by whomever is in front of me at the time. When I think out loud, people wonder if I'm really going to act on what I'm thinking. Is the company really going to move to Hawaii? Are we going to launch a new HR product? Be careful when you ask what you think are harmless "what if" questions—your employees will wonder what if you really went ahead and did what you're asking "what if" about. Rumors start and pretty soon the whole company is distracted. Then you have to reassure each person of what you are really thinking and doing.

Now, when I want to brainstorm or ask a "what if" question, I first look around at who my audience is and who else is within earshot. Where might their minds go if I ask a theoretical "what if" question? It takes a lot of self-control to contain my idea if my audience isn't right. Even when it is, I preface loudly that, "this is just a 'what if' question, a loose thought, and I'm only doing research" and "I'm not making any decisions right now." I wait a moment for their minds to clear and then I ask, "What do you think of X?" I find that the feedback is excellent. Afterwards, I ask them what they would recommend. This is also an excellent way to involve people and to prevent unwarranted rumors.

This is similar to my recommendations on whom to ask for advice, yet it may also be useful to ask a "what if" question of otherwise unqualified people in the interest of market research to measure the general response to your idea.

Letting Go

Yikes! You've built your company from scratch, but it's reaching a point where you just can't do it all anymore and people around you are muttering something about you needing to "let go." Yeah, you'd like to, but what will happen? Your worst fears—certainly everything will go wrong. Or maybe others will pick up the ball and run with it.

Often when building our companies we have something to prove. We feel we are smart, competent, can do it better than the other guy, or our previous boss didn't get it—watch this. If you have something to prove, go ahead and prove it—it's productive motivation to work from. Temporarily. At some point, you will have proved your point. If you continue proving yourself for any of the above reasons, it's like continuing a sales pitch long after the customer wants to buy. It's really annoying. When you realize that you have established your proof, this is a time when you can begin to "let go"—allow others to come into being, allow them to prove themselves in the way you once did. What is the next step for you?

> ### I can't die. It would be bad for my image.
> — Jack Lalanne, legendary exercise personality

I have so much juice built up on proving my point that it's become a habit. You do this for ten years or longer and proving your point becomes your way of life. But when you realize you've proved your point, then you can let go of it and move on and do something you really wanted to do.

What is the position or point of view that I'm really trying to prove or hang on to? What happens if I let it go? As CEO, I can set it up so I can go in any new direction I choose. I'm hiring a COO, an experienced business manager, to run the operations of my company. Now I'll have more time to work on products, give seminars, travel and invent new things.

Business Black Belt Notes

- The old pyramid structure of management may not work for you.

- When you structure your business like the universe—in a circle or a sphere —information can flow in and out easily.

- You don't put people above or below you—you put them around you.

- Inform and include your team from the beginning if you want to maintain their support for your project.

- Differentiate between personal opinions and points of view.

- Introduce an idea, but let it float until all the ideas have been introduced—then you can more objectively choose the best idea.

- Use your perspective to guide your people to solve problems, so you don't have to pay for their mistakes or train them to wait for you to figure it out.

- Consider your audience before asking "what if" questions.

- Have you proved the point you set out to prove? Perhaps it's time to move on to the next thing. How can you set up your company to support you in doing that?

Meeting with a Purpose

Meetings without decisions are like foreplay without sex.

☞ **Who is going to do what, when, and where is it written down?**

We used to have a lot of meetings at JIAN. We used to hate them, because we were always meeting and not getting our work done. We weren't seeing meetings from a healthy perspective.

I'm sure meetings were originally devised for the right purpose, we've just lost track of that purpose. Actually, meetings are real time-savers. They're an opportunity to give the same explanation to several people instead of repeating it over and over again to each individual. Many people avoid meetings as a waste of time, and most meetings seem to be. I want to get away from this paradigm that meetings are a waste of time. If you look at meetings for what they really can be, you can put them to much better use. They become more pertinent, you get a lot out of them, and you will need them less often.

Instead of repeating yourself five times to five different people, put them all in a room and say it once. They all get it; you move on. Meetings should be designed in such a way that only the people who need to know are in the room at that time. We used to have one or two long meetings a week. Now we have three or four shorter meetings every week with just the right people who need to share information. In certain meetings, we just talk about pertinent subjects for the people who need to know. During general management meetings on Monday mornings, the management team gets together.

It's not so much show-and-tell, more like the Mission Impossible meeting. We all get together and figure out what we're going to do. Everybody leaves knowing who's doing what and what's going on.

Communication like this is very important. In many companies, the right hand doesn't know what the left hand is doing. In our marketing meetings at JIAN, the marketing manager, the controller, and our salespeople talk about our budget and about sales. No one from R&D is there so we're not wasting their time.

A meeting is a means of exchanging information among people to save time. Meetings need to be structured so that they're more efficient. At JIAN, we have agendas for our meetings. We have a list of action items we're going to talk about and we look at the list ahead of time so we know what's going to be talked about, what's coming up, and what materials to bring. Before we leave a subject, we have made a decision, someone's responsible for it, we know what the action is going to be and we know when the action is going to be taken. We don't just talk a lot about a subject and just move on to the next one without closure. A subject is not done without a decision that someone owns. We keep a list of action items and the people responsible for each item for next week's meeting when we go back and review. That way everybody knows they're on the hook and accountable. The secretary writes the notes, makes copies, and hands them out. The managers in the meeting can take those notes and give them to their staffs so everybody in the company can know what's going on.

Meetings are for decisions, not just for discussions

List the date any action item was put on your agenda. This way it won't remain there very long without causing severe embarrassment for its owner.

Having only five new items on each person's agenda forces everyone to prioritize. Sort by responsible person—when it's their turn in the meeting, you can review their progress on several actions at one time. Here's an example of the format we use:

Burke   8:30-8:55 AM   **Due:**

Current Action Items:
(These are things I'm working on right now and have a specific due date.)
1. x
2. x
3. x
4. x
5. x

Future Action Items:
(These are upcoming things I'm working on and it's useful for people to see what's coming up.)
1. x
2. x
3. x

New Items:
(These are the items that require a decision by the Management Team.)
1. x
2. x
3. x

Priorities
(These are overall things I'm working on.)
1. x
2. x
3. x

Announcements / Results:
(This is where I inform everyone of major events that have occurred.)
1. x
2. x

Decisions:
(This is a place for my notes on the conclusions that we reach.)

Requests:
(This is where I fill in specific requests that people have made of me.)
1. x
2. x

Action Items:
(These are the things that I will be responsible for next week and in the future)
1. x
2. x

Business Black Belt Notes

- Instead of repeating yourself many times, put everyone in a room together and say it once. In this way, meetings save time.

- Structure your meetings to include only the pertinent people without wasting others' time.

- Have an agenda for every meeting.

- Don't go on to the next subject until you make a decision and someone is responsible for it.

- Hand out the notes of the meeting so that everyone in the company or department has the big picture.

Hiring the Right People

There is something that is much more scarce, something finer far,
something rarer than ability. It is the ability to recognize ability.
—Elbert Hubbard, writer

☞ Before you hire anyone just to get some more things done, take some time to plan what you need done and who you need to hire.

The entrepreneurial hiring phenomenon

Here you are, building this business you started by yourself. Ideally, things are booming, which is why you're hiring an employee. You've got customers to take care of, you've got orders to fill, lots to do, and you need some help. You're so busy, and you need so much help that it's easy to ignore good hiring practices.

Here's what happens: A friend of a friend sends somebody over because you've been complaining about all the work you've got to do and how you wished you had some help. People start showing up on your doorstep, and since you are so busy doing what you got to do, you say, "Great, start here, work on this." And you hire them. Then somebody else comes along, and they can do a little something else, and you say, "Great! Go over there, do that." You start hiring these people almost indiscriminately because they solve what you see as your immediate problem, and that's just getting more done. You'll take almost anybody, because you're so desperate to get something done. The natural thing is to focus on your market, on your customers and getting the job done. Unfortunately, by doing only that, you shortcut the planning, selection, and hiring process.

To start, figure out what help you really need and what exactly you want each person to do. And then select the person who can best do the job.

Plan for complementary skills

Think about what would complement your skills and abilities. Maybe you're good at making the product, but not good at talking to customers. Sure enough, somebody comes along and says, "I can help you make that product." You hire them and then you go off and talk to customers. And there you are with somebody making the product when that's really your strength, and you're out selling, which is really not your strength. Although you should be busy selling, it's in your nature to work on the product, so you get in your employee's face and micro-manage production. To begin with, you really should have determined that you are good at making the product. Customers are buying the product because it's good. You need someone who can sell it better than you can. The person to hire should be a salesperson, so that you can make the product and let them sell it for you.

How do you find a good person? A Zen master would say, "When the student is ready, the teacher will appear." In your case, when the manager is ready, a good employee will appear. In my experience, I'm amazed at how I can spot a good person for the job when the job is clearly defined and I know exactly what I need done.

A choice must be made, and it goes something like this:

> *Who should do this job, them or me?*
> *If you've hired the right person,*
> *the immediate answer is them.*

Your hiring intention

When I walk onto a 747, I'm very certain that all of us on the flight are better off having the trained pilot fly the airplane instead of me. So, instead of walking up to the cockpit to fly the plane (manage), I go sit in back and relax. This should be your hiring intention. From the start of your hiring process, define the job and select a person to do it so well that you can relax. We sometimes lose sight of this reason for hiring people to work for us.

The job today. . . the job tomorrow

In the job description, figure out what exactly needs to be done. Some things need to be done immediately. Those are at the top of the job description. You may need someone to call on retail accounts now. You may need someone who can train retail salespeople. That's your problem today. Also consider what will need to be done in the next few years. You want to hire someone who can deliver what you need now as well as evolve and deliver what you will need in the future.

All the consultants and recruiters I've talked to say that the best judge of future performance is past performance. Education is not as important. What matters is that they have successfully handled what you want done before. Start with a list of the immediate things you need done. For example, if you need to hire a salesperson to train your resellers to sell your products—ask, "Tell me about your experience calling on retailers" or, "We need to train our resellers. How would you go about doing that?" The person you're hiring should have an answer to these questions. They're not giving up anything by giving you a detailed answer. One person I asked that question to said, "Well, that's what you're paying me for. If I answer that now, why would you hire me?" Wrong answer. I didn't ask her to do the job for nothing. I simply asked how she would go about it. I didn't want to learn how to do it myself, I wanted her to do the job, but I first wanted to get a feeling as to how she would operate. Her abrupt answer indicated to me that she would be difficult to work with.

You need to structure your interviews so you know what people would do on their own—left up to their own devices. That way, you can effectively delegate and empower people to do a good job. Otherwise, you'll never really know. Most people hire someone by telling them what they want done and trusting the applicant to respond honestly as to their ability to perform. "If I paid you a million dollars, could you run my company?" A better question for a COO candidate might be, "How do you justify expenditures?" I know what I think, but how and what does he or she think?

You are the casting director

The idea, at your level of the game, is to keep a constant watch for good people. This seems obvious, but our job (yours and mine) must be to recruit talent if we are ever going to build our businesses and keep our sanity. With almost every person I meet, I wonder to myself where he or she might fit into my company. With this thought, conversations take on a whole new meaning and importance to me. I pay much closer attention to people. I ask them questions based upon the assumption that they might be brilliant at something useful. Often, I find myself referring them to someone I know. You might even think of it like the card game "Concentration." You spread out all the cards face down on the table and take turns looking at each one—trying to remember which card is where to find a match and pick up the pair. This is how talent scouts and casting directors think and work—how they "discover" people. And it's an important part of your business no matter which industry you're in.

*Does this person improve your company talent pool
or do they take you back toward the swamp?*

Create a high-class problem

I define a high-class problem as having to choose between a variety of excellent options, each of which provides an outstanding result. Should you buy the Porsche, the Ferrari or the Lamborghini? To have this as your problem is an ideal situation. The idea is to have at least THREE enthusiastic candidates, all of whom are highly qualified for the job, who all fit your culture, and everyone likes each of them. If the decision is too simple, perhaps you haven't looked hard enough. I recommend finding a couple more candidates just to be sure that you cannot do better. If you are really pushing the envelope, there should be several candidates who are a perfect fit. When we hired our Director of Product Management, we had narrowed the field to several excellent choices to agonize over. I met with our management team as well as the people who would work for the new Director. Given some of the additional strengths these potential Directors had, we even had to reconsider a fundamental part of the company's future direction during the process and the choice was ultimately unanimous in favor of the person who could take us where we wanted to go. It was a wholesome agony to go through and I look forward to more of it.

You're not running a clinic

I often see the tremendous potential in people. If they only realized that they had _____ talent then they could do/be _____. I used to think I was just the right guy to bring it out in them. I used to hire people with the thought that I could transform them into the ultimate employee I was really looking for. Forget it. I was actually running a clinic for employee transformation. Truly great managers throughout history get "ordinary people to do extraordinary things." I'll still pursue that greatness, but for now, I'm training to be a master at hiring better people in the first place. Then I'll work with them. My current crew has been selected using this new philosophy, my life has gotten much easier, and we are growing more profitably. I now take prospective employees at face value—what have they done, what can they do right now with the skills and experience they have, where will their interests naturally drive them, and will their personality fit with our culture? (Read their resumes and listen carefully and you'll see and hear where they are likely to be attracted. It's better to choose people who will naturally gravitate into specific areas of your business as if it were their hobby.) The priority in hiring is having them do what they're currently capable of doing. Hiring them for their potential growth is a risky speculation and you probably don't have the time to give them the attention or the money for the workshops they need to bring it out. Sure, they can be all they can be and I often can see much more potential in them than they can, but they must be able to access and utilize their skills and abilities to be of any use as a productive employee.

When you must make room for someone who can do the job...

It's a worthwhile investment to put the energy and consciousness into your hiring process to enable yourself to make a good decision, but if you must to undo a past hiring mistake, here are a few ideas.

We recommend in our EmployeeManual*Maker*™ employee policy manual software package that you have a 3-month or 90-day *introductory* period (not *probationary* period) stated in the employee manual and in the offer of employment letter. The employee knows that there's a 90-day window where we both acknowledge that we can say good-bye with no consequences within that period. Once you go beyond 90 days, your situation can become more complicated.

> **Never carry someone longer than their mother did.**
> — Jay Shelov, management consultant

A small business, especially, cannot afford to carry anyone for very long. A big company may carry a number of people who aren't performing without suffering permanent damage, but as the downsizing trend indicates, they seem to be catching on too.

If and when you need to terminate an employee (I prefer to say, "let them go.") I think you must do it. You cannot be intimidated by the threat of wrongful termination or having a missing person in a key position. The wrong person—whether they're incapable of doing the job or poisoning your environment—can do more long-term damage than having no one in that key position. They're going to be more trouble to you by being there every day that they ever could by not being there every day. According to the second law of physics: "Two things cannot occupy the same space at the same time." While your emotional and intellectual energy is occupied (as well as that of your management team and other employees) with the problems created by the presence of the errant person, you will be unable to fully concentrate on doing what has to be done—including finding the ideal person to fill that position.

One of the keys to a successful termination is doing it with dignity. You must enable your employee to save face. Every decision you make and every word you speak, ask yourself, "will this preserve their dignity?" Violating a person's dignity is one of the fundamental driving forces behind an employee lawsuit. I have that on good authority from the attorneys who assisted us with the development of EmployeeManual*Maker*. Besides, what does a lawsuit cost compared with what it costs to preserve a person's dignity?

And, don't wait for them to really screw up to use that as your excuse for letting them go (unless it was a terminable offense as described in your employee manual). Although you probably have a hundred reasons for firing them, they can use that one reason as not enough to warrant being fired. Let me give you an example of a successful termination that I have now used several times.

I called the employee into my office and, after scanning my body for how I felt physically in that moment, told him that I had a sick feeling in my stomach because I realized that I just couldn't let this go on any longer... It just wasn't working between us any longer... I knew I was driving him crazy... I'm not getting what I really want... He wasn't doing what he really wanted to do... And, there must be a place where he would be happy... I'm really uncomfortable doing this, but I have to let him go.

Let me restate what happened from behind the scenes. First, I looked for my feeling in-the-moment to ground myself in preparation for our conversation. I needed to tell him how I felt—my actual physical body sensations in that moment were my true feelings at that moment. So that's what I communicated. Second, I looked at what my participation in our relationship was. It wasn't all his fault. And the truth was, he was miserable and he could be much more productive and happy somewhere else. So why bullshit each other any longer? The first person to act in a situation like this does both people a favor. We were both relieved and could retain the friendship and respect that had developed while allowing us both to move on. It's the job and circumstances that are the problem and—not the person. End the struggle, but preserve the person.

> **Deliver the good news on Friday.**
> **Deliver the bad news on Monday.**
> — overheard Hewlett Packard manager

This wisdom works like this: Giving an employee a raise or a great review is best done on Friday because they can enjoy the elation for the next two days and be enthusiastically ready to come back to work on Monday. On the other hand, letting an employee go is best done on a Monday or early in the week to enable them to settle their affairs, ask questions and generally complete things while the office is open. Anger and resentment can be dissipated by productive activity and conversation. Terminating them on a Friday allows them two days to smolder about how evil, unreasonable, etc. you are and build resentment.

As part of your termination conversation, tell them that, when they are ready, you'd like to sit with them and write a nice note (e-mail) to everyone in the company and you want to be sure that it conveys what they will feel good about. This way they'll know that you are interested in saying what needs to be said to everyone else and prevents premature gossiping.

Business Black Belt Notes

- What projects do you have that somebody else could do better than you, that don't need your direct personal attention?

- Past performance is the best indicator of future performance.

- Plan the job description carefully for today and several years out.

- Hire with the intention that they will fly the plane and you will sit in back and relax.

- Hire people at face value—they can do what they perceive they can do, regardless of the additional potential you think they have.

- Create a high-class problem—an agonizing choice between great candidates.

Hiring Friends?

*A friendship founded on business is better
than a business founded on friendship.*
— John D. Rockefeller, oil magnate

☞ By hiring someone because he or she is your friend, you can really paint yourself into a corner—here are a few ideas to consider if you are thinking of hiring one.

I'll just reaffirm the advice I'm sure you've already heard about not hiring friends. When you realize that you have to fire your friends, that's an ugly situation.

I hired a friend I'd known for some time. He'd gone to school, told great stories of the business activities he'd been involved in in the past, and so on.

Here's my mistake: Because he was a friend, I thought I knew him. I didn't really feel the need to check him out like I would anyone else. If I'd been cultivating my relationship with the guys who I knew knew him or called the people he had worked with, surely I would have gotten a different story. This guy was great at giving advice... I should do this, do that, or so-and-so should really get on the ball. He had some good ideas, but he would never act on them and make them happen himself. Apparently, he thought his presence, advice and friendship with me was enough to get by. Unfortunately, it was. I didn't evaluate his performance like I would anyone else because he was a friend. I thought he was a good guy and I kept him on because I thought I saw potential that would some day pay off, plus I was afraid that our other friends would think I was a jerk for firing such a smart guy. In the final analysis, he generated nothing.

Friends or not, you need people who will generate 10 times what you pay them. Whether your payroll is $5,000 or $50,000 a month, you can't afford to have slugs working for you. Friends cannot be considered special.

Another aggravation is that my "friend" was constantly pitching me on his activities. At social events, he would invariably bring up a low-priority business project he wanted to pursue and relentlessly discuss it after we had already agreed on his actual projects. Even our other friends and acquaintances would chime in by mentioning that I should pursue these pathetic projects they'd heard about. It was like Chinese water torture.

After I finally got rid of him, I then heard from several mutual acquaintances who confided that he was a great guy socially, but they never would have hired him. And, over the next couple of years I heard from others, who knew him personally as well as professionally, and told me a few more horror stories. Yeah, I was a jerk—a few phone calls to these people could have saved me tremendous aggravation and him a lot of embarrassment.

Why are they here?

If you must hire a friend, make sure your friend really wants to be there because of the business. You don't want them there if they think they're getting a free ride from you. "Oh yeah, I can get a job with Burke because he likes me; we're friends. He'd never fire me. I can do whatever I want." A good employee must have a passion for the business or for the job they do.

I've met few people with a passion for my business who have also become my friends. Most of my friends have a passion for what *they* are involved in. Because I'm passionate about what I do, I attract people who are also intense about what they do. What makes us interested in each other is that we can appreciate the passion the other has for his or her work. But we're not necessarily in the same business. So, when friends come along who want to work for me, I seriously question their reasons. I want to hire employees who have a passion for what our products and services are providing for our customers.

Hire only the smartest because you'll never get all the people you want.
— overheard Microsoft hiring credo

I can always find a place in my heart for competent people

No matter how much I originally liked someone, if they prove to be incompetent, I come to hate them. That sounds sick, but when you're doing business, have a lot of money on the line, have deadlines, people, and resources flying in every direction, you can't have somebody in the middle of all that who's incompetent. It drives everyone crazy.

Unless you get rid of your incompetent people (friends included) immediately, your other team members are going to say, "You are responsible for managing this situation. Do something about it." With any other employee, it would be easier. But if the problem is your friend, it makes things worse. Other employees can't talk to you about the problem because they know the person is your friend. You've created a barrier between you and the other employees who need to talk to you and to whom you should listen.

No matter what, use a contract

Recently, we were sued by a former employee. Someone who was a friend. He thought we owed him more than we did. But several years ago we didn't use the right contract to spell out our deal. How dumb was that? After all, we were friends. I don't care who they are, they must sign a contract with you stating clearly your expectations, how much they'll be paid and what qualifies for payment. A friendship can weather a disagreement over a contract to potentially do business together, but if you disagree after there is money on the table, it's likely the friendship will suffer irreparable damage. Understand, agree and write your contract presuming the business relationship will eventually end, but the friendship will be preserved. Even then, draw up a detailed agreement that especially covers their job responsibilities, results (sales volume for example), and projects to complete when you do part company. How much will you pay for an incomplete project? Or, how will you handle completing it? If they are getting a commission, be sure to spell out how long after they leave your company they will qualify for sales to customers they worked with. Agreements with these specifics are necessary for any employee or contrcator. (We sell thess contracts in our Agreement-*Builder*™ software.)

It's a small world and you may even be working in an incestuous industry. Building and nurturing healthy relationships is a must—they'll be back in a couple of years.

It's easier to end a working agreement when you can appreciate what the person contributed to the business. Then he or she can move on. You can give the person glowing references because they left for a calling to do something else and not because you got frustrated and had to fire them.

I told my mother no

My mother asked me once if I would hire the daughter of one of her friends. I asked my mother if she would be comfortable explaining to her friend at her annual Christmas party why I fired her daughter.

Maybe I was being negative, but I didn't want to hear about it the rest of my life, in case hiring her friend's daughter didn't work out. I have plenty of people to choose from and so do you. (Sure, there are exceptions—you'll know what to do.)

Business Black Belt Notes

- Don't get sucked into hiring friends. Choose first: your business or your social life.

- If you must hire a friend, do the same due diligence search on a friend as you would anyone else.

- Make sure when hiring a friend that he or she really wants to be there and has a passion for the business, not just because they want a free ride from you.

- Before you become friends with an employee, make sure he or she is a productive, long-term contributor to the business.

- Be sure you can end your business relationship and still preserve your friendship.

Interview Questions
Not in Anybody's Book

Hire smart or manage tough.
— Lou Adler, executive recruiter

☞ If you're betting the farm on key employees, you need all
the clues you can get. Here are a few questions to add to your
interview repertoire.

Tell me what you've done or
continue to do to educate yourself?

What people do to continue their education is very important. I am amazed
how many people have stopped learning in their field beyond their college
degree. For example, I have a degree in economics. Since 1979, when I graduated with this degree, I've studied little to nothing on economic theory. I
may read a magazine article here and there on some economic theory, but
generally I've done absolutely nothing with it. On the other hand, I've studied marketing, sales, and management. I'm much more valuable to a company as a marketing and sales person than I am as an economic analyst.

Consequently, if someone has a degree in marketing, I often wonder if
they have studied anything in marketing since they got their degree. Perhaps
they feel they had enough marketing in college and have studied nothing
since. Sure, their college degree provided them with good background. I

know for certain that a lot of marketing is not taught in college. In my case, economics was a good foundation for my further learning in sales, marketing, and business. My actual knowledge in marketing came way after college. Also, what someone has studied since college is a good indication of a continuing interest in learning. Further education shows me several things: They are interested in continuing to learn, they're improving their skills constantly, and they will probably continue to keep reading and learning.

Does your present employer know you're looking?

Compare the candidate who says, "Yes, my boss knows I'm looking," with the one who says, "No, please keep this confidential...." As a business black belt, you know that what a person does to or says about another will someday be said about or done to you. And, as you seek to improve your organization, wouldn't you prefer to hire an employee who honestly communicates their thoughts and feelings to you? I find that the candidates who respond like the first one above seem to be more forthright overall.

Here's the kind of person I'm looking for: They've spoken with their employer about their position and their interests–they've made every attempt to adjust their current job to their liking and they have openly involved their employer in that process. Obviously, their employer could not accommodate them and they are now looking elsewhere for a better fit. As their future employer, I'd like the opportunity to discuss their situation and work something out before they jump ship behind my back. If they jump ship behind the other employer's back, what else am I supposed to expect is going to happen to me?

I've had candidates who responded to ads because they were curious and hadn't been considering a job change, but I'm always interested in how they respond to this question. It's always a good one to ask. Also, if they haven't told their boss, when will they do so?

What do/did your parents do?

(Technically (legally), you cannot ask this question, but I try to find out some way.)
Wouldn't you like to know what influences—not shown on their resume—they grew up with? In my case, my father is a financial planner, and my

mother is an interior designer. I can't tell you how many dinner conversations I sat through listening about financial planning and interior design or about dealing with their clients. All of those subjects were constantly in my environment. I watched my mother work on houses through the before and after stages, and saw what could be done. I asked questions and she told me why certain colors went together, why certain fabrics went together, and why certain designs were the way they were. My father talked about financial planning, investments, and taxes. I wasn't wildly interested in pursuing either of these subjects on my own, nevertheless, they were in my background, and I learned quite a bit about them in addition to my college education and other experiences.

Now when I talk to and interview a potential employee, I always wonder what else they learned in their background that might be useful. For example, our Chief Financial Officer's father is an attorney, which makes her very useful in meetings when discussing legal issues and looking at contracts. Sure, she's not an attorney herself, but she asks many useful questions most of us don't think of (obviously, we seek legal counsel for finalizing any significant deal) and it's very helpful. You never know what extra benefits a potential employee may bring to your party. This informal education also gives you some indication of what influences them in their thinking, or what influences their point of view as they approach their job with you. You could even ask them how they might apply that additional life experience to their job now, or how it influences their thinking today.

Who are your heroes? Why?

The more important component of this question is *why*. But to get to that, you want to know who the hero is. That will at least access memory and thinking in the direction of inner goals and desires. Hopefully, these heroes display the characteristics of the kind of person you're looking for to fill the job.

Here's a current problem: [use a real life current situation here]. How would you handle it?

This is my favorite question to ask. Can the candidate think on their feet? Are they current with our industry? Do I like their thought process? What probing questions do they ask before offering a solution? This is real, not hypothetical, so you can get a feeling for how this potential employee is going to bail you out of the problem you're hiring them to handle. The more specifically they answer this question the better. Answers to a variety of these kinds of specific questions weigh heaviest at decision time.

Give them a test

We gave our product managers a writing test. We wanted to know how well they can write. After all, what we sell is the best way to handle a business task, such as writing a business plan, writing an employee manual, and writing a marketing plan. So, we gave the applicants a sample of some text we were currently working on (on disk) and asked them to bring it back edited the way they would do it. We wanted to see how creative they were, how much they were willing to change (they could have written and reformatted the entire page), how clear a communicator they were and so on. As a result, the people we hired were excellent. Also, we keep the same page to test new applicants for the same job and compare with our existing people.

Tell me about a mistake you made and what you learned from it

The bigger the mistake the better. A good candidate should smile and admit he or she has several doozies to choose from. A healthy attitude and answer to this question demonstrates to me that the person isn't afraid of being a little vulnerable and has plenty of self-confidence. It also seems that they are willing to face their mistakes and learn from them. This kind of person can bring a lot of good experience (mistakes that don't need to be repeated) to your business.

We hired an executive a few years ago who seemed to be the poster boy for that position. Slick, confident and very polished, he very adroitly dodged this question as if to say that he had never screwed up. Overall, we were so impressed with his charisma that we hired him. Big mistake. I can't say that this question should have given us cause not to hire him, but it and a few others should have been clues to look a little further and think twice.

Tell me about your vacations

What someone chooses to do on a vacation provides tremendous insight into other interests they may have. Instead of hearing about fantasies and something they may like to do someday, you hear about what someone actually did and what experiences they actually had. Vacations represent people's freest choices and give you some further insight into their natural tendencies. Ideally, you would like to have an employee in a job where they can apply their natural tendencies to do the right thing, or the things you want them to do.

Business Black Belt Notes

- Make sure your questions are relevant to the job.

- It's often useful to know what factors influence the thinking of your employees.

- Do they continue to educate themselves?

- Who do they admire and why?

- What do they do on their off time and how might that relate to your business?

- Are they up-front with difficult relationship issues like their job situation?

- Can they own up to mistakes, learn from them, and even teach others?

Let People Tell *You* What's Wrong So They Won't Tell Everyone *Else*

The one who needs to know the most is often the last to find out.

☞ You must create a connection with your customer grapevine, otherwise you'll never know trouble is brewing in enough time to deal with it inexpensively.

A government study concluded that if people *like* you, your product or service, they'll tell three people. If they don't, they'll tell 13. In fact, something like 15% of those people will actually go out and tell 20 people what they don't like about your product, service, or you. If there's a problem, they'll always communicate to someone else what their gripe is. They won't automatically communicate directly to you and give you the opportunity to fix the problem.

I don't know what the psychology of this is, but people often tell everybody *except* the one concerned. If customers can't tell you what's wrong with the product, then they'll tell everybody else. If anybody they meet is considering buying your product, people are only too happy to tell others not to buy it for their own reasons. So you've got to put yourself in a place where people can address you. Once they tell you, then they've let off steam on the subject and they'll cease to tell everybody else what's wrong with you, your product, your service, or your company. Create an 800 line that people can call with suggestions and address those things head-on yourself. Ask your employees specifically what kinds of loose ends they have, what kinds of things they think are wrong that could be fixed. If they were running the company, what would they tell you to do? Give them the opportunity to tell you directly what kinds of changes they would make. Let them air out their gripes instead of getting together in the conference room or with other employees at lunch, taking other people away from their jobs, and bitching to them about what they think should be done with the company and never tell you.

Is your door really open?

Make sure people can talk to you without being afraid you'll bite their heads off. Once you bite off their heads, they're never going to come back. Give people at all levels of the organization an opportunity to say things like "Well, you know, the color on that brochure is terrible." That way they won't go off and bitch to other people about it.

E-mail within your company is a great way to gather feedback. It's not as confrontational as a face-to-face meeting and encourages a "stream of consciousness" message that might suck out any other venomous problems brewing in employees' minds. It's *safe* when you are genuinely learning and interested in improving everything that you do or sell. Your responses will demonstrate appreciation and encourage further communication. You don't want to be the last to find out about the rumors circulating through your business.

What don't you know?

A gentleman in a seminar recently asked, "How would you foster more communication in your business in order to know what's going on?" And I said, "Ask questions!" I mean really find out by asking, "How do you feel about this? Do you think we are doing the right thing on this project?" Our software packages include an 800 number and a note from me that says, *"I would personally like to hear what you have to say. If you have a suggestion, idea, complaint, comment or success story... anything we can do to improve our products, service or better run our company to help you, I'd like your input. Please feel free to give me a call* (800) 898-5426"

Here's an example of a call I received a few years ago on my 800 number regarding one of our products—it's part of the feedback we get that helps us improve our products.

> *"I am using* BizPlan*Builder. It does not integrate properly on years 2 through 5 for the cost of materials, labor, other factors. And there is a problem on the interest expense allocation and income. All of these things have to be forced. It is a developmental program. To the uninitiated, this is trouble. In other words, the program does not take into consideration increase in sales from one year to the next year and apply the appropriate percentage of materials, labor, and fixed costs to the increase. It only applies a defined increase to the previous year's costs. Very, very interesting problem, very fundamental, needs to be changed, and quickly. Nice talking with you. Bye-bye."*

This is great stuff and we needed to hear about it! I would prefer to hear how wonderful our products are and how cool I am, but what if this person didn't call? How would we know to make this important change in our product? Then I wonder about other people who didn't call. What comments might they have had for improvements? We take these opportunities seriously and act on all of them, because we know that the few that do contact us represent hundreds of others who don't.

Your call makes a difference

Once I called another software company to order their product and their voice mail system finally transferred me to the sales department and then proceeded to lose me in an endless loop. I called again. Same thing! After ranting and raving to whoever would listen at *my* company, I decided to go to the source of my frustration. I left a brutal message on the company's voice mail system saying, in no uncertain terms, what a problem their system was and how it must be killing their sales. To make sure that my call was productive and served their company, I offered a workable suggestion that they could replay for the benefit of the salesperson who sold them the system.

(It gave them the ammunition they might need to make their case.) The company president himself called me back to thank me for letting him know that he had such a problem. He even offered me an extraordinary price on his product!

Once people have had an opportunity to communicate with you, they no longer feel a need to tell other people. They feel like they've made their statements, they've said their piece, and they can probably go ahead and recommend your product, knowing in the back of their minds that they've been heard. They've connected directly with the source. Conversely, if you take your problem straight to the source, you'll feel better and not contribute to negative gossip that will eventually earn you a reputation as a whiner. I felt good even though I left my message on their voice mail. Now there is no energy propelling further complaints of mine to others who can do nothing to solve my problem. This is a powerful way to keep a strong, positive, word-of-mouth promotional network working for you.

Business Black Belt Notes

- Provide a convenient, safe outlet for direct feedback—direct 800 number and e-mail.

- You need to know if there are problems, because you have the authority to make changes and improvements.

- Communicate your issue directly to the source—to someone who can really do something about it and not to those who cannot.

Note: The following two chapters are meant for you to copy and distribute to your employees so you can enjoy some expert, third-party support for what you need done.

Managing Creative Interference– Business Builder or Business Killer?

Never give an order that can be understood.
Always give an order that can never be misunderstood.
— Douglas MacArthur, W.W.II General

☞ Why can't people follow directions? Your clients and boss are your customers—listening to them and giving them exactly what they want will make you successful. After you've mastered that, you can anticipate what they'll buy next. Then you'll become wildly successful.

To be successful in business, you must provide what your customer wants. So why is it that I can specify with reasonable detail exactly what I want, and some people feel compelled to be creative and give me something different than what I asked for? Let's make sure you aren't losing business because your client thinks you're missing the boat.

My karma bites me in my butt

When I first started developing sales materials as my business, I thought I knew better than my clients what they needed. They would tell me what they wanted and I would "improve" on it to give them something different and better. If they disagreed, I argued with them. And I lost some clients. As I realized that I needed the money, it occurred to me that it was more important to make them happy than to do what I thought was right. (With clients, the right thing is to make them happy.)

Here's what works

First give your clients exactly what they ask for. Any discussion while they are specifying what they want should only be questions to clarify. Not challenges! If you feel moved to offer improvement, make a copy of the original in your computer, if appropriate, and add your changes to a *new* proposal. When you present your finished product, show them the one they expect to see first. Then mention that you had a few ideas and express your desire to discuss them. For example: On the brochures I was creating back then, I would type their headline on top and add a few of my own below. Sometimes they would see it my way and choose one of mine or we'd write a hybrid. When they said they wanted to keep theirs, I asked if they liked the type-style and was it big enough. There was never an argument that perhaps I was right. I offered advice and direction, but I made sure that I was not a pain in the ass to work with.

> How can you believe that someone is truly
> interested in helping you solve your problems
> if they won't take the time
> to fully understand your problems first?

Then, a miracle occurs

After about the third project, my client, who was too busy to explain what he wanted, said, "You know what to do, just bring back something that works." Because of his previous experience with me, he knew that I would give him what he wanted. Now he could trust me to give him what he wanted on my own.

When contractors consistently deliver something other than what I asked for, I have to continuously spend a lot of time re-explaining to them what I want. That gets old very fast. But how do you explain that to them? You don't have to. That's not what you pay them for. Just call someone else and maybe they will follow directions. Smart employees and contractors would be well advised to ask, in advance, how much creative license they have in the execution of the request.

The plan and direction must be clear

Sometimes I know exactly what I want right down to the minute details. Sometimes I just have a few parameters or requests that I want complied with. For example, a recent mailing piece had to:

- Weigh less than one ounce to minimize postage
- Show a large color photograph of our product
- Include the table of contents
- Tell the JIAN story

The creative team had to do the rest. I usually ask for three variations to compel the designers to take different approaches and to prevent them from coming to us and proclaiming, "This is it." There is no one way; therefore, I'd like to see three and usually we combine the best of each.

Combine Top-Down with Bottom-Up

As the CEO or customer of my employees and contractors, I often don't have time to explain why things should be done a certain way. I just know that certain things must be done a certain way and that's what I ask for—without giving an explanation for it. If I had time to explain, I would, and I'd love to explain later perhaps over a beer. This, of course, is top down. Specifying design parameters with room for additions works well as long as the designers/employees happily comply with the original specs.

Let's look at this from the bottom up. Regardless of what you are specifying, there are many details to consider and it's important to include the input of many people, like those who do the manufacturing, selling, shipping, installing, and supporting. I expect this input to be considered in everything we do and I won't object when someone points out that my desires must bend to the realities of delivering something that works.

If you are dealing with a boss, client or customer who thinks they know it all, hopefully, they will also expect, request and appreciate that this input is solicited. It's your challenge to deliver it all within your and their expectations. Sometimes you'll have to explain to your customer that there are other important factors to consider that may affect achieving their expectations. Most of all, it's important that your customer perceives that he or she is getting what he or she wants from you. You may be right, but your customer can go away. If you work for an employer, you may be right, but they'll get you on your review. The art is in maintaining the perception in your customer's mind that you are delivering what they want.

Business Black Belt Notes

- Do not replace what your client/boss has requested with your "improved" version.

- Add your improved version behind the requested version.

- Ask for any parameters or ground rules for a project.

- Ask that your employee or contractor show you at least one version of plan or design that is exactly your way.

- Ask for three variations on a design.

- Give your customers what they want the way they want it.

Taking & Giving Credit

Everything comes to him who hustles while he waits.
—Thomas Edison, Inventor

☞ Watch a skillful billiards player. It's easier to take credit for your skill when you've called your shot instead of just slamming the ball and hoping for it to fall into any pocket.

It's easier to take credit for your contribution to a project when you've staked your claim to it up front. My assistant came to me once and asked, "I'm doing all these projects... How can I get credit for doing them?" It's not so much that she needed to get paid for them, but she wanted to feel acknowledged for doing these projects to prove her value in a more tangible way, other than, "Oh yeah, you're great. You do all these important things." She wanted to know she did some specific thing and got credit for it after the fact. It's human nature. When something goes well, everyone wants to take credit for it. And, of course, when it doesn't go well, no one wants to take credit for it.

My response to my assistant was that taking credit and being acknowledged for something really came from accountability for the project. For example, we had an open house that was an extremely successful event. My assistant can take the credit for it, because when we first talked about doing an open house, she said, "I'll handle it," and she did. So getting the credit after the fact ties directly back to taking accountability for the project in the first place. This was her project and she took ownership of it. It was obvious who was going to get credit for it when it happened. There's nothing worse than to be quietly working on a pet project that you make a significant contribution to only to have someone else come along and act as if they made it happen and get all the glory. It's much better to fight over taking charge of projects and activities than to feel ripped-off after you've done the work. (If it's a failure or worse, a disaster, which is what most people fear, don't worry, no one will notice and your connection to it will fade and be forgotten—especially if you own up to it and demonstrate that you learned something and perhaps added to your company's knowledge base.) Even minor successes are worthy of a round of applause at a meeting and a good e-mail PR campaign as to your brilliance (even if you write it yourself!). Again, you must step up and take ownership of a project or activity in the beginning or formative stages and publicly pronounce your responsibility for it if you want the recognition for its success.

Business Black Belt Notes

- Call your shots first for maximum credit.

- Credit comes with accountability

- To get maximum credit for a success, publicly put yourself in charge of the activity.

To know and to act
are one and the same
— Samurai Maxim

If you feel like you're in control,
then you're probably not going fast enough.
— A.J. Foyt, race car driver

Blue Belt

Attracting Customers

The learning curve starts to get a little steeper here. You must continue to practice the basics. Learn to combine the basics into useful maneuvers. These are what you will use in the real world when it really counts.

Keep Your Eye on Selling

What have you done for your customers lately?

☞ As your business picks up momentum, it also picks up problems and you get further away from your customers. If sales drop, you're in trouble.

While flying airplanes, I'll be handling an emergency (rarely real—usually simulated by a diabolical instructor) and my concentration is fully inside the cockpit—going through the checklist procedures. I sometimes forget to keep *flying the airplane!* This is very easy to do and a number of good pilots end up in the dirt.

Although much more subtle and less life threatening, this tendency translates into business as well. At JIAN, we always see a fall-off in sales and cash flow when we focus internally—only on ourselves—and neglect what we are supposed to be doing for our customers. This is easy to do when you are growing rapidly, developing a unique business, and inventing your structure as you go. If you keep your attention on internal details for too long, you risk going out of business. Unfortunately, you may think you need to focus even more on internal details as your business continues to falter, which tends to increase your attention internally. That makes matters even worse. An unattended airplane will start a slight turn and eventually continue into a spiral dive. The most important component of getting out of this death spiral is to recognize your situation (head in the cockpit) and regain your focus on your core business (look outside).

Similarly, in Tae Kwon Do, when I think about what I'll do next or what I look like, my opponent clobbers me. When I focus on my opponent, I stand a far better chance of winning. By the way, this internal/external focus has dramatic effects on us personally. Do you notice that you have the most problems when you are thinking about them? This happens only in your mind. Try this on for size: Consider your personal problems. Dwell on them for a moment and swirl them around in your mind like you would swirl a fine wine in your mouth. Now, look up and focus your attention on something outside of you. A painting on the wall, someone walking by, things in the room—do you see that your problems vanish when you focus outside of yourself? Out here is where you can solve your problems, take real action, and make a real difference. My business really took off when I exchanged the energy (and anger) spent grinding on internal thoughts for that of constructive external action. You can look outside yourself at any time, first to ease your mind, then to do something about it.

Remember to get back to making the products or providing the services you are originally in business for. Like crashing pilots and bruised karate students, companies get into trouble most often during complex restructuring or financial negotiations, when they forget to run the business!

Your business will not carry itself

The biggest lesson I learned from my college do-it-yourself used car lot business was that I had to promote it all the time. Many days I didn't feel like it or I complained about the work I had to do. I would drive by a car with a For Sale sign in its window and not make the effort to stop and attach my flier inviting the owner to bring the car to my lot. I figured I was spending a fortune on advertising and that should cover me. Since then I've discovered that for a business to really succeed, every moment of every day counts. Every single customer counts—you need all the business you can get. God helps those who help themselves. Nature seems to favor those who are constantly demonstrating their interest in succeeding. Besides, you never know who will turn into your biggest, most vocal success story. You never know who will be standing around at a party telling a dozen others about his or her experience with you. (And if the story is negative, it can poison the minds of people who might have been thinking about buying from you!)

We fired our ad agency

We were paying $6,500 per month for an advertising (marketing communications) firm to help us with our marketing. The problem with paying a retainer is that now it is up to you to manage their activities to assure that you are indeed getting your money's worth. I recommend avoiding retainers for this very reason and letting vendors work for you on a project-by-project basis. This burdens them with hustling their next project in order to be paid.

For the amount of money we were paying the marketing firm, they should have personally reminded or notified me of all the work they had done for us. Don't hope that their account rep would tell my marketing guy who would then report to me. That's the way it's supposed to work, but I wouldn't bet my business on that. How often do you communicate with your clients, remind them that you are working for them, update them on your progress as slow it sometimes may be? All I want to know is that progress on my behalf is being made. Send news clippings and other things in the mail, fax notes, ideas, loose thoughts for their consideration, call from your car and leave messages after hours on their voice-mail system (if you don't have time to talk with them). All these things accumulate in your client's mind and add up to an impression that you are on the job for them. Because if you're not, a zillion (at least probably three) competitors are working them over trying to get your account away from you. Who can you call right now?

Even your invoices should sell

Even though your customer has already bought your product or service, they must be reminded to pay you. What you give them to remind them to pay you should remind them of what you did that was so wonderful to deserve immediate payment. You never know what mood a person is likely to be in when they happen to open your invoice. They usually get the invoice some time after the job was done and have mentally moved on to another problem. Now, your invoice shows up and can either remind them of what great things you did and that they were worth the money, or your invoice may start them wondering if you were worth it. (Goddamn! A thousand bucks?! For what?) You also want to get paid as soon as possible.

You can offer special terms like a 2% discount if they pay within 10 days, but I rarely see anyone take it. I'm happy to get my money between 30 and 45 days. If the time goes longer, I think it's usually because customers lost sight of the value I provided. And, if you are in a service business, you'll want them to pay you as well as call you back to do more work.

When I was producing sales promotional materials in Silicon Valley, many of my clients were companies run by engineers who believed that marketing was a necessary evil—after all, their products will naturally sell themselves. My contention was that a good brochure should sell the product without a salesperson's pitch. (At worst, a totally inept salesperson could act as a drone who delivered the brochure to the target.) So, I did what I thought needed to be done, whether or not the engineers knew they needed it or were willing to pay what I charged. In the end, they were happy with the finished product, but the invoices sometimes gave them heart failure. Then I reminded them of all the work that actually went into producing (engineering) their sales promotional materials.

The deal is done when their check clears your bank.

Itemize everything your customer got

Maybe you don't want to itemize everything you did with the price for each because it may look like you are nickel-and-diming them to death, so list everything anyway, but put just one number with it. I explain what usually unseen items mean. Itemize the items or activities you threw in for free. Remind your customer that a lot went into the work you did for them.

Here's an example of what my invoices used to look like:

XYZ Brochure
Salespeople to use at ABC tradeshow and for responses to inquiries

Concept Development	$1,500
Copywriting *(cover letter, brochure & envelope)*	2,500
Illustrations *(used my computer)*	NC
Layout/Design & Desktop Publishing	1,200
Order Form *(I modified one I had on file)*	NC
Photography *(Image: Disk drive on granite slab)*	700
Model *(my assistant)*	NC
Film	35
Separations *(converts photo into 4-color film)*	550
Mechanical Art *(press-ready—1 plate for each of 4 colors)*	1,100
Total	$7,585

The same ad agency we fired above would send invoices that simply stated a number:

May 1996 $5,500.00   Net 10 Days.

OK, I had a deal to pay them, but that invoice did nothing to remind me of all the wonderful things they had done for us that month. In the beginning, our agency gave us a lengthy proposal, which should have served as a reminder for all the services they provided. But, months later, when I saw just the solitary number, how quickly I forgot.

A customer sent us a copy of an invoice he received from his lawyers for preparing his living trust. It went something like this:

Attorney A confer with Attorney B	1.5
Meet with client	2.5
Research	.5
Attorney A confer with Attorney B	1.1
Attorney B confer with Attorney A	2.2
etc.,	
etc.,	
etc.,	
Sub-Total	$2,500.00
Postage	5.65
Copies	9.20
Total	$2,514.85

Miraculously, after about 30 to 40 line items of meetings, phone calls and conferences, the total legal fees worked out to exactly $2,500. And then there were extras like postage and copies! Why do you think the client went ballistic? In this case, itemizing backfired because it itemized in painful detail what the lawyers did, not what their client got. It would have been better if they had listed the various documents that were included and what the documents meant to their client. All of this could have been created from a boilerplate template usable over and over again with very little effort.

Don't let yourself be written off

It's very easy for a company (perhaps a client or customer of yours) to need to find ways to save money and go on a witch hunt looking for expenses to cut. In our case, our CFO, who got the marketing firm's invoices, but was not involved in marketing, singled the above invoice out as a possibility for elimination in order to save money. Combine our lack of memory for what was done with the neglect mentioned above and you can probably see why we felt we could live without them. Don't let this happen to you.

Business Black Belt Notes

- Remember to run your business while you work on it. (Fly the airplane.)

- Look outside.

- Focus on what you are doing for your customers more than on what you are doing for yourself.

- EVERY customer and potential customer counts.

- Check on your customers regularly—let them know you're working for them.

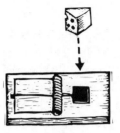

Marketing

Create an environment where sales can occur.

☞ **Have your customers think it's their idea to buy your product or service.**

Most people fail in marketing because they're too bashful to market full out. If you really have confidence in your product or service, if you really believe in what you're selling, there shouldn't be any problem in pulling out all the stops to let the world know what you have and why they need it.

When I first started learning marketing, the idea was to get customers interested enough so they would call; then you could give them a sales presentation. This leads to a multi-step sales approach, which means answering a call, answering questions, sending an expensive brochure, making several sales presentations (taking one or more hours each), making follow-up calls, sending more literature and follow-up letters, and so on. That's fine if you have nothing better to do than give sales presentations to anyone who'll listen. But I'd rather no one called unless they were really interested. Besides, how much time does this multi-step approach take and how much does it cost?

As a customer, I don't want to go through that tedious process either. I'm more concerned that the product or service does everything I want it to do, that the price is right, and that the seller will provide any service or support that I may need later.

Why not give prospective customers everything they need to know to make an intelligent purchasing decision on their own after they look through your literature? I look at our own literature and packaging and constantly ask, "Is there anything else I need to know to compel me to buy this product?" When customers ask questions, we use those questions as our cue to incorporate the answers into our literature and packaging.

Here's why: We can't be sure someone will always be available to accurately answer those questions by phone, in a retail store, or elsewhere. Customers want answers right now wherever they are—no matter what time of day.

And, here's the kicker: If people had all the information they needed, the unqualified customers wouldn't waste your time, energy, and resources. Look at your financial statements (or projections) and add up what it costs you to make a sale. *Anything* and everything you can do to minimize the number of steps in your sales cycle will make a difference.

Marketing is not an event but a continuous process.

The fact that customers usually buy from us on the first contact saves us a tremendous investment in our costs of selling. I want it to be a one-step sales cycle for your sanity as well as ours. This involves pricing, advertising, reputation, and constant study of what it takes to enable your customer to feel comfortable enough to place their order on their own. Instead of $100, we would need to sell our software for $300 to pay for the additional selling expenses, and our profits would be about the same. Even if your sales process involves a sales contract and presentation, approaching your marketing with this intention will make a dramatic improvement in your results.

Sell to the person who ends up with the product

Who actually buys your product or service and uses it for their personal benefit? This is the person to whom you must direct your advertising and marketing, especially when you have a limited budget.

Dealers and resellers also see these ads! You don't need to spend big bucks on industry promos trying to convince dealers to sell your products. We've spent a fortune on marketing programs aimed at dealers, but still I think it's more important to convince your ultimate customer that they want your product. If the world wants it, you can bet that dealers will line up to sell it to them.

When JIAN first wanted to get into retail, we pulled a dirty trick. Our ads included our 800 number, but we also stated that our products were available through leading retail stores. Although, they weren't—yet. A few frustrated customers called and said the stores weren't carrying our products, but we made them happy by shipping to them directly. At the same time, the store buyers would call and want to know how they could carry our products. The problem we created only lasted a few months. We had a special package ready for the stores when they called, and the customers got free overnight shipping, and sometimes we even shipped to the customer via the store.[9]

> *No one can write decently who is distrustful of the reader's intelligence, or whose attitude is patronizing.*
> — E. B. White

You've got three seconds to grab their attention

OK, you've got your customers' attention (there are lots of creative ways to do that), now what? This is where most marketers goof. I've been in more than one meeting where there was general agreement that people are stupid. You know, use eighth grade language. The trap is to follow-up your attention-grabbing headline or graphic with something meaningless. Meaningless doesn't sell. It doesn't leave a lasting impression that can be built upon by another ad or promotional campaign. Meaningless doesn't give your salesperson a head start with a new customer. I assume something different...

I assume that people are intelligent, but *distracted*. They've got a lot on their minds, a lot of other promos are going on around them and they don't have much time to focus on any one thing. Given this assumption, your message better make a point quickly and, although you may not always compel your audience to take immediate action, at least you can plant something useful and memorable in their minds. I recommend a specific benefit or advantage that your product or service delivers. Rather than using worthless drivel like, "Our employee manual software is the finest on the market. You'll see when you distribute it to your employees. Look for it at your favorite software store..." Say, "With 120 employee policies and 30 benefits fully scripted in warm, friendly, plain English, our EmployeeManual*Maker* software will keep you out of court and build a smooth working relationship with your employees." These are specifics an intelligent person can sink their teeth in to. Even if they don't buy right away, the message has a chance of staying with them until they are ready to buy.

Think about this the next time you're involved in the development of any message to your customers. From this perspective, you will write an altogether different promotion than you would if you assumed people are stupid.

The things we do to impress others
are the very things others find most annoying.

Do your promos get in the way of your customers?

People who brag too much call too much attention to themselves and less to their merits. The best martial artists I've known are usually soft-spoken and unassuming. The guys who talk a lot seem to do so to make up for a lack of performance. I always loved sparring with the talkers in karate class. The quiet ones were the ones to worry about. Likewise, your promotional materials themselves should be transparent to your audience—your customers just want your product. If they notice your ad or brochure, then it is ineffective. Do you want to call attention to your ad or to your product? Do you want your customer to buy your ad or your product? Think about this subtle distinction when you look at advertising and at your own ads. Too much attention to the ad itself competes with what it is supposed to be selling. I'm sure you can think of many memorable ads, but which ones spark your memory of the product?

Address objections up front

Let's face it, you already know exactly why any customer might object to buying your product or service. (If you don't yet know what the objections are, you'll find out very quickly after talking with a few customers.) Rather than have your customers get the upper hand by bringing them up first and putting you in a *defensive* position, I recommend beating your customers to the punch.

The Heinz ketchup commercials on TV make the hell we go through to get the ketchup out of the bottle (with too small an opening) seem like a benefit!

Bring up the possible objection as part of your sales presentation or lead with the objection as if it weren't a big deal. You know your customer will bring it up eventually and you don't want him or her to build a strong position on it. So address the objection early and positively:

> *"For the $1,000 you'll invest in this product, we've provided x, y, and z because they will be important in the long run for your business."*
>
> Not: *"Well, uh, we added x, y, and z and that's why it costs $1,000."*

Your customers will discover your warts soon enough because your competitors will surely tell them. But if your customers already know and have been properly educated in advance, they can withstand a competitor's pitch against you. Bringing out perceived negative points—but not at the expense of all your positive points—up front assures your customer that you are being forthright and honest, and will help build a solid relationship.

20 Questions

Originated to help develop advertising brochures and promotional pieces, these 20 questions are what most people will want to know about your business.

You can also include this template as an initial summary for bankers or investors. You should have the answers to these questions readily available when seeking a loan or investments for your new venture.

1) What type of business do you have?

2) What is the purpose of this business?

3) What is your product or service?

4) Who is your target audience?

5) What is the product/service application?

6) Can you list three unique benefits of your product or service?

7) What is the key message or phrase to describe your business in one sentence?

8) What is your reason for starting or running this business? (What's a nice person like you doing in a business like this? Here's where you can tell a heart warming story of why you are uniquely qualified to deliver the best....)

9) Do you have datasheets, brochures, diagrams, sketches, photographs, related press releases or other documentation about your product/service?

10) What led you to develop your product/service?

11) Is this product or service used in connection with other products or services?

12) List the top three objections to buying your product/service immediately?

13) When will your product be available?

14) Who is your competition?

15) How is your product differentiated from that of your competition?

16) What is the pricing of your product versus your competition?

17) Are you making any special offers?

18) What plans do you have for advertising & promotions?

19) How will you finance company growth?

20) Do you have the management team needed to achieve your goals?

(These questions are included on diskette with BizPlan*Builder*® and Marketing*Builder*™.)

Business Black Belt Notes

- Look at your entire selling environment. Consider how you can influence your customers and have them want to buy from you.

- Direct your marketing messages to the person who will buy and use your product or service—everyone in between (resellers et al) will be interested as well.

- People are intelligent, but distracted. While you've got their attention (about eight seconds), give them something worth knowing and remembering.

- Address objections up front in a favorable, positive way.

---

9   Much has been written on marketing. I've read a lot of it and I practice as much as possible. Rather than give you my version of marketing, I'll refer you to a variety of very well-written and informative books that I've followed very successfully. If you feel that this subject is a priority for you, run out and grab these books!

Ogilvy, David. *Ogilvy on Advertising*. New York, New York. Crown, 1983.

Ries, Al and Jack Trout. *Positioning: The Battle for Your Mind*. New York, New York, McGraw-Hill, 1981.

Ries, Al and Jack Trout. *Bottom-Up Marketing*. New York, McGraw-Hill, 1989.

Advertising:
An *Investment*, Not an *Expense*

Sell customers what they want, provide what they need,
and deliver more than they expect.

☞ Advertising is expensive as hell. Here are a few thoughts you can use to make your investment go a little further.

This is my favorite subject because so much can be done to make or break a business by how you present it. I hear many people say that their advertising doesn't work. When I look at their ads and ask how they track them, it's no mystery why they feel badly about their advertising. They rarely track which ads in which media generate results. Where did the money go? What did it do?

First of all, let's look at a point of view: When you invest your money, you expect to get a greater return. When you spend your money, you buy something of value; but the money is gone and is not expected to come back worth more. This is a psychological concept that is useful to consider in a variety of situations, but in the area of marketing most people think of it as a *cost of doing business* and therefore something to be minimized. If you look at marketing as a business investment, then you would seek to invest as much as possible in the highest yielding vehicles. (By the way, I recommend changing the words: cost, price, expense, etc. in your promotional literature to 'investment'—it will send a subtle message to your customer that they will get more than the price of your product or service back.)

Where are the fish biting?

The first step to maximizing your marketing investment is to determine which vehicles reach the right audience. We started out by placing many one- and two-column-inch classified ads in a number of computer and business magazines to see if people would call. It was cheap enough to have many small ads in as many as 20 publications to test where we should consider expanding our presence. To make a classified ad work, you can't just send over some copy and allow your ad to be buried in a sea of text. We used "display" classifieds, which means we sent a fully designed ad (as much as you can in a microscopic classified). Here's an example:

Business Plan on Diskette
90+ pages of text you can edit.
Lotus or Excel financial templates
$99 Visa•MC•Amex (800)-346-5426

These worked fairly well to get us off the ground. The reversed headline helped to grab people's attention. Anyone with a computer who was even considering writing a business plan was sure to call.

Prepare a *script*—leave nothing to chance

Because the ad didn't tell much, people called for more information. At first I just stumbled through my pitch and answers to their questions trying to say something that ultimately made sense. Every time the customer said, "Oh, I get it," I wrote down what I'd said that worked—exactly as I said it. Pretty soon I had compiled and perfected a bullet-proof script I could use over and over again with about an 80% success rate. People would call as early as 5 A.M. and they'd say, "I saw your ad, could you tell me more?" (I'm in California and they would call from the East Coast. I trained myself to spring awake sounding happy to hear from them.) Since I had my script on a clipboard along with order forms near my bed, I could just read to them.

(If you're going to wake me up, you're going to give me your credit card. Four out of five times they did.) Later, the people I hired to answer calls also used this script and we even incorporated much of the text into our brochures.

How many ads should you run?

Advertising sales reps tell you that you need to advertise at least three times to effectively test an ad. That's nice, but your ad should indicate a degree of success (or failure) on the first run. If you're not sure, run just one and see what happens. If you're confident in a particular publication, a monthly magazine for example, go ahead and sign up for the full 12-month run. If it works, you'll have saved a lot of money on the rates for the first issues. If it doesn't pull, then discontinue your ad schedule as soon as possible and pay the short rate (the difference between the rate for the number of ads you ran and the rate for the discounted quantity rate). Here's why: If you conservatively ran a few ads before jumping in for the 12-issue rate, you'd pay the full rate for a one-time or three-time rate. You wouldn't save money until you went for the 12-month schedule. If you went for the 12-month schedule right away and your ads worked, you would continue. This way, you get your discount up front and pay the higher price only if it doesn't work! You don't want to penalize yourself when you're successful. Be sure to discuss this strategy with your ad rep first, to be straight with them in case they may need you to sign an irrevocable 12-month schedule, in which case you must go the distance for 12 months no matter what.

Test your ads—make them call!

I'm amazed at the number of ads I see that give the advertiser absolutely no indication whether the ad is attracting any interest, either through the publication or in what's being advertised. Unless you've got zillions to spend on ads and don't care to be efficient, always make an offer to the reader to contact you for something, like a free catalog or more information. Better yet, have them call to place their order. Nevertheless, you need to know if the advertising medium is putting your message in front of customers and the only way to be sure is to ask for some kind of response. Make it easy for customers to buy from you—use an 800 number, accept all major credit cards, offer a no-risk, money-back guarantee. In fact, develop a unique guarantee appropriate to your product or service. Rather than offer a vanilla-flavored, 30-day, money-back guarantee, JIAN uses "Our 60-Day Get-the-Job-Done Guarantee" because people buy our software to handle a specific business project. We want them to succeed using our product rather than fool around looking for another product. Look closely at ads you like and watch your mail for other examples and good ideas.

Turn your risks into tests

The best way to know if your ad works is to track it. Now that you've put something in the ad that will compel people to call, make sure that your ad is tagged with some kind of code number. Don't expect people to have the magazine in their hand and say, "Oh yeah, I'm reading the June issue of *Success* magazine." In case the customer says, "My friend tore your ad out of some magazine," you're covered because you've put in a code number. By the way, that's how we learned that *Success* magazine was a very effective news magazine for JIAN. If we hadn't tried it *and tracked it*, we probably never would have known. I wouldn't have been able to quantify exactly how much business came in. If I'm going to take the risk to try a publication, I'm going to learn whether or not it's a fertile place to find customers. Internally, we call it a Sales Source Code, but in your ads, you want to appeal to your customer: Discount Code, VIP Code, Priority Code, etc. You might even use an extension on your phone number, but I think that makes you look small time. Some people even say, "Ask for Susie." Susie is the code for the ad. I start losing trust in companies that play these kinds of tricks, however. Customers aren't stupid, they can handle the fact that you want to track the source of your sales.

You need to know how much a particular ad pulls and when. I recommend using a different number for each ad, even if the same artwork runs in the same magazine. If you change your artwork or message, you'll want to track the results. You'll know the results of your marketing month by month. Keep track of your results using a spreadsheet. Maybe it does nothing the first month but pulls like crazy a month later. We have some ads that inspire a call as much as a year later.

Business Black Belt Notes

- You must measure the results of all of your sales and promotional activities to learn what works and what doesn't.

- In direct response advertising, the priorities are A) the media in which you advertise (for direct mail, it's the list you mail to), B) the offer of a good deal, and C) creative design and copy—in that order of importance.

- Use copies of your brochures before committing to a large quantity of four-color printed literature. Ask for comments and suggestions in real sales situations. Incorporate answers to questions customers ask.

- Track all ads, mailers, promos. etc. with a code number and put them into a spreadsheet that you review monthly.

How Right is Your Price?

If 10 percent of your customers don't complain that your price is too high, then your price is too low.
— Anonymous

☞ Pricing is a touchy subject, but to a good sales and marketing person, it can be a useful tool rather than a subject to dance around.

As a young salesman, I was always afraid of selling something for a high price. My boss at one time screamed at me, "You're too chicken-shit to *sell* the product!" Obviously, I couldn't really grasp that our product was worth what we were charging. Many people in sales suffer from the dilemma of not being able to afford their own product, so they project that same fear onto their customers.

There's a saying, "Those who can't sell give the product away." I did that because I didn't fully understand the value of my product, service, and all of the materials as well as emotional factors that would compel a customer to buy from me. Given that, how could I make sure my customer fully understood the value of everything that was included in our price? So when you set a price on something, you must consider all of the factors in your customer's universe where your product or service provides value. All things considered, what would it be worth to them to buy from you? The effort you invest here will pay off in your ability to sell at higher prices and generate more profits. Just make sure your promotional materials and sales training also incorporate these value factors. In the case of JIAN, we know that an entrepreneur or business owner would pay an outside consultant anywhere from $1,300 to

$7,000 or more to write them a business plan, a fair price for the work involved. Having written a number of business plans myself, I have a sense of how much work it's going to take. And we remind customers in our literature of the effort and time they'll save by buying the product. We can easily sell BizPlan*Builder* for $100 because we know that we're giving people more than $1,000 worth of value.

If you were your customer, how much would you pay?

You don't really want to price your product or service based on its cost to you. In other words, your cost of goods is not relevant to the price of your product or service. I was standing in an art gallery when I overheard a guy telling his girlfriend that he couldn't believe the artist wanted $30,000 for a painting. The canvas and paint could only cost a few dollars, he told her. Obviously, he didn't understand art customers. The value of the painting has nothing to do with the cost of canvas and paint. Software provides a similar example. The cost of goods for software is about $5 to $10, yet people will pay $100 to $500 and more. In our line of products, you get thousands of dollars of expert advice for under $100. You couldn't touch it for that little money any other way. That $100 investment is a no-brainer. As a businessperson, I'm in a situation where I'm selling based not on my cost, but on the fact that our customers will leap at solving an otherwise huge business problem for only $100.

For JIAN's project-specific management tools, it makes sense to charge a little more. We can then afford to include all the ingredients a business owner needs to build their company. The products we sell form the central nervous system of a business—this is no place to opt for the cheap version or a brand new, unproven product. Respecting the importance of the subject matter our products address, we need to do a lot of research, stay on top of law changes, trends, and business practices so we can provide the best information to our customers. We don't want to cut corners here in order to sell a $100 product for $49. I'd rather see our customer leverage his or her $100 investment in our software into millions of dollars—which most of them do. We can also afford to promote our products with a respectable marketing program to let people know these tools exist. Looking at your business, how can you build this profit-building thinking into your product development or service delivery as well as your sales, marketing and customer service?

Also, we've added our own touches that make our products special. Figure out how you can make your products and services special by adding your own touch, the *art*, which gives it a significant boost in value. Personally I can't stand big words and legalese. I hate being confused, so one of my special touches is to write our products like advertising copy—it's simple, quick to read, clean, and compelling to action. This is one of our secrets to our successful products. It's taken a long time for me to come to this, and we pay extra to have our products edited with this in mind. Our business-owner customers can leverage this magic in all of their business documents. And it works!

Picasso once scribbled on a piece of paper and asked $10,000 for it. Someone complained, "It took you 30 seconds to do that!"

"No, it took me thirty years," Picasso replied.

True story

One of our software resellers, a major player in the computer software retail business, was selling BizPlan*Builder* for $69.95 when everyone else was selling it for $79 to $89. At first, we thought they would ruin our market as everyone would run to this store, that our price point would erode everywhere, but we discovered there was no appreciable difference in sales through this store chain. Apparently, this reseller was underselling most of their products, and as a result, they were posting horrendous losses at the time. Since then, they have raised their (and our) prices, their profits are now good, and our software is selling better than ever.

Include your price in your advertising

When I become interested in a product or service, the next thing I want to know is its cost. One school of thought is to not state your price in your advertising. The theory goes that customers will be curious and call or circle the number on the reader service ("bingo") card. Then you have a chance to get in front of your customer and give them your pitch. As a customer, I'm seldom that curious. I'm more concerned that the price is indeed out of line, the seller is playing games or is holding out on me (what else aren't they telling?). I'm a big boy, I expect to pay for what I get. The way I figure it:

If you are afraid to list your price,
you are afraid it might be too high.

The following ad from Lamborghini demonstrates they have no fear of the price of their automobile. Everyone knows it's one of the most prestigious cars available in the world—the big question they answer is "What does it take to have one?" If they aren't afraid of their price, why should you be afraid of yours?

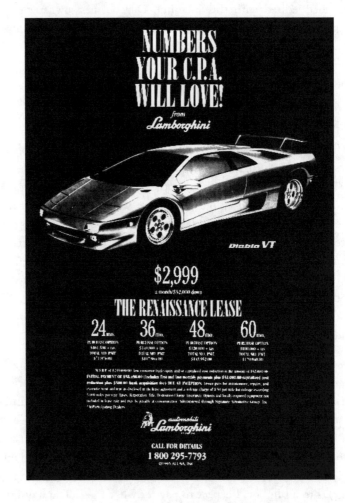

$2,999 a Month / $52,000 Down

I want one! The price actually gives me a goal to shoot for. On the other hand, a wealthy person may look at this ad and think, "Hey, I can afford that!" Until then, they may have only wondered in passing what it would take to have a Lamborghini and may have even been embarrassed to ask! (The people at Lamborghini request that you call for an update on price and financing.)

Not printing your prices in an expensive color brochure makes practical sense if you will be changing your prices, making special offers, or using the brochure for resellers as well as end-user customers. At least, include a current price list somewhere along with the brochure.

A common pricing calculation mistake

As long as we're talking about pricing, let's look at the math. You have several ways to price a product. You can base it either on cost or mark it up based on a target profit margin. (Remember that if you want to earn 30 percent on the selling price, you would *divide* your cost by .70 (1 − .30 = .70), not multiply your cost by 1.30. For example, $100 / .70 = $142.86. The $42.86 profit equals 30% of $142.86. On the other hand, $100 x 1.3 = $130; the $30 profit is only 23% of $130.)

See what everyone else is asking and charge a little more

By charging just a little bit more (even if it's just 5%) than your competition, you will often be perceived as offering higher quality. If you've done your homework, people will often think, "Why not pay a little more to get the best one?"

People who buy the good stuff are more fun to work with. It feels better and is more fun to make or do something right. A higher price enables you to make a better product. Make it the way it should be made; offer a service the way it should be done. People will usually invest a little more to get the good one. There's too much junk in the world. The last thing we need to be doing is making more cheap products that will break and litter the planet, or offering cheap services that will tick everyone off because something wasn't done right. How do you feel when you drive a cheap car? When you use a cheap tool? Sit in a cheap chair? Eat cheap food? Wear cheap clothes? What are you saving your money for? Save it for a cheap funeral.

One more thing

Assuming your product or service can be purchased through the mail or over the phone, a very effective way to determine the best price is to use direct mail testing. This is very simple, much more reliable than focus groups, and is much cheaper. Simply mail batches of 3,000 to 5,000 mail pieces which are identical except for the price. 3 to 5 thousand names should provide a statistically respectable result. You can mail 4 to 5 or more batches with each batch promoting a different price point in a range. For example: $49, $59, $69, $79, $89, and $99. I like this much better than focus groups that will give you theoretical numbers, whereas a direct mail test will provide the reality of real customers voting with real money.

Business Black Belt Notes

- People who can't sell give the product away.

- Maintain your respect for the value of your product or service.

- Price things by understanding the value of your product/service and how your customers will benefit.

- Find out what your competitors are charging and charge a little more.

- Include your price in your advertising.

- If practical, use direct mail to test your price.

Salespeople

Most people already want to buy.
Good salespeople simply engineer the deal.

☞   The sales techniques we learned in the past are appalling and ineffective, yet many people continue using them—let's revisit the sales process in order to make it less painful for everyone.

When focusing on breaking a board in martial arts, we're taught not to focus on the surface of the board, but to focus on a point about six inches beyond the board. That way, we're sure to punch through the board and effectively break it without breaking our hand.

Similarly in sales, you must think beyond the point of closing the sale (the board). Focus on working with your customer when your product is already installed or your service is being performed (beyond the board). This is more than just a simple optimistic technique of visualizing yourself closing the deal. You must focus beyond the point of sale.

De-emphasize the close

Most sales anxiety exists around closing the deal. That is the magic moment when all you can hear in the room is your customer's pen scratching across your purchase contract. It's the moment every salesperson longs for and the moment most customers want to put off until they are absolutely certain. Your customer has all of his or her senses on red alert and any fear, anxiety, doubt, or bad energy oozing from a salesperson will be detected at this moment. That's why it's crucial that your energy, vibes, aura, urgency, strategy, etc., span the entire sales spectrum to bridge the moment of completing the sales transaction.

The Sales Cycle

The entire spectrum of selling includes finding a prospect, working with them to purchase your product or service, then working with your customer to enjoy your product or service. The "close" is a thin sliver in the middle that can be bridged easily if you spread your energy over the entire spectrum and take the spotlight off the closing point of the sale.

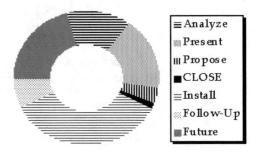

Closing the sale is simply a formality of paperwork to list everything purchased and to record the method of payment.

Close the deal?

Before we go any farther, we need to address something that has been nagging me for years. "Closing" the sale is an asinine term. You're not opening or closing a sale. When you complete the sale, do the paperwork, and sign the contract, you are actually confirming the terms for the business you are going to do together. That's hardly *closing* a deal. Subliminally, the salesperson would take the money and run if the relationship was closed. Actually, now the customer expects more attention than ever. There is much to establishing a relationship with a customer or client to the point where they'll trust you with their money, their project or your word on your product. You must build enough inertia in your selling that it carries you easily over the golden threshold of completing the sale. I believe that customers can tell if your a closer (meaning: your done...) vs. interested in their satisfaction as an important component of your pride. You'll know when people are buying from you and referring their friends to you. Closing, in this case, is a word that I feel is fatally misapplied to the selling process and is unhealthy to all parties involved in the sale.

We may not be able to change the words used in the sales process to new terminology that will transform salespeople throughout the world, but at least we can be aware of the potential unspoken fear that may prevent our customers from doing business with us.

Focus on making your customer happy. Relax. A sale can happen but business is not about the sale itself.

If you have a deal hanging

Most people who have a deal hanging are doing the deal for the money. But what are you providing the customer for the money they're spending with you?

Customers seem to subconsciously react to salespeople who need to make a deal and are motivated primarily by money. A commission is a great way to reward a salesperson for their effort, but the best salespeople become absorbed in the benefits their customer will enjoy from the product or the service. Much like the best musicians who get lost in their music, the best martial artists flow with their opponents and let go of the mechanics of what they're doing. When you're absorbed in your deal from your customer's perspective and doing everything you can to solve their problems, you'll be tremendously effective, appreciated, and eventually, rewarded. You call them up as often as you like and say what you need to complete the deal, because it's in the best interest of your customer.

My friend Jill had a deal with a phone company worth $300,000 that had stalled. She kept calling to ask "Where are we on the deal?" Her contact wasn't returning her calls. I advised her, "What you need to do is think of reasons why this person is buying from you. What benefits are they getting from this? Get off the money you're going to make and go back to what the customer is going to get by placing their order." The customer needed to get software installed for their users to work with. They needed to have their word processing and spreadsheet software updated so everybody used the latest stuff. She needed to concentrate on those issues, get on the side of the buyer, and work with the buyer on the buyer's problem.

This idea alone can get a stalled deal going again. This can make a difference between getting a deal or losing it to a competitor. Nothing can help you if your competitor is coming from this "ground of being" and you're not.

I recommend taking a moment and using my situational reminder memory technique. Plant this process in your mind in preparation for your next deal. This concept is key, and the primary reason for the turnaround of my career. Different thinking took me from making $15,000 a year to making a lot more every year.

Most purchases are not single transactions like going to the grocery store. Many things happen along the way, many details need to be followed up and questions answered. You need to prove that you can do the job. Credibility must be built. Your customer must feel that you really understand their problems and interests. Whatever you're selling them must easily solve their problem and save them money.

I think a salesperson often goes into a sales meeting or an initial sales call with a customer and listens to how they're going to solve the customer's problem. The prospect of selling something that really solves an important problem is very exciting. But in the process of making the sale and as months go by—the sales cycle on some of these items takes a long time—you (the salesperson) can lose sight of your original enthusiasm. Always go back to what it is that you're doing for the customer and keep that in mind. Keep thinking of ways to work with your customer. Put your commission second, and your customer is going to be interested in doing business with you.

Jill acknowledged that this was the single biggest factor in her deal going through. By the way, she cleared $20,000 in net profit for herself.

I see it all the time. I can tell when a salesperson only wants to make money. When he or she is not really interested in the sale for my well-being, I get nervous. I have now put my finger on this as the fundamental flaw in most people's sales presentations. I feel that they're there to make a sale and my best interests are secondary to them. Some people say they never do that. If that's true, then your sales must be skyrocketing. If your sales are not coming easily and they're stalled, then I suggest that you revisit the solutions to your customer's problem.

Engineer the deal

I was visiting a friend in Colorado who really wanted to buy a new BMW 325i. She was ready to trade in her old car, she had the money, good credit— everything. So I suggested that we go look at the cars. The BMW dealer had the perfect car—red, convertible, and loaded. The salesman was very nice, gave us the keys, and told us to enjoy ourselves. After driving around for a while, she obviously didn't need to be convinced that this was the right car for her. The salesman ran the numbers, checked her credit, and then, over the next two hours, tried to come up with the paperwork to put this deal together.

What went wrong? That car dealer could not engineer a transaction and generate one document that incorporated all the terms we agreed upon! A spreadsheet showed the lease vs. purchase comparison and included the desired down payment along with the number of months to get the desired monthly payment. There was a problem with the leasing document. My friend knew she wanted the car, she didn't need an extra sales pitch for lease. All she needed was a single document to incorporate her personal information, the car's identification, places to fill in the price, some options, taxes, financing calculations, subtract the allowance for the car she was trading in and calculate her drive-off payment (if any). And it all should have squirted out of a laser printer in one good-looking document with the particulars in **bold print**. The sale should have gone like this:

Ma'am, here are the keys to your new BMW, and here's the purchase order complete with all the numbers we agreed to. We're giving you $x for your trade-in. All we need is a check for the down payment, your signature here, and the keys to your old car. . . and you're ready to go.

Even if she had a few doubts and was slightly fearful of completing the deal, while her emotions were hot and with a little coaxing, she could easily write her name a couple of times and drive off in the gorgeous, brand new car of her dreams! It didn't happen that way. They couldn't get the paperwork in order while we were hot. We left without buying the car.

An airplane as an impulse buy!

Here's a different story. I've fantasized about owning an airplane almost all my life. But they're expensive, I had no practical reason to own one, I should have spent my money on more practical things, blah, blah, blah. Nevertheless, I had learned to fly, went to airshows, and looked at all the *Trade-a-Plane* ads. One day I saw a good-looking plane for sale at a nearby airport, so I called the broker who had it, went to see him (just to check it out), and a couple of days later he took me for a demo flight. It was great; I was in love.

We went back to his office to talk more about it. He wanted to know what I liked and what I didn't like. He told me it needed a few things, I wanted him to add a few things, and he agreed to take care of them. I asked about financing, so he brought up a screen on his computer. He filled in my name and the specifics of the airplane including some financing options. While he was at it, he filled in the things he would do to fix it and the things I wanted added. I knew I wanted a mechanic (someone he didn't know) to look it over, so he typed in a provision for that. When he printed it out, the entire deal was spelled out on a single page! With a nice place for my signature next to my name typed out. I knew the price was right, the details were in order, I had an out if the mechanic found problems or if I couldn't get a loan, so I signed it. I haven't had a minute of remorse since and I'm still excited about my airplane (a 1980 V-Tail Beech Bonanza V35B). Despite the fact that I still needed a tie-down space at my local airport, insurance, special training, and a loan, the entire transaction, including flying the plane for an hour, talking about airplanes, and telling war stories, took less than three hours. The fact that the broker could produce a single, comprehensive document made an otherwise monumental sale go down like it was an impulse buy. I still dread going to lease my next car.

Salespeople are the customers of the marketing department

I suggest that you debrief your top salespeople as an ongoing part of your marketing program. Imagine incorporating your most successful sales pitches, developed and used by your most successful people, into your marketing materials. I'm amazed at how companies neglect this opportunity. I remember being a top salesman in a company and calling the marketing department to make a suggestion or comment about what to include in our brochures. You can probably imagine their response. They said they had already done their market research. Really? How? I called our other top 10 sales representatives—none had ever been interviewed by the marketing department. Don't the salespeople talk to customers every day? Isn't the idea to introduce your product or service to as many qualified prospects as possible, to pique their interest and reduce the length of the sales cycle? I think your top salespeople can provide useful information on this subject to the people who spend millions on advertising, direct mail, and retail merchandising.

I'd recommend having your top few salespeople review your promotional materials while they are being developed, not after mechanical art is complete and on its way to the printer. Sure, this takes a little extra time, but when you print 1,000 to 1,000,000 copies, where every single one makes an impression on a valuable prospective customer, isn't it worth it? The marketing people are making tools for the salespeople to be more effective, so unless the marketing people are willing to make sales calls to get a real feel for what's happening out there, I recommend listening to the sales staff.

Tape your top salespeople in action

What better way to train your sales staff than to have your most successful salesperson demonstrate what he or she does to respond to customers, to have the customer purchase right away. Videotape them role-playing. Sometimes we record our telesales conversations for training purposes. Nothing is more powerful to train people than successfully selling a real customer in front of them. You can buy a telephone recording device for your tape recorder from a local electronics store (remember to comply with federal and local laws regarding recording telephone conversations).

Listen to yourself. Listen to how you listen (or not). Listen to how your responses sound. This is something you might think you don't need to do. It's very easy to fall into that trap. This is a rare opportunity to be a fly on the wall and listen to yourself in action when you're talking to a real customer. Play it back when you're not engaged in the conversation and you'll discover things that need improvement. Subtle things—things that can make a big difference in your customers' perception of you, your product or service and your company. I heard how much I interrupted my customers with my quick responses to their cut-off questions! Insist that your salespeople listen to themselves for the same reasons too. The improvements are self-evident—they'll hear it for themselves and know exactly what to do. (It's amazing how we can be willing to allow the world to see and hear us, but we are afraid to listen and look at ourselves!) Try even copying yourself on a voice-mail message to hear how well your message comes across. Do you sell it well or not? What would make it better?

Trade show tip. . . Pleeeez!

Have you ever walked up to a salesperson just after they've had a cigarette and a cup of coffee? At trade shows, we make sure everyone working our booth has a breath freshener handy so they can talk to a customer without knocking them out. (Those little bottles of Binaca are great—gum is tacky.) It's difficult if not impossible for a customer to be interested in what you have to say when he or she can't breathe around you or your salespeople!

Business Black Belt Notes

- Envision beyond the sale—to a time when you have established an ongoing, working relationship with your customer and your product or service is successfully installed and operating.

- Simplify the paperwork, engineer the deal, and make it ridiculously easy for your customer to commit to the purchase.

- Tape yourself making (or losing) a sale—review it as if you were the customer.

Selling for a Change

*You can lead a horse to water,
but you can't make him drink. . .
Try salting the oats.*
— Anonymous

☞ **Selling is often not just convincing someone to buy your product
or service but to change what they already have or what they are
doing now.**

Some customers are already interested in changing to something new and
they know they need to buy your product or service. Others need to be made
aware that something new is available and that they should upgrade as soon
as possible. Either you sell the customer your product or service or your customer sells you that they don't need it. Either way, a sale occurs. It's your
job to convince them to purchase your service or product. But after you educate them and they still won't buy. . . what's the problem?

As you already know, most people are afraid of change. Where does the
fear come from and why? Like many people, I developed a fear of change during childhood. Looking back, I sense that *changes were not necessarily improvements in my situation, rather they were dictated and initiated by others for their convenience.* Perhaps the changes were not ones that I would have made. As a
child, things were not in my control.

You don't need to be a psychologist to see that my mental association
with change was somewhat negative. Perhaps you had a similar experience.

Fortunately for me, my reaction later on in life to all of this was ultimately to take control of things and make changes that suited me. I developed the ability to make changes that improved my situation. To this end, I'm relatively easy to sell to because I like to invest in improvements. Some people, on the other hand, still resist change because they're afraid that the change will actually make things worse. These people are difficult to sell to.

Some customers avoid change because they aren't sure how they got as far as they have. They think they were lucky and they don't want to rock the boat. Any change at all could upset everything! Without getting much further involved in the psychological details of the fear of change, consider it as a possibility behind your customer's resistance to buying.

Customers have to change what they have been using or doing

Out of your customers' mouths come all of the classic sales objections and excuses: "I can't afford it. I don't have enough time. I need to think about it. Blah, blah, blah. . ." These standard sales objections mean nothing and simply mask the real fear of taking (or accepting) action.

Selling is offering someone the opportunity
to improve their situation.

Position your offer in such a way that the change (i.e., improvement) it will make in your customer's life is obvious. Work with your customers to make them feel in control of the change so it will improve their lives. This is more than selling benefits, because you could pitch benefits all day long only to have your customers still be afraid to go forward. I like bluntness: "Will this make an improvement that you're looking for?" or "Do you feel like you are in control of what's going on here?" The answers may reveal a few simple things you can do to complete your transaction. There won't be any more sales objections. Remember that this is an attitude adjustment on *your* part.

Appeal to the inner brat

Because I've studied marketing for so long, when I become a customer, I become a hyper-sensitive, critical-of-the-sales-process lunatic. I'm a sales and marketing perfectionist who's always trying to do everything right. As a customer, I'm always gauging my own feelings, thoughts, and emotions toward a salesperson or a marketing tactic. I walk into a store to buy something and I become a six year old child. All week long I've been selling, I'm now the customer, I've got my money, and it's my turn to buy. And dammit...

I want service, I want what I want, I want it now, and I want it my way

We haven't matured much when it comes to our turn to be kids in the candy store. Since most sales are based on emotions (logic just provides the justification after-the-fact), our emotions as a buyer have probably not matured much either. If you've ever worked in a public service job, like a restaurant, gas station, or retail store, you've likely seen this to be true. As a salesperson you have to work your sales approach to appeal to this spoiled child in everyone. My initial reaction when I see a spoiled brat is to think about strangling them. On the other hand, being more interested in making the person happy and completing the sale, I remember to appeal to their good side and satisfy the child before they become the brat.

I know I'm successful if I can please my customers and make their inner child happy immediately, regardless of their demands. As the person selling, look at how happy you get by helping people have what they want. Remember the chapter on getting out of people's way? Give them what they want.

To really study marketing, learn what appeals to you and incorporate whatever works with you to compel you to spend your money. Make changes to what doesn't work for you in your own presentation to your own customers.

Business Black Belt Notes

- A customer's real resistance to buying something may be because they feel out of control about making a change in their life.

- A customer can be like a spoiled child. The salesperson must make the customer happy immediately.

- Study what appeals to you and incorporate whatever works into your own presentation to customers.

Why Should I Buy from You?

The reputation you build for the future is more valuable than the profit you earn today.

☞   Your character plays a crucial part in completing a sale. It's much easier for customers to buy from you when they buy because of you, not in spite of you.

One of the most profound personal experiences I ever had was imposed on me during a workshop. This time, fourteen of us were in Hawaii for six days with the founder of the workshop company.

I was working as a salesman for Texas Instruments, selling electronic components. I was having a hard time with sales and being a salesman. I was very frustrated and I had an attitude problem. I'd read the most popular sales books and attended both private and corporate sales seminars, but I was still having trouble making sales. Something was really wrong for me and I couldn't put my finger on it.

The most difficult thing was that I knew I had to get past my bad attitude to get to the other side. On the one hand, I wanted to say, "Screw sales." On the other hand, I knew I wasn't going to advance in life unless I understood what I was going through and dealt with it.

So I registered for the "Master Course." On the first day, I talked to the workshop leader about my dilemma. I explained my attitude about being a salesman and selling.

He asked, "Why should I buy from you?" It seemed like a simple enough question to role-play, so I said, "Because I work for T.I. and we've got the best stuff." He replied, "Can't I buy the same things you sell from someone down the street?" Hmmm. That was one of the biggest things that made me crazy. Other distributors of similar products were everywhere, so I didn't have anything special going for me. Truthfully, I wanted to have an unfair advantage and I didn't have one. I also wanted it to be easier to have people buy than it really was.

Again he asked, "Why should I buy from you?" I answered, "Because my prices are better." He replied, "Don't give me that. I can get a good price from any of your competitors. Don't you think I can find a competitor who's hungrier than you are and can give me a better deal?" That was Pet Peeve Number Two. I was losing orders every day because of our prices (I thought).

His question came at me again. I said, "Because we give better service." He responded, "Yeah, but think about it. Wouldn't your competitors tell me the same thing?" They would.

When I heard the question again, I panicked. I was desperate. I was going to say that I had better quality. But everybody could say that, so quality wasn't an issue. My problem was that I couldn't think of a good reason. I'd gone through price, quality, brand name, delivery, service, and all that stuff I'd been taught, but nothing was working. It just didn't make sense. I could respond to all those questions and give a good pitch to explain why my company, service, quality, and prices were better, so why wasn't I doing well in sales?

Relax, think about it for a week

The workshop leader could see that I wasn't getting it, so he suggested I relax and just participate in the workshop. He'd ask me the question again later. As it turned out, the workshop was about how we are reflections of other people—others are reflections of ourselves. You know, *it takes one to know one.* But this course imparted that concept at a higher, deeper gut level where it had everyday meaning. Who you talk to reflects what is really going on with you. Other people are our mirror. We are not cameras, but projectors. It took five days of this seminar for me to really get my own truth of that, but it finally made it to my gut, and to this day, the truth of that sinks deeper and deeper. It's very useful knowledge to train yourself and learn from everyone.

By the last day of the workshop, I had completely forgotten about my original problem. I had a great time, a great tan, and a variety of interesting insights into human nature. We were all saying good-bye, when the workshop leader turned to me and asked, "Why should I buy from you?"

"Oh yeah!!" I remembered and replied with complete understanding, "Because you want to do business with *me*."

"You got it," he said.

My response came out of nowhere. After doing the seminar, it just suddenly seemed so obvious. This is the number one reason people will do business with you. Or not. Everything else is secondary.

Being successful because people want to do business with you carries a lot of responsibility. Your reputation is on the line. You owe it to yourself, your future career, and your customers to sell the best possible product for the best possible company. You also need to be very well informed about what your product does and does not do. That's how you give the best value to your customers.

We've all been watching TV pretty much since it came into being. We've all watched commercials as they've evolved. We've all seen and heard a variety of sales pitches, scams, and rip–offs, to the point that we are fine-tuned to fending them off. A clean, straightforward sales representation is refreshing, unique, and effective.

My product won't work for you

Now that I was so immersed in the fact that my customers were buying from me, I could be really honest with them. If a product was not good for them, I could say, "In fact, a competitor has what you really need." It blew my mind when I told a customer to buy my competitor's product, but I felt better about it because I was doing my customer an honest service in the interest of getting them what they really needed and making them happy. (That's another reason to always know about your competitors' products—not just to prove yours are better but to know where they fit.) One customer later told me how relieved he was that I stopped pitching my product, because we both knew I was swimming against the current. As a result, he knew he could rely on me to seek his best interests. He wanted to do more business with me with other things. He did, plus he sent me referrals.

I've said this before, but let's look at it again

In this chapter, I'm putting my finger on something that you may have had a feeling about but weren't sure that you could actually do. You know when a salesman is giving you the run-around. You just have a bad feeling. When a car salesperson introduces himself with "If I make you a deal today, will you buy it today?" a sense inside you says, "Whoa, I'm just starting to look at cars. Does this mean you're not going to help me?" (The salesperson is trained to qualify you—are you really a buyer or just a tire-kicker? How much time should he or she invest? Unfortunately, the cynicism comes across.)

We need to overcome the inherent conflict of interest in sales. Get rid of the idea that you don't make any money if you don't sell to a customer now. Selling needs to come from an interest in helping your customer first and making money on the deal second. This makes a world of difference in sales success. After I started doing that, my sales doubled immediately and I started enjoying my work.

That's the difference between a good salesman and a bad one these days. Until you get this fundamental point, you're never going to be a really successful salesperson. The ones who do get this are excellent. Sales seem to come easily to them. This new breed of salespeople can be honest and make money in the process.

Like a said before, I can tell in a heartbeat now if a salesperson is coming to pitch me because he or she wants the deal or if he or she thinks they have something I could really use. Sometimes it doesn't matter and I buy regardless of a sleazy salesperson, because I want to buy the product or service anyway. Unfortunately for them, these people are very forgettable. On the other hand, if I'm looking for something really important or expensive, I want to work with my kind of salesperson.

It's OK to cop to your pitch

If you don't recognize that they're buying from *you*, then you could be making a sales pitch at them. If you catch yourself making this mindless pitch, you can always turn things around and get your customer back. You can always dig yourself out of the hole and come clean. Try asking them something like this:

- Am I pitching you too hard on this?

- I've talked perhaps a little too much; where are we?

- I've thrown a lot of numbers at you; does this make sense?

- I went off on a tangent there; did I even come close to answering your question?

- Maybe you shouldn't buy right now. Let's talk about your situation— maybe I can send you in the right direction.

This is not a sales *technique*. It's as simple as doing the right thing for the person in front of you and not what's necessarily most profitable for you, regardless of what's best for them. That's manipulative and it's what gave salespeople a bad reputation. Not only will you sell more, but you'll feel great about what you sold. You'll be happy to see that customer again, knowing that what you sold them did them a service. That customer will be happy to see you again because you steered them in the right direction. They're also happy to refer you to their friends and family. I don't care how much you spend on advertising, if people give you a bad reference, business will be tough.

This, I think, is a very honorable attitude. It's not arrogant or showing off. Your sales representation has a matter-of-factness to it. It's not about having a positive mental attitude or psyching yourself up. You know who you are and that commands respect, separates you from the sales yahoos, and attracts people to you because they want to do business with you.

Business Black Belt Notes

- People buy from you and everything else about the sale is secondary.

- You owe it to yourself and your customers to sell the best and to know all about your product and your competitor's products.

- A good salesperson has an interest in making the customer happy first. Then the money will come.

Manufacturers' Reps

You don't get paid until you come through.

☞ Here are some things to consider when hiring and managing a virtual sales force.

Manufacturers' representatives are especially useful when you can't afford your own sales force. Reps also may know many things about your business that could help you. You can hire people as your reps who have established relationships with customers you'd like to do business with. It's important to choose reps who sell non-competing products to the same customers. In other words, your products would extend the reps' product offering to the same people who buy their other products.

Strategic Marketing Partners (a highly motivated and successful rep firm for computer hardware and software) consults with us on many techniques and strategies for establishing sales through many important resellers. SMP is an example of a dream rep firm and are the reps we use today. These people know the business, know the players in the industry, know how to structure good deals, and are straight shooters. No wonder they make a ton of money and many people like and respect them.

On the other hand, some reps just call to find out how much has sold in their territory so they can calculate their expected commissions.

Don't be fooled into thinking these guys should just know the business and will be out there banging on doors and slam-dunking sales. Your contract should be very specific and spell out all your expectations. (We have the latest version of the one we use included in our Agreement*Builder*™ contract development software.) Clearly state that commissions are not paid until the sale is complete. You may even stipulate that you must first collect on sales. Also, sales to distributors may not count as sales. In the software industry, we consider a sale to a distributor as merely a transfer of inventory from one warehouse to another until the software is shipped to a retailer. Distributors want to be able to return excess inventories. You can get burned by a huge return especially near the distributor's fiscal year-end when they want to make their books look better. Some companies and salespeople drive their numbers up by "stuffing the channel" (i.e., convincing the distributor to place a larger than necessary order only to have it returned in a few months). To make matters worse, distributors will offer to place a large order if you'll give them a discount. If it makes good business sense, do it but make sure it's non-returnable, and consider the likelihood that they'll place a reasonable order at your regular price in the near future anyway so it may be worthwhile to wait. Also, your accounting firm may not allow you to recognize sales to a distributor until the distributor has sold your merchandise through to your dealers. Even then, the dealers may return excess stock to the distributor and it may be returned to you.

Manage your reps

Don't be bashful about making a specific list of activities you think your reps should perform. Be up front with them, and follow up regularly by providing news clips, product success stories, customer quotes—anything and everything to keep in front of them—interesting things to inspire them to promote your products.

Our sales executive several years ago thought our reps were "professionals" and didn't need specific direction. Instead, they needed him in their faces on a regular basis. Rather than provide them with leads, product training, information, motivating case histories of customer successes, and little-known but useful facts about our products to stimulate them positively on a regular basis, he would harass them only for higher sales and to book orders by the end of the quarter. This drove them crazy and cost us a fortune in unnecessary travel and entertainment expenses. Eventually, we terminated those reps. I regret this happened, because most of our reps could have been managed more effectively and we would be farther along today. We also terminated the sales executive.

Ideally, to avoid confusion and to assure accurate payments, consider a rep firm that handles relationships with your distributors as well as your individual dealers. Otherwise, the reps who sell to the dealers want to take orders directly and coerce the dealer not to buy from a distributor. Dealers often prefer to order through distributors because they have an established line of credit, the ability to ship to multiple store locations, and the availability of multiple products at the same time. You want retailers to buy through distributors for these same reasons, as well as the fact that distributors have the leverage to collect from the hundreds and thousands of retailers who are sometimes slow to pay. Your rep firm should handle your product line through distributors and retailers to avoid any conflicts, with the added bonus that the rep firm can recommend and coordinate complex special promotions between distributors and retailers.

Business Black Belt Notes

- Reps should buy you important relationships and save money on selling.

- Fax interesting info to keep your reps up to date and interested.

- Your rep firm should handle your product line through distributors and retailers to avoid any conflicts.

- Sales to distributors may not count until product has sold through.

- Remember to include your reps in market research and ask them for recommendations for product as well as promotional material improvements.

Sell to Those Who
Influence Your Customers

The least movement is of importance to all nature.
The entire ocean is affected by a pebble.
— Blaise Pascal, French mathematician & religious writer

☞ It's crucial to your success that industry experts endorse you, your company, and your product or service—remember to include a marketing campaign to these important people.

Remember to market to the people who influence your customers. At JIAN, we call this the Influencer Channel and treat it with about as much respect as we treat the Retail Channel.

Think of your customer as looking in all directions for assistance

In our business, our customers are influenced by many factors and come in contact with many people. Earlier, I described marketing as creating an environment where sales can occur. Respected people who influence our customers are an important part of our environment. Investors look at business plans all the time and are always asked about business planning. Therefore, we promote BizPlan*Builder* to them in hopes that they'll recommend it. We also promote to bankers, CPAs, management consultants, and others so they'll be aware of our products and recommend them to their clients.

Ideally, they'll outright tell their clients to buy our software because it will make everyone's job easier. The investor and banker prefer to deal with a business owner who is thoroughly prepared. A business consultant prefers that clients do all the prep work on their own and use the consultant's time more efficiently for more important matters (besides, consultants want to work on the more fun stuff like strategies and creative tactical things).

Second best is when our potential customer may be considering our software and asks a banker, investor, or consultant if they've ever heard of JIAN or any of our software packages. In that case, I'd like to think the expert responds with "Oh yeah, those guys are great. I've heard good things about their software. I know several people who've used it and were very successful. Sounds like a great idea." Worst of all would be "I've heard of [competitor] and they're good, but I haven't heard of [your company], so I don't know." I think it's crucial that you determine who the influential people are in your business and make sure that they are aware of you, your company, and your products or services. Materials directed at them should be more technical in nature because they will be more aware of any requirements in greater depth and they'll be more interested to know that you've done your job right so they can honestly recommend you to their clients.

Support your influencers' business

Since you want the influential people in your business to recommend you, be careful not to promote your product or service as a replacement for them! We never say, "Buy EmployeeManual*Maker* and you'll never need a Human Resources professional again." As the saying goes, "It's not nice to call a witch doctor a sonofabitch." We want HR professionals to recommend our software to their clients and many of them do because a) they don't want to have to write the manual themselves, b) they know their client will appreciate their interest in saving them money, and c) the HR pro can invest more of their time in helping their clients with more serious, specific problems that will ultimately serve their client better. We want these people to like us.

Ideally, you want all of your customers' trusted advisors to be aware of your products or services and recommend that your customer do business with you.

Business Black Belt Notes

- Surround your customer.

- Leverage your marketing by promoting your products or services to those whose professional advice your customers trust.

You can find a directory full of Professional Business Advisors familiar with our software on our website: www.jian.com

Say "Thank You" and Promote Yourself

The heart has eyes which the brain knows nothing of.
— *Charles H. Parkhurst*

☞ Salespeople use thank you letters as endorsements to sell their products and services. Include a brief promo in the letter you write and you'll expand your sales force.

Certainly you've been shown numerous endorsement and thank you letters by customers who have previously purchased a product or service from the salesperson pitching you his or her product or service. American Express as well as thousands of other companies routinely run ads featuring real people who are successful with their product. *Success* magazine ran an article on BizPlan*Builder* featuring a couple who started a successful child care center in Atlanta, Georgia. Not only did we get hundreds of calls for our software, the couple got hundreds of calls for their day care business. How did we find out about them? They wrote an unsolicited thank you letter to us. Of course, we were thrilled to receive it and it was a great success story that proved the value of BizPlan*Builder*. When working with *Success* to develop a case history feature story, we naturally promoted our thankful couple for the article. Take a look at the following letter and you'll see a perfect example of a genuine thank you letter that works wonderfully to sell his products too.

SAFE·MAN

May 4, 1995

Mr. Burke Franklin
JIAN Tools For Sales, Inc.
1975 El Camino Real, Suite 301
Mountain View, CA 94040-2218

Dear Burke,

I recently purchased your BizPlan Builder program to put the final polish on our company's business plan. Our company manufactures a product called Safe-T-Man which is a life-size, personal safety companion that offers a proactive defense against car assaults and home burglaries. Its design resembles a strong, intimidating man that, when properly positioned in the home, car or recreation vehicle, gives the appearance that the home is occupied or that the driver is not alone in his or her vehicle.

Since criminals and carjackers tend to target people who are alone and who appear more vulnerable, Safe-T-Man can make a difference during that split second when a criminal is targeting his next victim to attack. Safe-T-Man looks like a rugged, 180-pound man, yet weighs less than a baby. He has a life-like face and hands made of latex, a full head of hair and a body stuffed with polyfil.

By using your program, we have identified and corrected several omissions in the first draft of our business plan. I think we will have an award-winning plan once we are finished. Thank you for publishing such a helpful piece of software.

Very sincerely,

Christian LesStrang
Vice President

Look at how well this letter works. He raved about BizPlan*Builder*, and now I'm using the letter to prove my point—at the same time, Safe-T-Man gets a whopping promo as I use it as my demo for you in this book as well as for our promotion of BizPlan*Builder*.

Be specific in your acknowledgment

Notice that he first thanks us for specific reasons. These reasons are useful to your suppliers' salespeople and customers because they are important features or benefits that need highlighting. This makes your letter and story more desirable for broad use and promotion. Next, he brilliantly sandwiched in a promo for himself that makes one interested in what he has to offer. This also serves to help the salesperson say, "See what these guys are doing? It worked for them." What if the salesperson is showing the testimonial to someone who turns out to be interested in a Safe-T-Man? Who knows who might also get interested in your featured product or service in the same way?

This could be a lot of free promotion for very little effort and it's also a good Karma payment that may generate some good letters from your customers that you can use.

Business Black Belt Notes

• Write thank you letters to your suppliers. It supports them and builds your relationship.

• Include a brief, compelling description of your product or service in the middle of the letter.

Using Competitors for Fun & Profit

*Look around for the sucker.
If you can't recognize him,
it's probably you.*
— An anonymous poker player

☞ **Believe it or not, competition can actually improve your business.**

I analyze my advertising results because I invest a lot of money and I want to know exactly what is paying off and why. We graph our ad results by media month to month. We also keep copies of all of our ads. One day I decided to take out all our ad "tear sheets" for one magazine (it was the classified section), lay them side by side on the table, and compare them to the bar chart showing total sales from this magazine for each month. Why was there a spike in sales after a particular month? Why was there a significant dip in sales after another month? Were these seasonal things? Did we say something or design our ads differently between these months? Were there any other factors?

After considering all the possibilities and finding nothing, I decided to see what the trends were when our competitor appeared in the magazine. Then I found something. When our competitor appeared on the same page, our sales went up! When they appeared right next to our ad, our sales went even higher! Why? Customers would call and ask, "How is your software different from your next-door neighbor?" We had good answers for that and we took their order four out of five times. But I still couldn't come up with a truly reasonable answer for why our sales would increase when the competitor's ads were literally next to ours. I thought sales would surely decline because customers had another option.

One of our product advisors provided the answer: Having two ads side-by-side actually provided more selling area that caught people's eye before they turned the page. There were two messages enticing people to buy business planning software so it increased the likelihood of being seen. We had more customers seeing our ad. Once they saw it, they would call and order. Our competitor was actually helping us expand the awareness of business planning products.

> *Competitors are like castor oil.*
> *At first they make you sick, then they make you better.*
> — Unknown

When you are the leader, look inward as well as listen to your customers

The biggest advantage to using your own products yourself is the fact that, while your competitors are imitating you, you're breaking new ground and solving new problems. Since you're never alone in your problems, your customers will appreciate your innovations as well. You are taking your destiny into your own hands. You enjoy the unique capability to solve problems and pass along your solutions to the world. And with competitors who copy your ideas, you can always be sure they will never get ahead of you.

Don't try to put your competitors out of business

I strongly recommend that you erase the focus of trying to put your competitors out of business, even as a marketing strategy. It's bad karma—what goes around comes around—and the effort in this direction will likely come back around to bite you. Instead, focus on delivering what is best for your customers. Do it better than your competitors do, but keep your focus on your customers.

*If we devote our time disparaging the products
of our business rivals, we hurt business generally,
reduce confidence, and increase discontent.*
–Edward N. Hurley,

What do your customers think of your competition?

I travel a lot on United Airlines and belong to their Red Carpet Club.
However, I recently flew on another airline. So when I missed my flight due
to a gate hold for a previous flight, I hoped to spend the two-hour layover in
their First Class Club. I was politely turned away unless I spend $50 for a
single visit or join the club for $300. Since I didn't fly much on that airline,
I didn't expect the privileges I enjoy as a Premier passenger on United. But
before I ever achieved that status, I recall several times being allowed to use
the Red Carpet Club free of charge. When I finally became a member, it was
only $150 for a full year.

If the people at the other airline occasionally checked the practices over
at United, I think they would modify their policies and perhaps entice me
and others like me to become more regular passengers.

Have you checked your competitor's practices lately? Or are there people
out there like me writing books where they mention your mistakes to
the world?

Business Black Belt Notes

- Competitors may actually help to expand the universe of your interested
  customers.

- In the long run, competitors who copy you will never get ahead of you.

- Focus on your customers and only peripherally your competitors.

- Keep an eye on your competition because you need your customer's
  perspective.

Leave Your Pitch
On the Phone

The truth can be told in two minutes or less.
— Paul Larson, founder, Summit Organization

☞ We can use our voice mail systems to produce virtual conversations—
people no longer need to talk in person to make their point.

I get messages on my voice mail all the time from salespeople saying things
like "Hey, I'm in the marketing business. Give me a call. I've got some ideas
for you." They leave their number and hang up. Most professional salespeople,
especially from the old school when I was learning sales, would tell you never
to leave your pitch, never tell people what it is, always let them be curious,
always go for the appointment so you can get in front of them and see them.
I'll tell you what, these days I don't want to see anybody unless I really have to.
I want to hear what the gist of their idea is right then and there on the answering machine or voice mail. And, I don't want to spend another 20 minutes or
a half hour on the phone listening to what they've got to say. I recommend
leaving a pitch on voice mail. If they've got a good idea, they can leave the outline of it on the machine, then I can call them back. I've done very well myself
leaving my first presentation or proposal to people, in a summary form, in five
minutes or less on voice mail. And they've called back saying they were
intrigued with my proposition. Or when I called to follow up with them,
they've said, "Oh yeah, I remember, that was an interesting idea and I wanted

to talk to you about it." If they weren't the right person, they forwarded my message to the right person and I'm spared explaining it again. They could even forward it to several others as well, and my presentation is multiplied.

But when I get a message and don't know what the call was about, I just figure it's going to be some salesperson with another cockamamy idea that I'm not interested in at all. So my default response, when listening to these messages that request 20 minutes of my time to present something to me, is to hit the Message Delete key.

Leave your number as soon as possible

I often punch the Save key if I don't have time to return the call. However, I will absorb the message and keep it as a reminder to call later. Usually I'll remember what a call was about and re-listen to the message to grab the phone number—please don't make me listen to the whole message just to get your number. If you leave your number earlier on in the message (and repeat it again at the end), I can go back to your message, grab your number and call right away.

One more thing

I often pick up my messages while I'm driving. When leaving a voice mail message, leave it loud and clear enough to be understood from a mobile phone over static, weak signals or road noise. Also, be sure to enunciate your name and phone number. I can probably call you back right then when I have the time, but I can't look up your phone number when I'm driving.

Business Black Belt Notes

- Spell it out on voice mail. Tell the recipient what you would tell them if they were there in person.

- Speak clearly enough to be heard over road noise and a bad cellular or international connection.

- Always leave your phone number; the recipient can call right back without having to look it up!

Be Part of a Virtual Company

You're either part of the solution or part of the problem.
— Anonymous

☞ Promoting yourself or your services as a component of someone else's virtual corporation can be to your advantage.

A virtual corporation can be thought of as the coordination of existing services to deliver a product or service without building a company infrastructure. For example, the making of a feature film is an act of a virtual corporation. The producers bring together all those people and companies listed in the film's credits to make the movie. Then they all go away until individually called upon to work on another film.

JIAN's virtual company

We use the services of a manufacturer's rep firm with seven to eight sales reps who call on the retailers who sell our software. BINDCO in Redwood City, California, manufactures our software packages. They print the box and reference manual, duplicate the disks, put the labels on, assemble everything, shrink-wrap the package, warehouse, and ship. A merchandising firm in Chicago provides people who go into the retail stores in cities all over the United States and Canada to restock the shelves, provide inventory reports, and educate the store staff. We use a telesales firm in Los Angeles, with an unlimited number of telemarketing people we could bring on-line at any time 24 hours, 7 days a week. Our ad agency in San Francisco develops promotional materials. We also use a media broker in Minneapolis to get deals on advertising space. Using these companies allows us to focus on our core competency of developing business tools. And as you can see, we don't need everyone to be nearby.

This is not rocket science. The idea is to bolt on outside services to build your company and efficiently expand your capabilities. Perhaps you've been called by salespeople who pitch you these services.

But let's talk about the flip side

How do you pitch yourself and your services to other companies as a strategic or virtual partner to them? I've seen many salespeople come to me who just don't have the full picture together.

For example, one company prints our box, dupes the disks, and does everything to produce our package. But sales reps call me constantly and say, "We're a disk duplication house." Someone else calls and offers to print reference manuals. Others call to tell us about their assembly services. I think you get the picture.

Compared to the arrangement I enjoy now with BINDCO, these other guys just don't offer me the whole picture. They still need me to coordinate and manage. I don't want to assemble it. To successfully sell yourself as a virtual division or component of your customer's company, come in and offer the whole enchilada.

No finger pointing

An integral part of your sales pitch must be, "There's no finger pointing. We take full responsibility." In an age of disclaimers, anyone who offers responsibility for successfully completing a job or delivery of a product is golden. John Wade at BINDCO never makes any excuses. When we order 20,000 copies of BizPlan*Builder*, they go wherever they're supposed to go, come hell or high water, and the price remains as quoted.

With the previous company, they had a flood in their printing shop in Kentucky. They said, "We can't make that shipping date. We can move printing the boxes to Pennsylvania, if you'll pay an extra 70 cents each as an 'up charge' for the service to get them there. I think I can get them to you on time." Unacceptable. Not my problem. But we needed 20,000 packages shipped, so we paid the $14,000 and promptly dumped that printer as a vendor. That lack of responsibility cost them more than $900,000 in revenue over a couple of years time.

BINDCO, on the other hand, delivers the product no matter what. John doesn't blame some print shop in Kentucky. He doesn't blame some guy who makes disks somewhere else. He doesn't blame the book and box printer in Sacramento. If he's done some jobs that have cost him a fortune, and he's lost his shirt, I have no idea. If he had to pay UPS charges on pallet-loads of books from God-knows-where, I have no idea. All I know is that everything shows up on time as quoted.

If you can go in and pitch your business with that kind of certainty and take complete responsibility as a component or as a division of your customer's virtual corporation, I think you'll have a sale. That means you can leave nothing out—provide as much as possible to your customers/virtual partners. The key is controlling the entire process from bottom to top. Of course, in the process of completing your complement of services, you can and should use your own network of virtual company resources. I see very few people doing that and the ones I do see are very successful.

Business Black Belt Notes

- To provide services in a virtual company, you must provide the whole enchilada.

- What else do you need to offer in order to provide a complete service?

- Take the entire load off your customer and take full responsibility for delivery.

Working the BS Factor

**Short as life is,
we make it still shorter by the careless waste of time.**
— Victor Hugo, author

☞ **Some things are more trouble than they're worth. Sometimes you can put a direct cost to them. Sometimes it's just a feeling. Either way, it's always an angle to consider.**

I look at a lot of deals these days in terms of profitability, cash flow and the bullshit factor. I also use the bullshit factor in sales strategies. In these days of incredible business complexity, technological confusion, government bureaucracy, etc., business bullshit is playing a bigger and bigger part in our daily lives. I define the BS factor as the un-quantifiable emotional considerations surrounding a deal.

These are everyday things that affect decisions and steal time, and they can be used to your advantage when you include these consciously in your sales, marketing, and product or service design. In fact, the BS things are often the fundamental basis for my business. For example, in the software business, many people duplicate disks, print manuals, make boxes, assemble packages, warehouse, and ship... but few do all of the above and do them well. Having tried to manage a variety of vendors for each of these services, I learned to appreciate having *one* company handle all of it for me. I could save money by handling it myself, but the added BS isn't worth it. Our vendor knows this and structured his company accordingly.

Likewise, what can you include as part of your service that minimizes BS for your customers? We recently replaced our packaging for BizPlan*Builder*. Usually what happens is the 3,000 or so retailers as well as distributors and others want to ship back all the product with the old box in exchange for the new one. And the industry is set up to do that. Imagine the BS and cost this creates! In a stroke of genius, our Vice President of Sales decided to offer a $10 coupon for each product they didn't return. In the same letter, he pointed out all the BS the retailers would go through if they followed the normal pattern of returning the package. "You'll have to pull our packages off the shelves and have nothing to sell, take the time to box and ship them to the distributor, complete a Returned Materials Authorization form, deal with the accounting, explain it to and manage their employees, then double-check the entire process later! Or, accept $10 and proceed with business as usual." This worked like a charm and saved us a fortune in returned product.

Bring the BS to the surface

How can you work all the BS factors into your sales presentation? "In addition to [add the benefits] of our product/service, we handle/eliminate all the [list the BS factors] to make it easy for you [to do business with us....]" Put yourself in your customer's place—what would working with your company be like? And what can you do to rightfully take on your customers' BS and win their business?

Business Black Belt Notes

- Engineer and pitch your deal to demonstrate how it comes with minimum BS or removes BS from your customers' lives.

- Consider the BS involved in everything you do before you jump into a project.

*Infinite
patience
produces
immediate
results.*

— Anonymous

Brown Belt

Working *with* People

At this point, you are in a position to begin teaching what you've been learning. Preaching what you practice is an excellent way to further polish and engrain your knowledge and skills. This also forces you to live up to what you've been learning and prevents you from slacking off.

MBAs?

Use your intelligence,
not to prove how smart you are but to produce results.

☞ An MBA is a powerful tool that can be very useful, but it
guarantees nothing about the character of the person with it.

I run a company, so I've been asked many times if I have an MBA. The
answer is yes. Actually, I've had three. . . and I *fired* all of them. The lessons
I learned here cost me upwards of $165,000. What I say here may not be fair
to most people with MBAs, but unfortunately, my experience has been less
than desirable. (Yeah. . . that sounds polite.) A smart person packing an
MBA would be advised to use what I say here as market research. There's a
tremendous amount of agreement among successful business owners and
CEOs against MBAs, but only for certain reasons.

As I understand it, the MBA degree was originally created to provide a
crash course in management, finance, and other business topics for technical
people who were promoted into management positions. This makes sense. If
a brilliant engineer with a healthy technical education and experience is promoted to lead a group of engineers or an entire business unit, he or she needs
to quickly get up to speed on business, marketing, management, and finance.

Here's how I see them: MBAs are like racehorses. When you buy a good-
looking horse, you expect it to win some big prize money. So when it comes
out onto the track and just wants to eat, you've got to wonder when it is going

to run. Some MBAs have earned negative reputations with attitudes that they haven't had enough to eat yet. And pretty soon they're too fat to move.

One of my MBAs said to me, "Gee, Burke, I see my role as your advisor. I think you should hire some other people to do that work. . . . Well, I can't really commit to those sales and profit numbers, but I really think I'm worth $150,000 a year plus 20 percent of any increase in business, and by the way, I should get some warrants to buy stock in your business. And since my relationship with you is unique, can't I have them at a special preferred price?"

Aaaaaaaaaaaaaaaahhhhhhh!

Is an MBA another get-rich-quick scheme?

The people with MBAs I'm complaining about are the ones who come right out of business school and think they've mastered business. The danger word here is master. A master is one who has learned all that is taught and is now pushing the subject forward with their experience and insight. It's a horrible delusion to come out of MBA school and think you're a *master* of business administration.

> *Education is that which discloses to the wise and disguises from the foolish their lack of understanding.*
> — Ambrose Bierce, author

I have a black belt in karate. By most people's standards, if you're a Black Belt then you must be a master. But I'm here to tell you that if you're a Black Belt, all you've done is demonstrate an interest in learning the martial arts. You know enough to get your butt kicked, when to fight, and when you should just run away. It's readily and painfully apparent to anyone who gets a black belt that they're far from mastery. You're deluding yourself seriously if you think you're going to master the art of business in two or three years of school. How much can you learn from teachers whose interest is more in the study of business and who often have not run a real business or made any serious money in business themselves? I would feel better if MBAs embodied an attitude that they have demonstrated an interest in continual learning.

OK, so you want to hire an MBA

It's easy to lump all people with MBAs together and level a blanket dismissal or condemnation. It's just that it seems miraculous to me to come across an MBA with the attitude that he or she really wants to make a difference, will work to make things great, and is not there just for the money.

After my MBA experiences resulted in money down the drain, I tend to shy away from them. I've developed rapport with other CEOs who have been through the same thing. We all fall into the same trap. We all have these big expectations.

So, what would I do if I were looking at hiring another person with a MBA? I would scrutinize his or her work history to find out if they really performed the things touted on his or her resume.

In the interview, I would ask for examples of what was done. I would give examples of the work I need done right now and ask the person how he or she would go about it specifically. And, I would definitely double-check references. When looking at resumes and proposals, I look for danger words like coordinate, manage, oversaw, supervised, participated in, and so on, when a lot of credit for activities can be taken and not much was actually contributed. I want to see that he or she was actually in the middle of the project, doing it, that he or she had primary, hands–on responsibility. Otherwise, I'd just as soon hire the people he or she supervised to do the job. I want the job to get done, not someone to watch it get done. Words I like to see on resumes are wrote, lead, designed. It's apparent that someone's ass was on the line with complete responsibility for the outcome of a project. The person had his or her hands in it.

> **The best education in the world is that by struggling to get a living.**
> — Wendell Phillips, orator and reformer

Some people with MBAs think they're above work. They think they're so well educated they should manage others to do the work. But if you're just starting a company, you don't have room for people who are just managers. You need people who can actually do the work as well as manage and coordinate others.

Some people with MBAs think they know better and only want to tell you what to do. They want to come along and be the CEO's coach or the

CEO. Even if you're hiring a consultant, they must have specific tasks to complete.

You can't afford to pay people to stand on the sidelines and simply make suggestions. You want them to do what it takes to get a project done. If they're managing, it's their butts that are on the line as far as the completion of the project. They have no excuses for failure.

I've used people with MBAs as my trigger for this discussion. Actually, it applies to everyone you do business with.

Business Black Belt Notes

- An MBA doesn't automatically make someone OK—check out work records thoroughly before you hire him or her.

- MBAs sometimes make the mistake of believing they're masters of business.

- People with MBAs can be very slick. Like anyone working for you, hold them accountable for achieving specific results, figure what those results are really worth to you, and compensate them accordingly.

Stock Options from Hell

It's not ownership that I want, it's control.
— David Mahoney, former president, Norton-Simon

☞ Offering a piece of the action is a wonderful incentive and useful to minimize cash compensation for employees, but you must consider the angles before you give away the store.

This chapter was inspired after I fired an employee who had talked me into giving him options to buy stock in my company in lieu of a bigger salary. During the honeymoon and excitement of bringing in a new employee who seems to have promise for making things happen, remember to keep your head. Because stock options don't cost immediate cash, it's easy to feel generous and that was my mistake—amplified by a misguided friendship. Whatever you do, don't give anyone warrants without tying them to a specific performance goal and making the warrants vest.

I can't give you a complete explanation of stock options as incentives for employees, but this chapter will help you go about it in ways that will save big headaches and big bucks. Nevertheless, an option (or warrant) to buy stock is one way of compensating employees so you can pay lower salaries and save cash. Giving options to buy stock is their incentive for a much bigger gain from a future acquisition or initial public offering (IPO). Giving them *options* avoids a taxable event because you're only making a deal to sell stock in the future. Giving them the actual stock now is considered by the IRS to be a form of compensation. That's taxable because the stock has value; the employee has to come up with the cash to pay taxes on the value of the stock given to them.

> *He that is of the opinion money will do everything*
> *may well be suspected of doing everything for money.*
> — Benjamin Franklin, statesman and author

How many shares?

Be careful with how many stock options you give. We requested and were authorized 10 million shares. Sounds like a lot—that's the idea. Employees feel better getting 100,000 shares than they would if you gave them 10,000, but yet in terms of value, 10,000 of 1,000,000 is equal to 100,000 of 10 million. My attorney recommended to me that I never speak in terms of shares being a percentage of ownership. Steering all conversations where percentage is mentioned toward discussing only numbers of shares is helpful, in the event you must issue more shares and an employee's percentage will be reduced. Although you might use percentage as your initial calculation for the number of shares you want to issue, always speak only in terms of the number of shares (options) an employee owns. Also remember to imagine what would happen if you terminate employees. How many shares do you want them to have?

Always have them vest

Vesting means ownership transfers over time. Let's say that I give you options for 100,000 shares in my company. For all intents and purposes, you can buy those shares right now. However, if the shares vest over four years, that is, they vest at 25 percent per year, that means in the first year you can only buy 25,000 shares. The second year you can buy an additional 25,000 shares or 50,000 shares. The third year you can buy 75,000 shares, and the fourth year you can buy all of them. Usually, you never actually purchase the shares until your company goes public or is acquired—when you can simultaneously sell your shares. (For a fee, an underwriter handles the transaction. You are paid the net proceeds of current market value minus your original option price.) The catch is that if an employee leaves the company before he or she is fully vested, let's say after just one year, he or she is only eligible to purchase 25,000 shares. The idea is to entice them to stay on and fully vest, but if it doesn't work out, then they don't get the whole enchilada.

> *There's more synergy and fewer conficts in a company*
> *when everyone gets rich the same way.*
> — Dennis DeBroeck, attorney

Ownership by disgruntled ex-employees is minimized

When hiring the first few employees, you often take anyone you can get because you need the job done. They come along and enthusiastically say, "Yeah, I can do that." You say, "Great, I'll take you, " because business is doing great and things are happening.

You give stock in the business and everybody is in love. But you can imagine, as the company grows, if the people you hired in the beginning do not grow with you and the company goes in a different direction, you may have to let some of these people go.

Over three to four years, you may have four, five, ten, or more ex-employees who own part of your company. It can (it will) cause problems later. Generally, you must treat all stock holders alike. For example, I considered taking a dividend from the company, but if I'm going to pay myself a dividend as a stockholder, I've got to give my other stockholders an equal amount proportionate to the amount of shares they own.

This can be a major problem. Imagine distributing a $100,000 bonus. If you own 75 percent of the stock, you've got to pay out $25,000 to someone else. I don't know about you, but I would find that annoying if it went to disgruntled ex-employees. It wouldn't be so bad if the ex-employees each owned 1,000 shares of stock instead of 5,000.

How and when to cash in?

For the stock options to work as an incentive, you'll need to plan and communicate to your options holders some form of exit strategy. If you don't or won't, sooner or later your employees will begin to question the value of their options and express a strong interest in cash. At some point they want to eat the carrot you've been dangling on the stick. In a similar way, why would investors invest if they couldn't cash out sometime soon? Stock options can be a two-edged sword—great for hiring good people for less, but lousy if you want to keep your company private forever. I'm planning my strategy soon for a possible future offering, including what we'll do with the money and how my job may change. This is not the time or place to skimp on attorney's fees—work with an attorney who specializes in this area and has many war stories to tell. You can design something you'll like as well as make your long-term employees rich.

Business Black Belt Notes

- Request a large number of shares to be authorized for your company.

- Use a vesting period for all stock and stock options.

- Consider what happens if/when an ex-employee owns stock.

- Refer only to the numbers of options/shares an employee owns, not the percentage.

- For stock options to succeed as an incentive, you must plan and communicate your exit strategy.

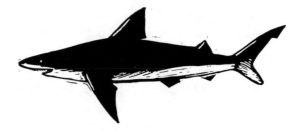

Lawyers,
the Care and Feeding Thereof

I never wanted to see anybody die,
but there are a few obituary notices I have read with pleasure.
— Clarence Darrow, attorney

☞ The practice of law is a combination of technical skill, strategy, and salesmanship. You must have all of these attributes in your legal advisors.

Not being an attorney, (although I think I've paid enough in legal fees to put myself through law school) I'm not going to give you legal advice. But I can recommend a few things to look for in contracts as well as in your relationship with attorneys.

Look for two important things in a lawyer. First, make sure that he or she is experienced and specializes in laws and practices relevant to your needs. Second, find one with excellent people skills. In other words, you want a skilled deal maker not a deal killer. I would happily introduce our customers, suppliers and other business alliance partners to any of the people in the law firm with whom we work.

Prospective customers are not bound by contracts and you don't sell to them in court where judges and juries make the purchasing decisions. Prospective customers don't have to buy from you, they can go somewhere else! I don't care what anyone says, practicing law involves salesmanship.

Lawyer or statesman

We filed an application for a registered trademark (®) with the U.S. Patent & Trademark Office (PTO), a government agency. JIAN had an intellectual property (trademarks, copyrights, and patents) lawyer who had a reputation for rudeness. A bully of a lawyer can backfire on you. When you use bullying tactics on people who work for the government, all you will get are problems. Imagine trying to throw your weight around at the Department of Motor Vehicles!

Just because the law is the law and people are supposed to act accordingly, you can't make demands and expect people to jump. Our application for trademark wasn't going through. Our bullying letters ran into a lot of red tape. After switching to a new law firm, who sent friendly letters and made friendly calls, it was amazing how quickly matters cleared up.

The difference was that the new firm "sold" the PTO on the simplicity of the solution to our legal problem; we took it upon ourselves to organize and explain the facts instead of demand that the people at the PTO figure it out because it was their job.

How can we make this work?

Some people characterize lawyers as deal killers. At least look for an attorney with a positive attitude. I used to think that finding fault with things proved how smart I was. Many people can point out problems, but the trick is to know how to deal with them. Ask your attorney how he or she would make something work. The type of lawyer you're looking for should help you do what you want to do. And they should steer you clear of obstacles that may create problems. After they've made every effort to assist and then recommend killing the deal, perhaps your deal really should die.

He who has the most documentation wins.

Paperwork is good

You want attorneys who are strong and tough, who can see through things in contracts, who have learned what kinds of things can go wrong in deals and relationships, and who will prepare contingency plans in the event something does go wrong. Perhaps I could have avoided a variety of learning experiences if I had invested in a good attorney's advice and paid more for a customized contract that suited my situation. Here are my favorites:

- A memory lapse as to the *deal* can be very annoying, especially when it seems crystal clear to you. Sometimes it seems like such a simple deal, so why bother to write it down? Perhaps a letter agreement will suffice, since you're sure you both will remember exactly what the deal really is. An attorney may point out a few other things that might occur and prepare you for them. . . like what if you've paid for programming and the programmer decides to move to Central America? Don't laugh.

- Your supplier has financial problems elsewhere and needs to make up for it with *your* deal. He starts telling you about the home he's building, the costs, the problems with the contractor... forget their stories, excuses, and BS, how much time does your agreement allow them before making good on the deal? And what can you do about it?

- An employee was negotiating his employment contract and asked for full medical coverage for his entire family. Can I legally inquire as to his or his wife's health or that of his family? This could be a can of worms. I said OK to him if the premium were no higher than anyone else's in the company. This was fair, and if a family member had some exotic disease, I wouldn't get blind-sided by an ugly expense. Besides, if he did that to me, I would have lost my trust in him and found a way to get rid of him eventually.

- They find out that they could have gotten a better deal elsewhere and want to come back and change their deal with you. There's always a better deal out there, but if you've started work on a project or have invested money based on a particular agreement, you need to be sure your deal is protected. An author of some of the text in one of our software packages was getting paid a 1 percent royalty, but came to my office one afternoon and informed me that he deserved 2 percent. Fortunately, I had a comprehensive contract that clearly covered me. I told him no. He talked to his attorney and was told that he had to comply with our agreement. . . whew!!!!

- Their idea of quality and completion differs from yours so when they deliver the finished goods, you're disappointed. This is tough, but try to quantify or compare the work to a known item as much as possible, so you can hopefully have a clear understanding of each other's expectations. It's best to do a small project together to get an idea of their standards for quality or completed work. Only then do you write a contract for a larger project.

- Business is good and there's a lot of money on the table. . . .
  Sometimes success can get ugly. When things are going well, it's easy to let things go without finalizing the paperwork. Perhaps you just got busy and let things go only to run into a disagreement later. Or maybe a small issue in an otherwise good relationship blows up when there's a lot of money at stake. A software author we worked with early on would never sign an agreement with us. We wanted him to work on further development and also allow the contributions of other authors. We were starting to make some respectable money on his product and wanted to promote it more, but it needed more input from other experts. When he refused to cooperate, we found another developer and replaced his content. . . . This cost him a lot of money over the next three years. Too *bad*.

Look for contradictions within your contracts

Agreements should be consistent throughout. It's one thing to pay your attorney to fight a bad deal or to defend your case. But to pay for their interpretation of how you or the other side might interpret the ambiguities in your own deal is a total waste of time and money. For example, we've shipped over $100,000 worth of software to a distributor who eventually managed itself out of business. Over two months elapsed before they paid our invoice, but they wanted to return everything of ours they hadn't sold. The first page of their contract said they could "return all unsold merchandise." The second page clearly stated that they could "return half of any merchandise they had purchased in the previous 90 days." Which was it?

The extra time and legal investment to interpret this contradiction and discuss it with the other side was a waste. (It took about three to four hours of legal review and conversation at $200 per hour. You can quickly burn up $600 to $800!) Even though we could have dealt with it before any money was on the table and made it perfectly clear one way or the other, we didn't do it because it didn't seem important at the time. Medium-sized mistake.

Clear up any contradictions in your contracts and set them straight before you make your deal.

Talk to your enemies

We were using the trademark for one of our products for several years when we discovered a registered trademark that was very similar. (We found out about its existence, but thought it was an abandoned product name.) Nevertheless, its existence on the books at the PTO prevented us from getting the coveted "®." We started the legal machine rolling because we wanted to protect the brand on our flagship product. Besides, this was a potential "skeleton in the closet," in the event we ever went for an initial public offering.

As it turned out, the name wasn't abandoned and we were the bad guys who infringed on someone else's trademark. We needed to make a deal. We spent a lot of money jockeying for position and trading paperwork through the attorneys. If you've never gone through this, it is a nerve-racking experience of uncertainty, expense, and the knowledge that you are working with human nature at its very worst—yours and theirs. You just want it to go away quickly and not cost too much.

I asked my attorney what this deal would cost and what our chances of winning were. He told me about $15,000 more and we had about a 90 percent chance of getting what we wanted. (That means that the other guy goes away and we own the name.) I asked if it was all right if I called the owner of the other trademark directly to see if I could make a deal. It was, so I called. I pointed out that even if he did want to use that name for his product, that it would only create confusion in the marketplace since we had already been advertising heavily for our product. I admitted to the owner that I was his enemy and he should confer with his ad agency. Fortunately, he had another name for his product and his agency concurred that it would be easier and cheaper if they developed his brand awareness using the other name. I purchased the name he owned for $10,000. I saved $5,000 in legal fees and I had a 100 percent guarantee of getting what I wanted.

You always have an open channel of communication with the other side. Most good attorneys want the dispute to be settled without a lot of drama; however, you should discuss first with your attorney the merits of direct contact with your opponent before contacting them.

Add it up

As a legal battle wears on, you and your adversary develop a common interest that can be worked into a motivating factor—you are both spending a lot of cash on legal fees. He or she would most likely want to make this nightmare go away as much as you would, so you have a mutual interest in working something out. As the legal bills add up, the animosity between you, as a percentage of your overall problem, becomes less and less a factor and he or she would probably like to talk with you, too. I recommend that you add up your likely costs in legal expenses if you continue to fight and weigh that against giving them what they want to settle immediately. (The certainty of a done deal, even if it involves making payments, is a tremendous negotiating tool.) Often, it may be cheaper to just pay them off.

Business Black Belt Notes

- Good lawyers aren't bullies; they employ the qualities of a good salesperson.

- Look for contradictions or any ambiguities in your contracts before deals are made.

- Do the math: Is it cheaper to pay than fight?

Consulting the Consultant

*A consultant is someone who saves his client
almost enough to pay his fee.*
— Arnold Glasow

☞ **If a consultant asked me to consult him or her on how to build
their business, here's what I'd say.**

To me, the word 'consultant' is a big turn-off. I often don't want to see consultants, talk to them, or pay their fees. It's a matter of semantics and an attitude, all in the word "consultant."

When I first started my business, Tools for Sales, I termed myself a marketing consultant and nobody wanted me. They all said, "I don't need one of
those." If you're a marketing consultant, I recommend giving your company
a name and listing several specific things you do either in a tag line beneath
your company name or as bullets on the back of your business card. A "marketing consultant" is way too general. For example: I called my company
"Tools for Sales." When people asked what I did, I told them I made data
sheets, brochures, and mailing pieces. . . you know, tools salespeople can use
to sell with. A potential client would think of similar things he or she needed and ask if I could handle them. "Do you do advertising or telemarketing
training?" he or she might have asked. I responded, "What exactly do you
need?" Then tailored my pitch to their immediate needs. The idea is to first
get them interested in what you do as opposed to what you are. You're much
more likely to have a new client or be referred to one.

The idea behind hiring a consultant is to bring in someone with expertise to handle specific tasks for a fixed amount of money and, when it's done, they leave. We've used these experts very effectively many times. The trick is to write down exactly what it is you're going to do and the price on what you're going to deliver. That way you're out of there as soon as you're finished. This is what we clients hope to get. Even though you may return for a repeat performance like handling my taxes every year, it's difficult to bring on a consultant if I think they'll stay forever or be difficult to get rid of. If you help me define my project completion criteria, cost, and timing—it's much easier to hire you to get started.

Big company expertise just part time

On the other hand, we hired one management consultant part-time who, if paid full time, would cost about $150,000 a year. However, we arranged that he come in two half-days a week and we get the benefit of a senior financial manager for $1,500 a month. In his case, we have enough ongoing activities needing his expertise to keep him productively busy. Some months it looks like he's done nothing. And other months, he's earned his keep for an entire year in one conversation. In his case, we have a Fortune 500 financial officer available to our small company without having to hire him full time.

If you come from a high-level job in a big corporation, possibly many companies would appreciate the sophistication you bring. Without looking for project after project or a full-time job, you might consider working one day a week for five companies or some kind of combination. They could afford you, you'd enjoy a variety of clients, and the sum total of your fees could add up to much more than a single full-time job. A small company could easily afford $500 a day which adds up to $120,000 per year and $1,000 per day brings in close to $250,000 per year.

That kind of consultant works very well. Especially with the virtual corporation model described in the chapter "Be Part of a Virtual Company." Small companies don't need and cannot afford to hire a lot of expensive employees. Clients can get as much expertise as they need and pay as they go. And, this concept is relatively easy to sell.

The first hour is free. . . that's it!

Many consultants get stuck pitching, pitching, and pitching, and giving too much away for free. How do you get your potential client to sign you on? The first hour is free—that's when you go find out what the problems and priorities are. Before the hour is up, figure out what small project can be accomplished for only a few hours of your time that your client can afford, maybe $100 to $500. This should be a project that by itself has value to your client whether or not you continue to work together. It could be a simple component of the big picture you want to work into. In my marketing business, I offered to develop a data sheet—something relatively simple, inexpensive, but useful and, in itself, complete. This gave my client a feel for working with me and for the quality I delivered. It's also easy for a client to commit to and pay for. And it's a painless way for you to gauge your working relationship as well as your client's responsiveness to your invoices. The next step is working on the next larger project.

Too many consultants come in and paint a big expensive picture, only to lose the opportunity because they fail to break the project into bite-sized and affordable pieces.

Business Black Belt Notes

- Define the project completion criteria, cost, and date.

- Assure clients that you won't stay forever.

- Can you provide needed sophistication on a part-time basis?

- Sell your services in stages.

- Sell your efficiencies.

Working With Programmers

Some of us are like wheelbarrows
—only useful when pushed, and very easily upset.
— Jack Herbert

☞ Working in the Information Age requires software development or modification for your business. Here are some ideas for working with the people who can do it for you.

You may not need a software programmer but just in case, here's the scoop.

Being in the software business, JIAN works with many programmers. When we've wanted to tailor a software package to create something specific for businesses, we've run into a few major problems with some programmers.

Many times when you buy a computer program, you get just the *executable* code. For example, when you buy Microsoft Word, you get a word processor. But you cannot go into Microsoft Word and change how Microsoft Word works because you don't have the *source* code. The same ordinarily holds true when you purchase the work of a programmer for your company.

In your contract with a programmer, you want an understanding that you own the work that the programmer does. This is "work for hire." Programmers are very proprietary about what they do. He or she may be reluctant to give you the source code of his or her work. If so, you may run into trouble in the future if the programmer isn't around to make changes. As I mentioned near the beginning of this book, a programmer working on a new software revision we were interested in suddenly dropped dead.

Some software programs, such as accounting packages, will include the source code because individual companies will need to tailor a program to their own needs. If you buy a custom program from somebody, you'd better make sure you get the source code from the programmer. If something happens to that programmer, you need to be able to hand it to another programmer so he or she can continue to update it.

> *Whatever you cannot understand, you cannot possess.*
> — Johann Wolfgang von Goethe, poet and playwright

Source code as hostage

Proprietary programmers see keeping the source code as an insurance policy to get paid. They become paranoid that we're going steal their code, cut them off, and no longer work with them. Unfortunately, it has probably happened to them before. But in JIAN's case, the exact opposite is true.

We terminated our work with one particular programmer because he was reluctant to give us the source code. We had to give up several months of work, throw away everything he'd done, and start over because we couldn't give his source code to another programmer or anyone else to evaluate, make suggestions, or offer improvements. I don't want to work with a programmer like this again. Without you having possession of the source code and the legal rights to it, a programmer can hold you hostage. I don't need any programmers like this because plenty of programmers will give me the source code.

Good programmers charge an hourly rate and give you what you want. They will document their work and they won't argue with you about it. If they show any signs of instability—get rid of them. Get a programmer who has a reputation for delivering what you want at a fair price.

They'll program for free!

Sounds great, but this can kill you in the long run. I've talked with a number of people who have programmers willing to create programs for a royalty on sales or for stock in the company. This deal is almost too good to pass up. And, it's too good to be true. Here are a few potential problems:

- Since you're not paying them cash, they feel they can make the program any way they want.

- They can work on it when they want.

- They don't necessarily have to deliver it on your schedule.

I now know that it's better to bite the bullet and pay cash.

I recommend thoroughly checking out any programmer's background with other people who understand software coding. Was the code "clean"? That is to say, was it efficiently programmed and documented along the way? (Good programmers include non-operating lines of documentation within the lines of computer programming code so that another programmer could follow the first programmer's design logic throughout the program.) If I was writing code for a royalty, I might not bother to leave tracks for someone else to follow.

Unless you thoroughly understand software development, the best bet is to work with a company that provides software design and computer programming as their principle business. They understand and can manage programmers. They will spec in a thorough Quality Control process and make sure that someone, in the future, can pick up and make improvements where the first version left off.

Business Black Belt Notes

- When working with a programmer, make sure he or she gives you the source codes.

- Programs must be designed to be useable from programmer to programmer.

- Design your program to be improvable from the start.

- Incorporate the right personalities—hire somebody who will give you what you want the way you want it.

- Make sure that you own all rights, title and interests to all software you have developed for your company.

Editors, Writers, & Reporters

Guns are always loaded. . . everything is on the record.

☞ Your approach to a PR interview will make a world of difference in what appears in print or how you come across on camera.

When I had my first golden opportunity for an interview with a business reporter from the *Santa Barbara News Press* in California, where I had started my do-it-yourself used car lot, I thought I had made the big time. I was very positive throughout the interview.

He asked me if there were any bad times, and I responded that when the weather wasn't good, people didn't show up. This was a big mistake. Guess what leaped out of the brief little article about my business? Something like: ". . . but, Franklin admits that when the sun isn't out, the buyers don't come looking." Santa Barbara is on the coast and it often takes until noon to burn off a morning cloud cover. Anyone who read the article was sure to remember (via their subconscious use of the memory trick I taught you) that their car wouldn't sell unless the sun was out. Consequently, as luck would have it, the next weekend was cloudy and very few people showed up.

How will it look in print?

When I go in to talk with editors and writers, I want them to rave about my product. I want them to say all this great stuff about my company. But what they always seem to be looking for is what I'm not telling them. I found out early on that everything you say to a writer can be in the article. So, before you talk to any reporter, imagine that everything you say will appear in print. Consider how certain responses will look if only individual sentences or statements used out of context are used. Especially be careful of your little offhand remarks. Know your facts, because reporters are very concerned with accuracy.

If your thinking is pure to begin with and you're doing the right thing in business, you don't have anything to worry about. But make sure you're preaching what you practice.

> **A journalist is a grumbler, a censurer, a giver of advice,**
> **a regent of sovereigns, a tutor of nations.**
> **Four hostile newspapers are more to be feared**
> **than a thousand bayonets.**
> — Napoléon Bonaparte, military leader and statesman

Train your employees to work well with reporters

Look what happened when Newt Gingrich's mother was quoted as saying that Hillary Rodham Clinton "was a bitch." It backfired on her and made her son, the Speaker of the U.S. House of Representatives, look like a jerk. It's a great example of shooting your mouth off without thinking about the consequences, especially when amplified by the media. I hope Mrs. Gingrich learned something from her mistake, but what if she had some coaching before she talked in front of the cameras? (I hate to steal the fun for reporters.) And what if you did too?

Either tell your employees that you are the only media contact or you should practice questions and answers with them in advance, in the event they do talk with reporters. (You may be away from your trade show booth and a reporter will come by for some news, for example.)

Uh, we do have a few problems. . .

You may even want to build in some deliberate bad news. In our case, our biggest problem in life has been explaining to people how ridiculously easy it is to use our product. But it's been tough getting that across. We tend to play down the problem of letting people know about our product before they beat their brains out developing their own employee manual or business plan. We play that problem down because we figure it's our problem and we'll just deal with it. In other words, control the downside—give reporters something to tell that you ordinarily wouldn't say but gives readers some insight to your problems.

Design for the media

"This product is so good, I almost couldn't find anything wrong with it," said one reporter. A good reviewer is looking for some limitations to report; some flaw to expose. I think you can and should make a product that no one can find fault with. I look at our products and wonder what could the press find fault with? Part of the design consideration for your product or service must include what will appeal to reporters. They maintain an excellent pulse on the market, so developing a relationship with them is highly valuable. Their product recommendations or their responses to your product can be more important than those of your customers. That's because a favorable review can be leveraged into a ton of sales. So designing and promoting your product for a favorable review is crucial.

For example, for years JIAN concentrated on the content of BizPlan*Builder* from the input of thousands of customers. But we seriously neglected the installation routine. We felt that it was easy enough to import the text of financial templates into any word processor or spreadsheet. Customers had a little trouble installing it but we didn't give it that much importance. We thought customers could figure it out and they'd be on their way to writing their business plans. We thought it was more important to our customer that we use our resources to focus on the content, not the razzle-dazzle of the computer.

However, some reviewers liked our competitor's installation routines and were sidetracked away from our superior content. I thought our superior plan would shine through. But customers read reviews, so now we have a powerful menu with a start-up and installation routine. We've even built in several additional features to help our customers get started even faster.

Editors as focus groups

*A news sense is really a sense of what is important,
what is vital, what has color and life—
what people are interested in. That's journalism.*
— Burton Rascoe

The moral of the story is to pay attention to what reviewers want and recommend that you do.

I never used to give reporters so much importance. I thought they had sleazy jobs, reporting mostly bad news. But after getting to know a few of them, I see a different perspective that needs to be appreciated. I had a recent revelation about editors, writers, and reporters in general.

Keeping balance in the universe

They're not really going around saying, "Bad news is good news." Their job looks to me like they're keeping balance in the universe. You've got all these characters—me included—advertising products and claiming their own is the best. The reviewers feel they've got to go in and find the truth. If they find that a product is great, they'll say it's great. But if you're doing something behind the scenes that's not great, they want to find it and expose it. They're concerned and really want to protect the public from any evil businesspeople who may be trying to cheat them.

Most writers want to tell you what companies aren't telling you. A company's advertising will tell you the good news, and the reporter adds the balance of the other stuff the company is not telling you.

When you read the articles *and* the ads, you get a more balanced picture. That's why it appears to me that their purpose in the bigger picture is keeping balance in the universe.

Most journalists want to tell the truth. They're not out to make someone look bad—unless the person deserves it. When you can appreciate this perspective on journalists, perhaps you can be at peace with what they do, make news that's worth reporting, and go on about your business.

Business Black Belt Notes

- Make sure your product or service design appeals to reporters.

- A favorable review can be leveraged into a ton of sales.

- Train your staff—how will their statements look in print?

- A journalist's job is to keep balance in the universe.

Red Belt

Getting
On
With
It

How long does it take to get a black belt? How long does it take to become successful in business? It's time to let go of these questions. It takes as long as it does. This is the time to refine everything you've been learning. Your must make your decision to go the distance no matter what.

Bankruptcy— Behind the Scenes

New meaning for the term, "Go for broke."

☞ Bankruptcy may be an easy way out of paying your bills, but it leaves you open to losing a lot more—and it's an opportunity for shrewd takeovers.

We had a license agreement to pay one of our software developers a royalty for a number of years on a product he developed for us. What we didn't know was that he had a bad habit of declaring bankruptcy to get out of paying his bills. We found out when an attorney called to inquire about his royalty agreement and to inform me that all payments were to be paid directly to the attorney. He explained that handling bankruptcies weren't normally his business, but it was his turn to handle one. We joked about it being the equivalent of being assigned to "latrine duty," but it was his job to clean up this mess. His interest was in settling the accounts and creditors' claims as soon and as painlessly as possible. In this case, all of our developer's assets were assigned to the court in order to pay off the creditors. Unfortunately, his royalty contract was now part of the court's assets to be handled by this attorney. Our royalty agreement was to pay out over several years, but the attorney needed to settle this case ASAP. To make a long story short, we negotiated $5,000 cash to buy out the royalty contract. This saved us about $25,000 in royalty payments. You see, he didn't care what the real value was, he just wanted whatever he could get now to get the paperwork off his desk! Declaring bankruptcy was a big mistake on the developer's part. I'm not going to dwell on the intricacies of bankruptcy, nor am I going to do any further research on the subject, but it sure looks like you lose a lot of control over your life and assets—beyond the advertised simplicity of getting out of paying your bills.

There's a special place in Hell....

for people who declare bankruptcy. Many people suffer and I feel much the way banks do. In fact, many banks are now immediately disqualifying loan applicants if they've declared bankruptcy in the last 10 years. It's the equivalent of nuking your financial future. I draw your attention to the word "declare" used almost always when referring to bankruptcy. It looks to me that you aren't bankrupt unless you consciously declare it. With a little effort and some creativity, I think you can find a variety of ways to pay off your obligations. Having and maintaining credit and credibility goes a long way in business relationships. Knowing that someone would declare bankruptcy as a means of escape warns me not to trust them—ever.

> *Many people dream of success.*
> *To me success can only be achieved through*
> *repeated failure and introspection.*
> *In fact, success represents only 1% of your work*
> *which results from the 99% that is called failure.*
> — Soichiro Honda, founder, Honda Motor Company

Business Black Belt Notes

- The bankruptcy trustee can sell your assets for pennies on the dollar just to get your paperwork off his desk.

- Declaring bankruptcy is a conscious act.

- Bankruptcy has a nuclear fallout of 10 years.

New punctuation:

I call it the *anxiety* mark.

Write It Like You
Would *Say* It

It should be possible to explain the laws of physics to a barmaid.
— Albert Einstein, physicist

☞ We can learn much to improve our everyday written communications by studying the techniques used by advertising copywriters.

In school, some of us BSed our way through essays and exams and lived to brag about it. In business, you need to make a point—someone needs to get your message and they have neither the time nor the interest in BS. You get no points for more words, no points for sounding erudite. Short and simple wins the day.

If you write the dense prose of an academic, you're less likely to communicate your message effectively. More than likely, you'll prove your intelligence, but unfortunately, you won't make your point because few will read far enough to get it. Besides, nobody talks like that! So why do we waste energy writing that way?

People often talk in their heads when they're reading as if they're reading aloud to themselves, and what they read comes across as speech. Fewer, specific words that make your point will take less time to read and will sound, in their heads, as if you're talking to them. On the other hand, speed-readers grab whole blocks of text visually and absorb the meaning.

With some simple writing techniques, you'll say more with fewer words and more effectively sell people on your ideas. They'll understand what you're saying more fully because they have less clutter to weed through.

Some of the best writers talk to you in print. Why do you think advertising is so effective? Ad copy is appealing because the writers try to make it as personal as possible. Ideally, you don't even realize that you're reading an ad. You're completely absorbed in the description of a product and you're imagining yourself using it. Advertisers want you to identify with what they're saying so you'll feel the need to buy their product.

The first few sentences should provide the flavor of your entire message. Is it going to be hype and bull (hyperbole), dense technical jargon, academic jabberwocky, or informative and clean? If the copy starts out clean, readers will likely continue reading. If not, they'll look for something else to do. Just make sure that your message is consistent in style throughout.

Use subheads to highlight important information

People skip around to get the message to avoid reading the whole thing. Subheads recapture your reader's interest. When I'm reading promotional literature, I'm always wondering, "Can I throw this out or is it worth acting on?" A short subhead (some people call them cross-heads) will grab your reader's attention and pull them back in. A full page of text is scary to look at.

Remember to word your subheads wisely. Assume your reader will scan your letter or literature and see only the subheads. Therefore each subhead must communicate an important point. The text following should elaborate, explain or substantiate the statement made in your subhead. Avoid wasting subheads on bland statements like, "Product features" when you coud actually state one or two features in the sub-head.

Tricks with punctuation

Writing as you speak is a different style than we were taught in school. One trick is to use punctuation between thoughts as visual bridges to minimize the words to read and process in your brain. Punctuation is like a traffic sign. You would cause confusion and accidents if you used or interpreted them in novel ways. A common language and use of punctuation promotes understanding. Use these tricks sparingly, so the intended effect is not lost.

How do you punctuate the way you talk?

- If you want to indicate a significant pause, an em dash, a comma, or a period is most commonly used.

- Use bullets to set your points apart, maybe even indent the whole paragraph.

- Use ellipses (. . .) to connect loose thoughts without extra words. According to most style manuals, three dots indicate that words have been omitted from this middle of a sentence. If a sentence ends with ellipses, you must use four dots (the last is the period).

- Em dashes (—) are also great for connecting two related thoughts together. They're also good for indicating a significant pause. Example: You're not writing because you have a writing assignment—you're writing because your life depends on it!

- <u>Underlining an important point</u> that is buried in the text grabs attention. (Personally, I like avoid underlining a lower case *g*. It doesn't look <u>good</u>.)

- One–word sentences add emphasis. "Help! I need your help with this project." Any use (let alone overuse) of this trick must be carefully and very specifically chosen.

- Put a note in parentheses (it's as if you were whispering something to your reader on the side).

- I frequently read contracts with run-on thoughts where the overall meaning becomes ambiguous because there's no indication of the pauses. Attorneys often dictate these passages, but the emphasis and inflection are lost when typed. Put commas in places where you want a pause in your thought. In the reader's mind, it will sound the same way you thought it. "Jian's business planning software is the best there is, and when you use it, you can bet that you've developed the best presentation possible."

Even if you start with a wonderfully written letter or memo, a page full of text, at first impression, does not look inviting to read. That's a bad impression for your reader to begin with. Combine these techniques to give the impression of an interesting page and something worth reading. Now.

Study your junk mail

Before you throw your mail out, study what catches your eye and what keeps your attention. I learned a lot when I studied The Sharper Image catalog copy, and I learned even more when I wrote their copy. The simple rule to remember is to write like you talk—how would you say it if you were explaining something over the phone? Read what you write out loud. How does it sound? Does it make sense? Here's an example of textbook writing compared to how I'd write it:

**When carrying out an analysis of your target market,
you will find the following components to be useful. . .**

Sounds a little stuffy, doesn't it? This was used in a book on writing business plans. If this is how one section goes, what kind of book am I going to have to deal with? No wonder people dread writing business plans. Perhaps the following would reach the same conclusion more simply:

Analyze your target market using. . .

Which is the easiest to understand? The idea here is to make it easy for your audience to absorb your message. Make them speed-readers. You don't want them all tangled up in prepositional transitions—they may be grammatically correct but are mental tongue-twisters to read. It's important to set the tone right away or else your reader can only assume that your entire message will be a bummer to read. Sure, I may break a few grammatical rules, but you understand what I'm communicating. When you write this way, you respect and entertain your reader.[14]

In fact, this informal talk/writing comes across as even more intelligent than something that might sound like a sales rep fresh out of school who's pitching you and trying too hard. Take the candy coating off! Give it to them straight. That in itself makes you unique. It also makes your message worth reading.

---

[14]   I recommend that you own and use these as fundamental writing tools anyway.

Shertzer, Margaret. *Elements of Grammar*. New York, New York, Collier Books

Strunk, William and White, E.B. *Elements of Style*. New York, New York, MacMillan Publishing Company.

I trust people to tell me what they like,
but not what they think everyone else likes.

Opinion or experience

When I was first writing this book, I put in things from my opinion and just made up examples to illustrate my point, but when I reread those parts they were boring. I realized I was just spouting an opinion rather than coming from real experience. I actually had an experience that prompted me to write each chapter, so why not use it?

The next time you listen to a public speaker, think about this: do they fascinate you with a real-life adventure or do they put you to sleep with a theory? When you speak from your own experience, you transfer that experience at the gut level—you were there. Wow, that really happened! You transfer your experience to your audience, and they share that experience. People are captivated. They learn, they're entertained, or they're persuaded. Using real life facts and experiences is much more interesting than samples. The truth is often more bizarre than fiction.

An opinion is a belief based upon incomplete facts. (Expressing an opinion as a fact is called propaganda.) Remember to make clear which are facts or first-hand experiences and which are personal opinions. It's OK to have and express a point of view. This book is full of my points of view. The opinions and theories I described in my early drafts ultimately led me to express real experiences and what they taught me—real things you can use to build your business.

Communicating effectively is crucial in all areas of life, not just in advertising. The next time you're writing an office memo, a sales letter, an promo piece, etc. imagine talking face-to-face with your audience. It works.

Business Black Belt Notes

- Write like an advertising copywriter.

- Write like you would speak to a friend.

- Use subheads and other punctuation techniques to pull readers in.

- Incorporate your own experiences.

Don't Read This!
The Trouble with Negatives

*When dealing with people, remember you are not dealing with
creatures of logic, but with creatures of emotion, creatures bristling
with prejudice, and motivated by pride and vanity.*
— Dale Carnegie, author & teacher

☞ Sometimes negatives work to grab attention, but their literal
meanings win out. Is that really the message you want to
communicate?

Consider what you just did. The title clearly stated not to read this, but here
you are reading. In fact, you probably jumped right to this section. Leaving
aside a discussion of our perverse desire to do what others tell us not to do,
let's look at the impact of negatives on our thinking and our productivity.
This isn't going to be a discussion on positive thinking. It's actually about
using positive words versus negative words.

To this day, I remember many of the suggestions written in *Think and
Grow Rich* by Napoleon Hill. However, I don't remember much of anything
I read about what not to do.

If this chapter grabbed your attention because it said, "Don't read this,"
what do you think happens when you say, "Don't forget?" To demonstrate
further: If you were to say, "Don't think of a banana," of course, you immediately and automatically think of a banana. Where did the "don't" go? It
seems to disappear and we act upon what the action the "don't" refers to.

We're not helping ourselves or others by unconsciously saying things like "Don't forget to send that FedEx." So, "forget" is actually the subconscious command that stays in our minds. But if we were to say, "Remember to send that FedEx," we're actually assisting the other person by giving them a positive mental command. (I suppose that saying, "Don't remember to send that FedEx," would have the same effect.)

Always mentally translate from a double negative to positive. So, whenever you think to yourself or when someone tells you, "Don't forget to . . .," remember to simultaneously transpose that thought to "Remember to . . . ." Consciously implant the positive form of suggestion—it's the command your mind will follow.

Use this illustration as a tool to measure effectiveness:

A

– ——————————————— 0 ——————————————— +

In the simple graph above, the middle is zero or neutral, negative is on the left, and positive is on the right. If you were to say, "I don't want to lose more customers," where would you plot this statement in terms of its effect on your way of thinking? Somewhere near A because you haven't put a positive thought in your mind. In this case, your situation won't get any worse—you won't lose any *more* customers. It might move from A toward zero, but not into the positive because the statement is not positive. At best, you can reach neutral or 0 because stopping a negative only prevents your situation from getting worse. However, if you said, "I want to sell to more customers," then you're focused on the positive action you can take—you can go from A to the far positive end of the scale. The sky is the limit as to the possibilities available to you for improving your situation. This is powerful self-programming as well as successful communication with others. (Don't try it tomorrow at work.)

Take a hint from successful direct marketers

I mentioned this before. We've all heard "You learn from your mistakes." I began to wonder when I would start doing things right, because I had made a lot of mistakes and was pretty miserable. Then a wealthy and successful gentleman pointed out that I had been focused only on learning from my mistakes—and not from my successes. There are an infinite number of ways to screw up and fewer ways to be successful. (Why are there fewer successful people on the planet than unsuccessful people?) In direct marketing and mail-order, we constantly test everything: products, lists, offers, freebies, headlines, copy, and so on. We constantly look for what pulls the most and we discard what doesn't work. We make notes of what didn't work for us only to remember what we tested.

This won't affect your golf game

If you play golf, for example, remember this thought when you're about to hit the golf ball over a pond. Think to yourself, "Just hit the golf ball over the pond, but don't look at the pond." "Pretend the pond's not there." Or "Don't think of the pond." Of course, you'll sink the ball into the water. The obvious focus should be to aim the ball at the green, not to *avoid the pond.* Let the pond be there, but focus on the green. Focus on where you want to go, not on where you don't want to go. There's a big difference between avoiding what you don't want and focusing on what you do want. This concept applies to everything in life.

If we made a list of 10 reasons why businesses fail and another list of 10 reasons why businesses succeed, which list do you think is going to propel your business forward? Sure, you can learn a lot from other people's mistakes and avoid things that don't work, but you can learn a lot more from other people's successes.

I read an article entitled "10 Reasons Why Most Businesses Fail" in a prominent publication that catered to small companies. I went berserk! I happen to know that the author's own business had failed, and he didn't even list that reason why! Reading this article is what inspired me to write down some ideas that eventually evolved into this book. I hope it's more helpful to you in a positive way.

Business Black Belt Notes

- Use positive words instead of negative ones.

- In your mind, automatically replace "Don't forget to..." with "Remember to...."

- If you use negative goals, at best you won't get any worse.

- Focus on what you want, not on what you don't want.

- You can learn a lot from mistakes, but you can learn a lot more from successes.

Afraid of Getting
Your Idea Ripped Off?

*This telephone has too many shortcomings
to be seriously considered as a means of communication.
The device is inherently of no value to us.*
— Western Union internal memo, 1876

☞ **Although you must play the game of business, expressing your
ideas will take you farther than keeping them secret.**

People come up to me all the time at trade shows and say, "I thought of that
product" or "I could have done that." They could have, but they didn't.
Instead, I'm the one running a successful company because I took the action
and followed up on my idea.

You've probably heard from your friends that your idea has already been
thought of. And probably it has, but so what? In reality, what are the chances
of someone else actually becoming more successful with the idea than you?
Unless a direct competitor with manufacturing and marketing wherewithal
gets a hold of your new product design or service plans, you probably don't
have much to worry about. In fact, if you openly show off your idea, you'll
likely get a lot of excellent feedback. But first, let me explain why you're safe.

Let's say 100,000 people thought of your idea. If 10 percent actually take
action, there are 10,000 people working on your idea as you read this. You
know how easy it is to get distracted from your project by higher priorities—

other tasks, other ideas, emergencies, urgencies. So let's say 10 percent of 10,000, including you, manage to stay focused and make it past the other things in life.

Now there are only 1,000 people who've actually built a prototype and who are scrambling to beat you to market. But there aren't many people who are good at marketing. Let's say that 10 percent of them are. So, now we're down to about 100 competitors. Not very many are likely to mount a significant campaign against you. Plus they need financing. Maybe 10 percent of them will get the money together to launch their product.

We're down to 10 people who have stayed with the project, raised some money to launch it, and have some marketing savvy. But do they have a decent product? Does it really work? Is it pretty? Many things can go wrong here. Of course, you are going to do everything right and remain the one person who has the winning product and a commanding position in the marketplace.

Enough people have won this game, so you can too. Don't be put off by your fear of competitors beating you along the way. You've just seen the unlikelihood of that. I had this same fear myself. I thought for sure someone else would beat me to market. Too many projects get over engineered and run out of gas along the way. You can see why it's important to keep your idea and the execution of it simple. The world is full of inventions that made a difference and made their inventors rich. It was a matter of perseverance and belief in their concept. Actually, maybe only 100 other people start out with a similar idea. Do the math and the reality of the probability of your success leaps exponentially.

Here's a chart to summarize:

People with the same idea	*100,000*
Get past their miscellaneous distractions	*10,000*
Actually build a prototype	*1,000*
WRITE A BUSINESS PLAN AND RAISE MONEY	*100*
Get into production and to market	*10*
Actually have a successful product that people buy	*1*

This is meant to show you how good your chances of success really are if you're committed to creating and marketing a good idea.

I can tell you, but I'll have to kill you

Many people say, "I've got this really great idea, but it's secret. I can't tell anybody. Someone's going to rip off my idea."

In order to come up with a really convincing, full-blown sales pitch, you've got to make sure all the bases are covered. How do you do that? The best thing you can do is talk to people about your idea. You never know when someone could give you valuable feedback or advice on the subject.

I was once talking to a woman who had a really dark tan, as if she had been in a tanning booth. I said, "Wouldn't it be great if they just built the tanning lights into shower stalls? You take a shower every day anyway. You might as well get tan while you take a shower." The woman thought it was a great idea and said, "I think I'll go do that."

Do you think I'm worried that she ripped off my product idea? No. If she did, great! By sharing my idea, I got a response from someone that acknowledged its worth, almost like market research. People are so busy doing the things they've got to do. They've got their own information and knowledge applied to their deflector shields. The reality of someone stealing another's idea is so remote. Even if I went to the company that made lights and said, "You really ought to make a shower light so people can get a tan while they shower," they still would probably never do it.

> *I have traveled the length and breadth of this country*
> *and talked with the best people, and I can assure you*
> *that data processing is a fad that won't last out the year.*
> — The editor in charge of business books for Prentice Hall, 1957

The truth is I'm never going to do anything about the tanning light anyway. I hope someone does do something because I could benefit from this idea myself! Besides, I've made a karma deposit. Someone will inevitably come along and give me a million-dollar idea that I could implement.

Get out there with your idea. You want lots of input, qualified and unqualified. You want the feedback and you want to gather lots of ideas.

You're formulating your product and doing customer research. It's OK to tell people about it. You never know when someone might have a good insight.

As for my lights in the shower stall, someone might say, "You know a problem you might have with that is people might be afraid of getting electrocuted." That's important to put into the design criteria. Then I need to refer to my "We're Full of Solutions Looking for Problems" chapter to thoroughly understand the problem and to find out how to design these things so people aren't going to get electrocuted in the shower.

Now I've even written about my "shower–tan" idea for all the world to read. I'm not worried about someone stealing it. Although I'm not qualified in construction or electrical manufacturing, I could have a prototype built and start a business on this idea. However, I need to focus on my business software publishing company. So take this idea and run with it. Perhaps you already thought of this very idea. In this case, I'm an example of one of the thousands of people with your idea that will do nothing with it. Chances are you will actually do a better job and get it to market. "

This works for services as well

When I have an idea (usually a marketing idea) for somebody, I call them and give it to them. Some people would say I'm just giving away the idea for free so someone else can act on it on their own without me. That's fine. For example, you go to a doctor and ask him what's wrong with you. He says, "You need your appendix out." Now, what am I going to do, go home and take out my own appendix? I don't think so. (Though, it does inspire a product idea: 'SutureSelf™'—your home self-surgery kit complete with instructional CD and comprehensive Help! menu....) I'm going to go back to the doctor who told me I needed my appendix out and have the doctor do it. I'm certainly not going to do it myself.

When you give an idea to someone, they'll likely need your idea *implemented* by someone—that's why they'll hire you. Maybe you'll even come up with more useful and valuable ideas you can put to work for their benefit. Your generous gift of an idea is your promotional foot in the door. Just remember to explain how easily *you* can make it happen for them.

Note

Although I suggested earlier that you have little to fear, I still wouldn't go blabbing to your competitors. Be sure your employment agreement includes an "assignment of inventions" clause that includes rights to intellectual property developed by employees. A template covering this is included in the JIAN EmployeeManual*Maker* ™. See the back of the book for details.

Business Black Belt Notes

- Your idea likely won't get ripped off—even if you show it off.

- People are too distracted with other things in life to be a very big threat to your success.

- The chances of other people succeeding at building a prototype, writing a business plan, raising the money, and getting into the market are slim.

- When you talk about your idea, you're doing market research.

- People may like your ideas, but they also may need you to implement them.

The Easy Way
To Spec a New Product

When you make the world tolerable for yourself,
you make a world tolerable for others.
— Anaïs Nin, author

☞ Develop the specifications for anything new by first creating the brochure or package that would inspire you to buy it. Then go make it.

This concept is so simple. I'm blown away that no big name marketing guru hasn't plastered it everywhere. I guess you can't charge exorbitant consulting fees without the long process of analysis, testing, discussion, and a 10-pound proposal. You can't charge much for results that look too simple. But here's how to get them anyway.

Create your ad, brochure or package first. The idea, of course, is to make your product or service do what your brochure says it will do. This is what customers will see and what they'll buy from. If the ad, brochure or package is exciting, functional, "speaks" to your customers and addresses their problems, then it's likely you'll have a successful product or service.

Would YOU buy this product?

What would *you* need to know to feel comfortable buying your product or service? How does it work? What would *you* need to see? What kind of environment does your product or service belong in? Test your promo piece on friends and potential customers. (Do not actually place an ad in any media yet, unless you would bet your life that you can deliver by the time customers call to order it!)

This entire process is a lot of fun to do. It keeps things simple and embodies the essence of your new product or service. It's also the surest way to develop a new product or service that customers will buy and not a fabrication by someone who's out of touch with reality. Plus you'll save a fortune on market analysis, consulting, and advertising.

Reverse-engineer the process

The secret to this is to just do things backwards. Instead of doing research, engineering, drawings, and then the marketing, take your idea and work backwards. Develop the brochure first, then do the research, drawings, and engineering. (For some assistance, refer to "20 Questions" on pages 218-219)

A variation on this theme is to design your retail package. If you were in a store with no knowledgeable salespeople to offer advice, what would the package need to show and say to compel you to buy it? If possible, buy your competitors' products for comparison. In the event that your designer, product manager, or engineers disagree with your outrageous requirements, you can show them exactly what you are up against.

Here are a few suggestions:

- List all the bells and whistles in order of importance to your customer.

- Include a drawing or photograph illustrating your product's use.

- List the applications and uses your customer will enjoy.

- Include a price and maybe a special offer.

- Fabricate some quotes you'd like to hear from your customers.

- Try out a few choice headlines.

At JIAN, we've also developed a product plan for this purpose. For example, we wanted Marketing*Builder*™ to be a Windows or Mac software package that would develop a market analysis and marketing plan as well as a sales plan, and we also wanted a bunch of useful spreadsheets for analysis and tracking. We included sections to capture marketing ideas, a wish list of features (we constantly add things and make them available on our website), ideas as to who might be interested in strategic alliances, promotional advertising, specialty items, and other tools that will make it more useful and easier to use. If I bought this package for my own use in my business, what would I want it to do and have? Everyone at JIAN had access to this document on our file server so we could all add our comments and ideas directly without a complicated series of meetings, discussions, and a paperwork system for capturing suggestions. We worked this plan over until we were thrilled with the possibilities and the honest feeling that it's a no-brainer purchase decision. Only then did we begin to actually create the product.

Such a promo piece/product plan also serves to define your product expectations for your product managers, engineers, vendors, bankers, salespeople, and shipping department. Generally, everyone is clued in. Plus, you never know who's going to come up with great ideas for improvements along the way.

Business Black Belt Notes

- Write your ad or brochure first.

- If it's a retail product, create a mock-up of the package

- What would the ad or brochure need to show and tell for you to buy it?

- Make your product or service do what your brochure says it will do.

- Allow as many people as practical direct access to your promo spec.

Planning

The plan is what you follow
until an extraordinary opportunity comes along.

☞ What's the use of a plan if circumstances will change, new opportunities will arise, or you simply don't know what to expect?

I've always had a resistance to planning, yet my company's most popular product is about business planning. Many people out there probably wouldn't buy our product because they resist the planning process. They may not write a business plan because they don't want to plan at all; they want to "wing it." I think I know where this comes from. The plans I've seen have always been ones that seem to lock people in. I suspect many people think that plans tend toward rigidity, rather than provide a framework for action given what you know now, while allowing for extraordinary opportunities and bargains to come along the way. Does the extraordinary opportunity further you toward your goals and is it the right thing to do, or does it take you off track, and waste money, time, and resources? Planning prepares you for this.

With the right kind of plan, we could say, "Here's this extraordinary opportunity. . . . In fact, we've even been planning for this opportunity, and here's where it fits in." That way, the opportunity can be put into context with our environment and resources. We won't start acting on it without having other necessary things in place to support it or forget another more critical priority and go off on a wild goose chase wasting time.

I'm afraid that most people think of planning this way: "OK, let's lock everything in place and don't mess with the plan. I want this to stay the way it is and this is what I know I can do." In a way, that is the purpose of planning, but at the same time, it's got to foster some creativity and opportunism.

Visionaries use plans to explain to everyone else what to do

I don't want to undermine the goals of the company already in place. As a visionary, I'm used to some resistance to my ideas so I must find ways around that resistance. When I'm involved in planning, I don't have to have a plan imposed on me that I don't like,and I know that we can always tweak it so it works.

If you had a system in place allowing you to plug in possible opportunities so everybody feels good about including them, then if somebody comes up with an extraordinary opportunity, you can see where it fits in. If there is no place for the idea, you can forget it with no hard feelings. The person who came up with it doesn't feel bad either. Having my ideas constantly rejected would be my reason for quitting, and I don't want people to quit. I want them to be able to incorporate their ideas and bring their extraordinary opportunities to the table.

I think that is the big reason BizPlan*Builder* is so popular, because it's the kind of dynamic plan that doesn't lock you in. To be more positive, it's the kind of plan that keeps you on track and maintains your business priorities while allowing you to take advantage of extraordinary opportunities.

Can you plan for opportunities you'll need?

I say yes, even though you cannot yet clearly define what the opportunity must look like. Not knowing will have you looking and shopping along the way so you will know it when you see it.

For example, we created our entire line of business software on the basis of word-processing and spreadsheet templates, or prewritten text and financial projections you can edit or adapt to your business and situation. You simply use your own (familiar) software to make your changes. You don't have to learn any new programs, you can do something useful with the software you already own. This idea has worked wonderfully since early 1988. As the world changes, competitors emerge, and new technology becomes available, it is possible as well as desirable to improve this product model. Competitors felt that they could compete with us by adding the graphical software interface and making the process easier. Although they added little (usually their content was sadly lacking), their products appeared to be easier to use and more friendly. So, we have built into our plan to incorporate a new Windows® technology and an intelligent template navigator system to make our products even better. Until technology we liked came along, we held off and shopped for years until we found it. We build these opportunities into our plans knowing that they will come along as we need them.

Why following a *Budget* can cost you

Let's look at this another way, because opportunities come along all the time. In fact, just because you've taken action and your machine is in motion, extraordinary opportunities will come along. This happens to us repeatedly in marketing. We get these extraordinary opportunities for promotional ideas, but some people say, "It's not in the budget and, therefore, we can't do it." I think that these ideas would make money and pay for themselves. To say we can't do them because it's not in the budget drives me crazy! You must enable yourself and your co-workers to seize these opportunities. If you (and they) are stuck to a strict budget, you'll try to rob one budget item to fit in another. You must analyze the opportunity on its own merits to determine the investment you're willing to make AND the expected revenue it will generate. (Remember to add the revenue to your sales forecast.)

A simple method is to set a percentage for each category. For example, 10 percent revenue from dealers can be used for dealer marketing programs. Our marketing VP is held accountable for keeping his dealer marketing expenses to 10 percent, but he can make his own decisions to fund programs he thinks will pay off. This way we focus more on ROI for each activity rather than hard budget dollars. So, build into your budget a line item for extraordinary opportunities, whether it's a plan or a budget. As time goes on, that fund will get bigger and bigger. You'll plan it bigger and bigger, because you'll see the extraordinary opportunities that come along. Then with the growth of the company and its sales, everybody's budget gets bigger.

Luck: When preparation meets opportunity

I think the biggest thing we all take for granted and sell ourselves short on is our ability to *generate* extraordinary opportunities. By virtue of the fact that you're there, you've taken action, you're down the path, and you've created the space for an opportunity to occur. Usually, we call it luck. Part of the preparation in building a business, like taking a trip, is getting part way down the path and seeing opportunities along the path; but you must go down the path in order for them to appear. If you never make a plan, you won't take the first steps to making something happen and to create the extraordinary opportunity.

The mind as a transceiver

In the study of quantum mechanics, scientists have discovered a tremendous amount of space between the neutrons, protons, and electrons that make up atoms. What holds all these particles together is energy. Solid matter looks solid, but actually if you were to view it at the atomic level, there's a vast space between the particles it is composed of. We underestimate how much energy we have in our minds to manipulate the energy between the particles. In other words, scientists are discovering that we can indeed influence matter with the energy from our minds! Our mental transceivers can be tuned to a radio station so we can hear music or news, opportunities, problems, solutions, etc. (messages from Nature). If it's not tuned consciously, as if our radio is tuned between stations, then we hear just static. We must therefore clear our minds and focus—like tuning our transceivers—on what we want to happen. Then we can apply our energy toward the results we want.

Business Black Belt Notes

- Plans are great for explaining what everyone should do.

- Plans must be flexible to allow for taking advantage of unforeseen opportunities.

- Set budgets using percentages rather than hard dollar figures.

- We create luck by taking action.

- Planning is like tuning your mental radio to a station so you can hear the music. Otherwise, you'll get just static.

How to Turn Your Idea Into a Business

High heels were invented by a woman
who had been kissed on the forehead.
— Christopher Morley, author

☞   A well-written business plan is the only real link between fantasy and reality. If you want to build a business out of your idea, the place to start is by writing a business plan. Here's what you need to know.

Let's talk about business plans

Since 1988, my company has been refining and marketing a software package for developing business plans. Let me share with you a few things we've learned along the way. It's often the act of writing, rather than a concern with style, that prevents us from writing business plans—we simply can't get started or keep it going. Yet, here's a dozen reasons why a finished plan is a very useful tool to use with the following people:

1)   Associates: to establish agreement, direction and purpose...

2)   Bankers & other financial resources: to provide loans for equipment and materials...

3)   Business brokers: to use as a brochure when selling your business...

4) Employees: to align their efforts with yours and promote your vision of your company's potential...

5) Investors (angels, institutions, or VC): to convince them to supply cash for growth. The better job you do on your plan and the more prepared you are to answer their tough questions, the more control you'll keep...

6) Friends & Family: to convince them that you really do know what you are doing and have matured beyond their past memories of you... This is a bonafide business proposition and not a request for a hand-out...

7) Small Business Administration: A business plan is a must with an SBA loan application...

8) Senior executives: to convince them to approve and allocate company resources. Get buy-in from your management team...

9) Stock or partnership offerings: to use as the basis for preparing a prospectus or offering circular to sell shares or partnership units to raise money...

10) Suppliers: to establish credit for inventory...

11) Talented people: Any smart prospective key employee wouldn't touch a start-up without reading a good business plan first. Persuade them to join you...

12) Yourself: to collect your thoughts, analyze your business, set goals, and make decisions. Use it as your "brochure" to promote your business concept so you don't have to explain it over and over.

They laughed at my ideas. . . until I showed them my business plan

It's hard to take a business seriously when nothing is written down about its structure, future direction, or its position in the marketplace. That's why a business plan may be the most important document you'll ever write.

Simply put, a business plan is a written document detailing the operational and financial aspects of your company. Like a road map, it helps you determine where you are, where you want to be, and how you're going to get there. If it's well written, your business plan will keep you in touch with your goals, potential risks, and likely rewards. Moreover, it may be the crucial factor in convincing investors or company management to give you the financing you'll need to realize your dream.

Whether you're seeking a loan, looking for an investor, soliciting management, or simply using the business plan to manage your business growth, the ideas outlined in this chapter provide some useful tips.

Just because your vision is obvious to you, it will usually take considerable effort, explanation, and selling to convince others to support you.

Why write a business plan?

The first and most important benefit of a business plan is that it gives you a path to follow. A plan sets the stage to make the future what you want it to be. A business plan transforms your fantasy into a reality. It enables you to realize what is really involved in building a successful company. Others will see that you have your head screwed on right and that you're not being unrealistic. It also takes your non-linear thinking and coordinates it into a logical progression of concepts following one after another.

A plan makes it easy to let your banker in on the action. By reading or hearing the details of your plan, he or she will have real insight into your situation if the bank is to lend you money. Likewise, potential investors can review your plan to gain a better understanding of your business and to determine if the investment is worth the risk.

A plan can be a communications tool when you need to familiarize sales people, suppliers, and others with your operations and goals.

A plan can help you develop as a manager. It can give you practice in thinking about competitive conditions, promotional opportunities, and situations that are advantageous to your business. Such practice over a period of time can increase your ability to make wise decisions.

A good business plan saves you money and time by focusing your activities, giving you more control over your finances, marketing, and business objectives.

How do you start? What will you say?

You've gone over the idea a hundred times in your mind, so this should be easy. Yet, the written description of your business is often the most challenging to prepare. You stare at a blank screen unsure of your next step. Or you may not understand how to assemble the necessary components into a complete and cohesive document. The elements of a business plan consist of two parts: the narrative and financials.

The narrative covers where you are now, where you're going, who the managers are, how you're going to get there, and why the reader should believe you.

What kind of plan is best for you?

There are typically three types of business plans you may need:

- A **Complete Business Plan** is necessary when you need a significant amount of funding. You'll need to explain your business concept in detail to potential backers, strategic partners such as major corporations, or potential buyers of your company.

- A **Summary Business Plan** is a shorter format that contains the most important information about your business and its direction. A summary plan is great when you're in a hurry. It's usually about 10 to 15 pages long and is perfect for many bank loans or simply to gauge investors' interest.
  A summary plan is also good for attracting key employees or to convince friends and relatives to invest a few thousand dollars.

- An **Operational Business Plan** is the internal planning document for an ongoing business. It's excellent for focusing the talents of key managers toward a common goal, and therefore should be updated at least annually. Plus, a good operating plan can do wonders for any executive's career.

Components of a business plan

There may have been a day when people read business plans cover to cover. Not any more. When they get close to giving you the money, they might, but first you have to grab their interest and answer their questions. I recommend organizing your business plan like a reference guide allowing readers to turn directly to the information they want. Different people want to know different things; some things are more important to some people than to others. The components of a successful business plan and a brief description of each section are described below.

Title Page

The title page of your business plan provides the name, address, and phone number of your company and the CEO. For your first impression, make a bold, clean visual statement about your company.

Table of Contents

Ideally, your business plan will be a *reference guide* to your business and not a novel or thesis. Number your pages. I highly recommend starting a new section on a new page. Colored tabs dividing each section makes your plan immediately appealing and easier to use. When I recently reviewed a number of plans during a contest at San Diego State University, I was immediately drawn to the one with the color tabs—the other judges admitted they were too.

Executive Summary

This is merely a synopsis of your business plan and summarizes the highlights. However, it is the portion of your plan that will be first read by investors. You had better get to the point and be interesting—explain why your business will make money and is a great investment. (For bankers, it should demonstrate common business sense and that you have the where-withal to pay back a loan.) If you lose readers here, forget having them read any further. You should write this summary after you have completed your business plan and keep it to no more than two to three pages.

Company Direction

This is a snapshot of the present stage of your business, plus a picture of where your business is going and what it will look like, with the goals and objectives on how to get there.

Vision/ Mission

This is the part that, throughout history, has made the difference between great leaders and failures. (Regardless of their purpose, good or evil, selling their vision made the difference.) Your vision comprises your emotional drive to build your business to be something great that others can support and share in.

Objectives

Where are you going, what will it take, and what are you going to do with the money? Investors want to know how and when they'll make zillions on their investment in you.

Company Overview

This section provides basic information about your company: structure, management, staffing, and strategic alliances. What is the present situation in the world and how does it affect your business?

Management

Who have you hired to do the job? In a way, you are providing a mini-interview with your management team members to assure an investor, banker, or corporate manager that you have lined up the right people to make your project go. This section is one of the most crucial. The only thing that will ensure success is the day-to-day activity of intelligent people in the driver's seat. Nothing else is as important.

I recently was a judge for the San Diego State University business plan competition where 20 schools sent teams to pitch their business concepts. As I listened to their presentations and reviewed their plans, I was amazed at how these almost college graduates expected us to believe that they had the management experience and skill to run operations, marketing, and finance of their companies. It would have given them tremendous credibility if, instead of trying to convince us that they had enough experience, they outlined their intentions for hiring experienced managers to run key areas of their businesses. Although this was a college exercise, they were promoting real businesses. Put yourself in an investor's or banker's position. Would you give $50,000 to $5,000,000 to inexperienced people who try to convince you of their experience, or to people who demonstrated the sense to hire competent managers?

Product / Service Strategy

This section reviews your current product or service and what makes it unique and competitive. Your future research and development and production plans are part of your product strategy. Engineer types have a tendency to overemphasize this section—save that for a demo when the investors request it—great products and services have died without a good business model and the right people to run it.

Market Analysis

This section helps you understand and define your market, the demographics and psychographics of your target customers, competitor's products or services, and both business and environmental risks. Who are the people out there who will buy from you and can you efficiently sell to them?

Marketing Plan

The world will "beat a path to your door". . . only if they know who you are, what you've got, and where to reach you. This section includes your advertising and promotion, pricing and profitability, selling tactics, distribution, public relations, and business relationships. This should not be treated as something you'll work on later. It's a key component that affects everything you do.

Financials

This section addresses your ability to make money in your proposed business and how much money you'll need. Your company's capital requirements and the profit potential are analyzed and demonstrated here.

Are your financial projections believable?

Many people think a set of financial projections is a business plan. Numbers lie or can be used to distort the facts. Most experienced financial people know that a financial projection, no matter how honest and forthright it is, does not present the full picture. I've talked to thousands of bankers, investors, and customers. They've emphasized how important it is to address the state of your market, describe your product or service in detail, understand and formulate your marketing strategy, carefully outline your promotion and sales plans, and most important, introduce the management team responsible for using the capital and driving your business toward success. According to the money people, all of this information provides credibility for your financial projections.

Nevertheless, the financials demonstrate the viability of your business, whether it's a start-up or an established company. Different financing sources look for different things and emphasize different areas—you must be prepared for all of them. All of them make a difference to the success or failure of your business.

Financial assumptions—the crux of your pitch

All the quantitative components of your business converge on the assumptions page. You must build a case that your product or service will succeed because you have plenty of hungry customers who you can economically reach and sell to. How much will sell and how much does marketing cost? How much will production and fulfillment cost? How much will payroll cost? The narrative portion of your business plan builds the case for your assumptions. Your assumptions are the key components you must sell investors. Your financial projections are merely a mathematical representation that plays out what assumptions have been made. Remember: garbage in, garbage out.

What you and your investors must agree upon are the assumptions that feed your projections. With assumptions such as "Sales will double next year for product A, while product B will triple in sales," and "We'll save 15% on manufacturing costs by buying the new laser guided machine," an investor, by intuition or experience, may disagree that sales of product A will double. Maybe he or she thinks sales of product A will increase by only 75 percent or the cost savings with the new machine will only be 10 percent. Plug in the assumptions the investors believe and rerun your projections. Although we've modified ours considerably to show more clearly what's going on, most financial statements are similar and readily interpreted.

Your deal may be won or lost in the assumptions. In fact, the entire presentation of your business plan is about establishing and proving the assumptions that drive your financial projections. Every one of them should withstand the challenge, "How do you figure that?" This is critical! If the picture still looks good, maybe the investors will go for it. The value of your company (hence your share price today and the percentage you'll retain after an investment) is predicated on the *perceived* future value of your company. Your assumptions versus those of your investors can drastically alter the outcome of your financial picture and their perception of your business. Also, if your assumptions are way out of line, then you lose credibility. "What else is out of line?" they may wonder.

The supporting financial statements include the following:
- 12-Month Budget, including your Start-Up Requirements

- 12-Month as well as a 5-Year Income Statement

- 12-Month as well as a 5-Year Cashflow Projection

- 12-Month as well as a 5-Year Pro Forma Balance Sheet

- Break-Even Analysis

- Sources & Uses of Funds Summary

- Sensitivity Analysis showing Pessimistic, Planned and Optimistic scenarios

- A projection of your company's value after five years is also very useful. (It's also amusing to see what your company will be worth after five years of hard labor.)

I've never met an investor who believed in anything beyond five years—their financial attention span is fairly short and they want to be out with their profit in less than five years. Investment performance, measured in return on investment, takes time into consideration—the more the sooner, the better they did. The idea is to get 'em in, make 'em rich, get 'em out.

Your reader's perspective

In addition to providing a large amount of data, you must show your personality and spirit, and those of your management team. You're attracting interested people who can help you. The tone and credibility projected in your business plan will determine their response. How will your reader perceive you and your business and take action ($) on that perception? Remember this and be prepared.

Investors are often heard telling one horror story after another about a business plan "stubbing its toes" on its way into their office. One opportunity is usually all you'll get to demonstrate your competence and the feasibility of your project to your investors, senior executives, or clients. These are influential and powerful people. Don't waste their time, bore them, or leave them feeling dissatisfied with your work. Show them that you know what you are doing. Think in terms of return on investment. Show that you can project your company's earnings. Prove that you can execute your plan.

Business Black Belt Notes

- You must proceed down the path to attract the opportunities you need.

- A business plan is a comprehensive brochure that sells your ideas.

- A business plan takes your nonlinear thinking and coordinates it into a logical progression of concepts following one after another.

- The description of your business, market, competitive position, and so on all provide credibility for your financial projections.

- The deal is won or lost in your assumptions and your ability to sell them.

The Money People. . .
Who Are Ya Gonna Call?

*The meek shall inherit the earth,
but not its mineral rights.*
— J. Paul Getty, businessperson

☞ People will give you money for your venture provided it furthers
their agendas. Know who you are selling to if you want to speed
the process of getting cash.

There's a good reason why most business plans are never funded. Your idea
has to make sense, your business model to develop, market, and sell your idea
has to make sense, and you and your management team have to demonstrate
that you have enough sense to succeed. Fall short anywhere and your plan
goes in the trash.

Investors

Private investors are individuals who usually have earmarked a portion of
their portfolios for risky, high-return investments. Venture capitalists are
expert investors who specialize in a few industries. They perform sophisticated analyses of your opportunity and structure the deal to cover their interests. They solicit other investors and institutions to entrust earmarked por-
tions of their portfolios and make those investments in potentially high-

return opportunities like yours. Everyone who plays this game knows and accepts the risks and they use the following guidelines:

- How are you unique? Proprietary technology—a patent, process, trade secret, or something that can be protected from competition demonstrates uniqueness. Regardless, you must have a unique product, process, or something special that can make a lot of money.

- Can I bet on the management's track record? Investors usually bet on the jockey, not the horse. You must assemble a proven management team. A venture capital firm usually wants to invest at least $2 to $3 million or it's not worth all the effort. Since the stakes are higher, they want to see an experienced management team capable of capitalizing on your unique situation. These people are masters at sizing up management. Any attempt to convince them that an inexperienced manager can do the job will only damage your credibility. It's much better to describe the management competence you intend to hire. Investors want to be assured that the business will continue if something happens to the founder.

- Will I get a five to ten times return? For the risk, most investors expect huge returns. When you project your income statement, their investment should enable you to do big things that will catapult your company forward. Often they look at the "J curve," which projects the difference in growth (revenue and profits) of your business with and without their investment. The upward curve in the 'J' is the point where they write you a check.

- What is my exit strategy? When your company grows to $20 million, goes public in four years, and sells to a larger company, investors will want to know when and how they'll get their money out.

- Does this fit my niche? It's likely you'll get a warmer reception (and a more valuable partner) if you choose an investor who already has a portfolio with many companies in your industry or market. They already understand the common difficulties and opportunities in your industry, and they may be able to provide much synergistic assistance for your venture.

Get their attention. Show an aggressive yet believable plan within the first two to three pages. They see a foot-high pile of business plans every day. Sell the financial assumptions, the base figures that drive the rest of your projections. Prove that sales will grow and costs will drop.

A couple of things to consider before looking for investors

Often, when starting a business, many people think they need investors. I always wonder how much you can do without investors. Instead of spending your time trying to sell a portion of your business to investors, what if you invested your energy in selling your product or service to customers? Obviously, if you need expensive capital equipment to get going, you'll need cash, but what if you could get the equipment or to use it without cash? Having no money compels you to be creative. I'm in favor of exercising my creative talents as far as possible before taking on investors.

I'm also in favor of starting small to experiment with what works with customers. We often create simple desktop published brochures, photocopy them, and use these as sales tools with real customers before we commit to a run of 10,000 to 100,000 expensive full-color brochures. It never ceases to amaze me how many changes and improvements we make after we start showing customers our materials and then answer their questions. Other ideas include renting space in a customer's building in trade for your services. You may even win their business with an offer like this. A friend of mine runs his graphics business in the spare offices of a public relations firm in downtown San Jose, California. And, he gets a nice location, extra business and the use of an attractive, competent receptionist.

Big bucks can mean big mistakes

With a lot of money in your pocket, you can make big mistakes. Unless you've tested your marketing materials, refined your business model, and know how your customers will respond to your product or service, you may be tempted to put a lot of money behind some invalid assumptions.

You really want to know what's working and what's going to work before getting money to expand. If your business doesn't work out, the investors will own your business, you'll still not have enough money to make the necessary corrections, and if you need to ask for more money, your position is weak. You don't want to go out whole hog and mail 500,000 mailing pieces without testing. If you have no money, you can mail only 5,000. Then, if you lose it, you've only lost 5,000 mailing pieces, not half a million. Keep testing everything in your business on a small scale. Then when everything is working, you can build on it with a big investment. You'll also be able to promote your business to investors with greater confidence and come from a very strong position.

> *To be successful, keep looking tanned, live in an elegant building (even if you're in the cellar), be seen in the smart restaurants (even if you nurse one drink) and if you borrow, borrow big.*
> — Aristotle Onassis, Greek shipping tycoon

Bankers

If you're looking for a loan or line of credit over $100,000 or SBA-backed financing, you'll need a business plan. Bankers are almost the opposite of investors. They loan the money deposited from people who've been guaranteed to get it back with a little interest. The money was deposited with the idea that there's little risk, so bankers won't risk it. Bankers use the five Cs: Credit, Character, Cash flow, Collateral and Capacity—when evaluating a loan. They also look at a company from a deliberately pessimistic point of view to minimize the risk, so you must have good answers to their questions to demonstrate that you understand the issues.

Zen and banking

The old saying is that bankers will give you the money when you don't need it. This echoes the Zen philosophy: When you really want something, you don't get it. (And you can't not want something in order to get it.) When you completely let go of something, it comes to you and you have it. When you don't need money, bankers seem to want to give you money. That's the way the world works.

So, the more you try to get bankers to give you money, the more they don't want to give it to you. (The more you throw yourself at investors, the more they turn away.) That's because nobody wants anyone who's desperate. Let's look behind the scenes.

The nature of the banking business

 For example: You ask for a $100,000 loan. The way the banking system works is that they mark up the money they pay depositors by about 2% (the spread). In the backs of their minds, they're looking at you and considering, "What if you can't pay this $100,000 loan back?" Remember, in business you have to make up any losses from profits, not sales. So, how much profit is lost if they lose your loan? Two percent at $100,000 is all the profit from five million dollars worth of loans. So if your loan goes bad, that means they lose the equivalent of all the profit they would make on five million dollars worth of loans they've made elsewhere.

They want your first born

Now you can imagine why they scrutinize every loan. They look at how much business they would throw away if something went wrong with yours. That's why they're going to look at everything about you, including your character. Your credit history plays a big part here. They want to be sure you're the kind of person who's going to pay back the loan. They don't want to get left holding the bag because they'll lose all their profit. That makes it even more imperative that you know what you're doing in your business.

So what do you do? You've got to show them a track record. You need to prove that you can pay your loan back no matter what. That's also why they want collateral—it's insurance so they won't have to take it out of their slim profit.

Prerequisites for a bank loan

A bank wants to see a track record of profit for the past three years which also means you have to have been in business for at least three years.

Banks are looking to finance growth, not cover for inefficiencies. Show them how you'll use the loan to improve efficiencies in your operation. For example, buying a printing press will save money over buying printing if you spend a fortune on printing. Then the loan would make sense. However, if cash is short because you're slow to collect receivables, then the loan doesn't make sense. If you could collect your receivables faster, you wouldn't need the loan.

They prefer a debt-to-equity ratio of less than 3 to 1. This is a banker's measure of risk. Bankers hate risk. The debt-to-equity ratio compares the amount of what you owe to what you own. Banks expect that you will repay your loan out of cash flow—show that you'll generate enough cash (not just profit on paper) to repay your loan. If you can show that the loan improves cash flow, so much the better.

> *Sandbag your projections by just enough*
> *to assure that you hit your numbers.*
> — An anonymous banker

If you can hit your projections then apparently you understand your business and have it under control. You should have solid financials based upon conservative assumptions. Future projections should be conservative and show steady growth with profits over the next five years. Too much hype and too much projected growth equals too much risk.

Part of your financing package should always include a reasonable explanation of anything unusual in your credit report. I recommend including this explanation up front in your financing package because inevitably they will ask you about this unusual item on your credit report and you'll have to address it. If you want to speed the process of your financing, have this answer prepared in advance and include it with your package. If nothing else, at least a half page explaining the situation. For example, right now my TRW report has grown to about seven pages since I started my business. It got that way because bankers, investment firms, and finance firms have looked into my TRW report over the years for credit cards, limit increases, leasing, equipment purchases, and a number of other things. Every one of those inquiries appears on my credit history.

Five years ago, I had a pager that I rented from Pacific Bell, and one month I missed a payment on that pager. I thought I turned it in and made my final payment, but because the phone number was wrong, they added to my TRW a debt of $27 that they say went to collections. The $27 stopped the process of buying my house. It came up when we got our credit line, it came up when we got our SBA loan, it reared its head again when we got our credit increase. Every single time, I needed to explain why this $27 in collections on a simple pager was on my TRW report. The banks questioned nothing else. (Seven pages worth of TRW and the only thing that really disturbs anybody is the fact that a $27 pager payment was on there for collections!) Obviously, when I first heard about this debt, I immediately sent $27 because that was infinitely cheaper and easier than trying to argue with the company. Nevertheless, for all future lenders, I prepared a half page explanation of why my $27 pager payment is on there.

Use your business plan as a brochure, a tool to coach the loan rep to sell your company internally. Believe it or not, bankers want to know about your market, so include a strong analysis of your market as well as a sensible marketing plan. Back up your sales projections by demonstrating the demand for your product or service and your ability to reach and sell to customers who will ultimately provide the cash to repay your loan.

When you talk to your banker, remember to remain calm and sane. Too much entrepreneurial enthusiasm frightens bankers. This is a matter-of-fact deal, business as usual.

Friends & Relatives

When you ask those you know for a loan, the first hurdle you must overcome is your reputation and all your past sins. You might no longer do the foolish things of the past that maybe some friends and relatives have indelibly etched in their memories. Your new business plan will update your friends and relatives to the current you and prove that you are responsible with their cash. You must reposition your past as a time full of rich learning experiences from which you will now earn yourself and others a fortune.

You'll probably have to work extra hard to prove that you know what you're doing. Thorough market research will help demonstrate that your business makes sense.

I think it is important that you make it clear that you are in charge. Accepting an investment from family and friends opens you up to a variety of emotional hooks and distractions beyond that of most investors. The last thing you need is loved ones telling you how to run your business.

An advantage to having friends and family invest in your business is that it keeps the money in the family or community. If it's a failure, then you run less risk of repossessions and you enjoy some slack, but you'll have to pay everyone back or make good. Otherwise you'll never hear the end of it.

Finally, you'll need to overcome any emotional entanglement as you present your plan. I was very annoyed by most of my grandmother's questions before she gave me $5,000 for my do-it-yourself used car lot. Don't be distracted by your emotional reactions. Certainly any questions are reasonable and any investor would ask them, so treat your friends and family with the professionalism you'd present to a stranger. This will be key in overcoming past indiscretions and proving your maturity to manage your friends' and family's cash well.

Senior management

If you haven't taken the plunge to go on your own, consider the benefits of having the company you work for right now back your ideas. Management wants to know what resources you'll need. How long before payback? What's the risk? A thorough business plan helps you justify your program and gain your management's sign-off. And you can design your plan so you can collect a percentage of your success.

The first thing you'll probably hear is "Great idea . . . write me a proposal." This is where most good ideas die. Of course, we promote BizPlan-*Builder* for just such a purpose and I recommend including your name in the footer of every page lest someone else claim your ideas as theirs.

Obviously, what you must pitch is your ability to expand company sales and profitability, and your projections must show sufficient return on investment (just ask your boss how much). Management will likely want to be informed of key milestones and they'll watch you like most investors. In the next chapter, I elaborate more on the possibilities of pursuing business development within your company.

Employees

Sure, you can tell each one exactly what you want them to do, but if you want a high-performance team, you need to paint the whole picture. Many a manager has come close to the funny farm because he or she tried to wing it verbally. Now you can take your time to write a comprehensive plan your people can buy into and follow. Plus, you won't have to explain your plan over and over. BizPlan*Builder* makes it easy to engineer changes in your company and engage everyone's support.

Before asking for money. . . one last thing

Remember that soliciting investments for your business may actually constitute selling securities and falls under the jurisdiction of the Securities and Exchange Commission. You may be *personally* liable to your investors for any money they may lose as a result of their investments. (Regardless of corporate status, you sold them the stock, so you have to pay them back!) Use an applicable written Offering Circular or Prospectus for soliciting actual investments when appropriate.

Business Black Belt Notes

- What would you want to know before investing in a business? Be prepared to answer those questions.

- Bankers must repay their depositors—with a 2 percent margin, they need a 98 percent assurance that you will pay them back!

- Treat your family and friends who invest in you with the same respect you would a stranger.

Intrapreneurship

You never know what you can deal with until you have to.
—DeAnna Sodoma, champion wheelchair racer

☞   You may not need to venture out on your own when you could do
the equivalent just as easily within your present job.

Should you jump ship or start a new business within your present company?
It's called intrapreneurism. It makes a lot of sense, and many people do it.
You keep your job, maintain your income, benefits, and job security, plus you
harness your company's resources: customers, accounting, marketing, good-
will, reputation, name recognition, and finances. After all, your present company's management knows you and you know them. It can be a perfect environment for incubating your new company.

Think about it for a moment from management's point of view. It would
be expensive to hire and train someone to replace you. Or worse, they could
lose you to or have you become a competitor. They're better off if they support you. Plus, you'd be expanding the company and adding to its profits. If
you structure your deal so you get a percentage of the action (increased profits), you can do as well as any independent business owner, but with the
"safety net" of continuing income, less risk, and fewer sleepless nights!

Obviously, this may not work if your business idea is completely outside
the scope of the company's business, you can't stand the management, or you
have other reasons for not wanting to have them involved. But, I can't help

but urge you to consider this option before giving up a good job with a good company.

Another option would be to go to another company and propose that they invest in your project.

Management is always looking for good ideas and opportunities for profits, AND they need motivated people to make these ideas happen. More and more companies are promising to put the inventor in charge of the new business. Consider this option before you jump ship. Remember, with a comprehensive business plan in hand, if they don't go for your idea, you're already prepared to set sail on your own!

Business Black Belt Notes

•   Is it absolutely necessary to leave your job? Could you launch your business concept within your present company?

•   You could structure your deal so you could make as much money as if you went on your own.

What Are You Going to Do Next?

You know exactly what to do. You just don't do it fast enough.
— Robert Petersen, flight instructor

☞ **You really do know what to do.**

One afternoon I was flying the airplane home with my instructor. As we flew into the San Francisco Bay Area from over the eastern foothills, I was just sitting there enjoying the scenery. As airplanes are wont to do, it started to bank slightly to the left. I just sat there going along with it. Left uncorrected, this situation could have turned into a problem. Eventually, Bob, my instructor, asked if I was going to do anything about it. I casually leveled the wings and got us pointed more favorably in the direction we needed to go.

He said, "You know exactly what to. You just don't do it fast enough." I responded, "That's the story of my life." And, as I heard myself say that, I thought of a number of places where that was indeed true. Could I correct them as easily and quickly? I thought I could. There was no more information or a better time I could wait for. I just needed to make the move. I went back to the office and let a difficult employee go. I had been agonizing for months about doing this and so had everyone else. I was just watching the scenery but taking no action. When was I going to get the message and do something? We were all relieved when I finally leveled the company's wings.

Sometimes you can wait for a harmonic convergence (when all the planets align) where every aspect of a situation is perfect and the situation allows for easy correction. Usually, the situation will only get worse until you do something. Most of the time, however, you just cannot wait for the circumstances to conveniently make it easy for you to act on the obvious course of action. Sure, you'd like something or someone else you can point to to get yourself off the hook, but to be most effective, you must act out of your own free will with the knowledge and experience you have and without necessarily having other circumstances to blame. (Let someone go because it will serve both them and you to do so—don't wait for them to make a big enough mistake to justify your action.)

I would rather screw up than stand still.

This isn't to say that you want to leap in and make a mess, but the action you take sets up the next opportunity. Waiting and seeing does little to forward any action in your favor. If you are uncertain, then take very small steps and measure what happens. If you goof, it doesn't cost much. We've tried a number of things—products (make a package and go show the retailers), publications for advertising (run a classified to see if anybody responds), mailing lists (before mailing 100,000 pieces, test 10,000 names), etc. With any decision, the cost for waiting must be weighed against the cost of even the smallest mistake. Remember that sometimes the cost of inaction can be far more expensive than a mistake made trying to do the right thing... at least you did something and that has learning value as well as power in repositioning you for your next move.

You're already motivated

I do know exactly what to do next. I think you do, too. You don't have to do a hundred things next, just one thing at a time. Look and listen for the messages. Since you're building your business no matter what, rather than talk to you about motivating you, all I can say is that the information and experience you need will come from the action you take next using what you already know and what you'll find out by testing. Babe Ruth is famous for the 700+ home runs he hit; he also struck out more than 1,300 times. The idea is to get up and take a swing at the ball as many times as you can. And that means using what you do know, trying things out, learning from the results and keeping going.

> *Just you trust yourself, then you will know how to live.*
> — Johann Wolfgang von Goethe, poet and playwright

Business Black Belt Notes

- You already know what you need to do; just do it.

- Sometimes you need to take the action to compel the next thing to happen.

- From there, you will learn and be more successful the next time out, but get out again soon. And again.

- Trust yourself—your gut feelings—look for outside input but don't keep waiting for outside validation for everything you do.

Get a Life

Activities expand to fill the time available.
— Unknown

☞ When you proactively fill your time, you can prevent BS from filling it for you.

A friend of mine was complaining the other day that many otherwise great projects were going undone because he just couldn't get to them. And how was he going to have time with his family, go scuba diving, and generally do the other things in life that interested him?

Don't waste time on a time management consultant

My recommendation was to reverse the process. Instead of trying to plan his work time more effectively, what about planning his personal time more effectively? If the "Activities Expand to Fill the Time Available" law is true then you need to set your own parameters on time allowed for work projects. Plan your outside activities instead. If you want more time with your family, leave the office by 6:00 P.M. or whatever time that works for you, and make that your rule. All work must be completed by 6:00 P.M. Think about the experience you've had already with this. If you were leaving for a two-week business trip or vacation, isn't it amazing how you naturally know exactly what your priorities are, how fast you can complete them, and how miraculously efficient you are in getting everything done? You achieve a

Zen-like state of focus and clarity. What if your normally fun activities could be used as bookends to your work life?

Business Black Belt Notes

- Limit the time available to get your job done by establishing personal activities that provide motivating deadlines to get your work done.

What you learn after you think you know it all is what counts.
— John Wooden, legendary UCLA basketball coach

Black Belt

The Test

This is where it all comes together. Your black belt test is
your demonstration of your skills and your demonstration
that you can go beyond what you thought you could do. Make
no mistake, you are not invincible—there is much to learn
and, by the time you reach black belt level, you see how
much you don't know, but you've trained your mind and
body to learn.

20 Reasons Why People *Succeed* In Business

To any jerk who gives you reasons for why businesses fail...

I've come up with 20 reasons why you can succeed in business. Although no business fails for a single reason, no single reason in and of itself can make a business succeed. Ideally, you would incorporate all 20 things and more for your business to really succeed.

Things happen—miracles occur, phones ring, people are in agreement with you, people want to buy your stuff—it's not luck, but there are specific things you can do consciously and consistently to get bigger and better. Every chapter here describes small and large things to get your whole company operating in the "zone."

If you see something that needs to be fixed;
a wrong that needs to be righted
(and it's within your capabilities to do so),
you owe it to yourself and the world to do something about it.
— I wish I knew who said this...

1. You solve your own problem—with a vengeance.

You develop a solution to a problem that you have experienced. That solution becomes a product or service. What will drive this product or service to succeed is your empathy and compassion for the customers who have the same problem.

It's easy to find people with that problem and to share your experience and enthusiasm for why your product or service will, indeed, solve that problem and how good people will feel once it is solved. Because you have been through the same situation, you know exactly what it takes to solve that problem and can lead your customer to success.

2. You take a leadership position.

You are the expert on your product or service. At some time, the reason your customers are buying the product or service from *you* is that you know what you're doing, you're the expert, you're telling them what they need, and you're doing it the best possible way it can be done. You've taken the time, it's your industry, you know what's going on in it, and you're putting the best product forward that you know how to make. Leadership is having the confidence to do what's right, even in the face of uncertainty, disagreement, or being in an industry that's slogging in the wrong direction.

3. You assume that customers WANT to buy.

Do not assume that customers DON'T want to buy. Every sales training that I've ever taken assumes that customers don't want to buy. Listen to the language: "handling *rejection*," "*closing* a deal," "overcoming objections." I recommend looking at why customers do want to buy and reinforcing that.

If you've got a product that solves a person's problem and you can recognize a person with that problem, don't be bashful about talking to him or her. You can assume that the person wants to buy it. Your job as a salesperson is to prove that your product does, indeed, solve the problem. Then engineer a way for him or her to purchase it from you. Even if it's an expensive product or service, they want to buy it. It's just a matter of showing them how they can have it.

4. You offer quality over profit.

You emphasize is on the *quality* of your product, and your product's or service's ability to do the job and solve the problem the best way it can be solved, over profits. If there's a choice to be made between "Shall we add a little quality to the product?" and "Shall we sacrifice quality for better profits?" go for quality.

5. You are open to improvement.

You are open to ways your product, service or operation can be improved so your customer is always satisfied and buys more. You happily accept input and agree with your customers. You perceive criticism as constructive input for improving your product or service anytime someone has a question, a complaint, or a problem. This applies to you personally as well—there is no one else to blame.

> *They are learning to balance their interests in shaping the future with a prudent respect for the limits in their abilities to do so. They tuck, they weave, they dive—they ride with the river, rather than fight it.*
> — James F. Moore, CEO, GeoPartners Research, Inc.[10]

6. You always look for places to sell.

Always look for places to sell your product and people to sell it to—channels, stores, and people. Network, read magazines, and look for outlets where you can sell. Never be bashful about recommending your product to anyone.

7. You use direct-response marketing techniques.

Expect to take an order directly from the ad. Include 800 numbers in ads and take credit cards. The advertisements include quotes and testimonials from happy customers. The headlines introduce the solution to the problem, and the ad adequately explains the product and, most important, its benefits. Your ads and promotional materials are complete presentations in themselves.

---

[10]   As quoted in *Upside*, "Paradigm Shifts, Executive Leadership: Back to the Future," March 1996.

8. You know who your customer is.

You focus your products and services on who your customers are. What else would those same customers buy from you? How can you expand your successful reputation into another product or service that you could provide with credibility?

For example, JIAN is in the business management efficiency business (with an emphasis on cleaning up business practices worldwide). We have developed a reputation for a specific product line that we can "niche in" and claim as the best. If we added another product or service, it would be something our customers would expect us to provide. It would make sense to include it in a catalog and offer it with our other products to the *same* customers. Then we can build a following and build sales.

9. Businesses have karma too.

You are aware that businesses also have Karma and that the concept of "What goes around, comes around" applies to a company as well as an individual. It starts with the CEO and flows out from there. This attitude also prevents a company from getting arrogant about its success and treating customers badly. With everybody on the management team and every employee in the company keeping this in mind, when decisions are made by anybody at any level, the right thing will be done and the customers will be happy.

10. You are in business with people you just naturally like.

Probably the single biggest killer of businesses are bad relationships, when the partners or the top managers of a company don't get along. One of the beauties of being in business for yourself is that you can choose the people you work with. You might as well choose people you enjoy and trust, so the relationships will be long and happy ones.

Be sure you have agreements, so in the event you must split up, even that can be amicable. Don't be bashful about using an attorney to make sure you do this right.

11. You hire attitude over aptitude.

You look for people with heart before brains. You interview people carefully, paying close attention to performance (past performance is an indicator of future performance), ability, character, and personality. A good blend of different personality styles on your management team provides the best decisions. Any differences in personality or management style may cause friction. You may have heated arguments when necessary, but no one takes it personally, knowing that the end result is a better decision and a more efficient company. Everybody looks at it as a learning experience. Underneath it all, you genuinely *appreciate* each other's skills and abilities.

12. You invest in tools to get the job done.

Invest money in quality equipment necessary for the infrastructure, so employees can do their jobs most effectively. Perhaps more expensive, more efficient equipment, machinery, and supplies will enable your employees to more easily get their jobs done and be less distracted by problems. Plus, it makes everybody happy to feel that they're working with quality. It improves morale and keeps the focus on the purpose of your business.

13. All expenditures must generate cash.

Every time you spend money, your mantra is "Will this new purchase or investment generate immediate cash or not?" The key words are *immediate cash*, because that's what keeps a business going.

14. You keep going even while you are figuring things out.

You are able to make decisions without having all the information. Ideally, 20 percent of the information will give you 80 percent of what you need to know in order to make a good decision. Don't wait until you have everything you possibly need to know, because you may experience *paralysis from analysis!*

For example, I've been working on my ability to hire people. I still need to make hiring decisions while I'm in the process of improving my ability to do it. As I'm learning and working on it, I'm willing to make mistakes, yet the company moves forward anyway.

15. You take action and see. . .

. . .as opposed to "wait and see." You realize that you have to go ahead and make decisions to do something, even though you may not have found the best deal. You know that the longer you wait, the more it can cost you from inaction.

16. You're totally honest.

Don't fudge facts or figures. Be honest with your employees. Pay people what you owe them. Do what you say you're going to do. Always come through and maintain your reputation in a favorable way.

Often, a deal could be tenuous or you may need something from a new supplier in a hurry. Your reputation alone can pull you through. Or it may be a toss-up for a customer as to whether they buy your product or one from a competitor. If you give the customer a better feeling, they'll buy from you.

17. You maintain humility with success.

Maintain your interest and willingness to improve your skills, your products, your services—no matter how good you think you are already. Still play by the rules. There is much responsibility with success. Really great people look for ways to be even more constructive with the successes they enjoy.

18. You continue to train yourself.

Join organizations, take seminars and classes, and read books. Keep learning about your own job and different aspects of it, as well as different aspects of other people's jobs.

19. You have incredible will power.

No matter what the business is, it's gonna go, it's your thing, and you know it's going to make it. Even if your friends, relatives, and professionals tell you it's less than a great idea, you still envision its success and know you can make it happen. You are also very aware that people need your product or service.

I've read a number of business success stories, and what I find consistent about Henry Ford, Andrew Carnegie, Fred Smith at Federal Express, Bernard Marcus at Home Depot, Bill Gates at Microsoft, Steve Jobs at Apple, Lee

Iacocca at Chrysler, and Jack Welch at G.E. is that they have incredible will power and sheer tenacity to make the company succeed.

20. You're more interested in the game than the money.

Most wildly successful people have fundamentally been more interested in solving the problem than in making big bucks. Sure, they approach their business in a businesslike manner, but they are fanatic evangelists for what they are doing. Making money isn't enough of a motivator to sustain their interest, focus, and energy over time. Look into the backgrounds and stories of the wildly successful and you'll see this to be true.

It wasn't until I started doing what I really enjoyed, that helped others, that I began to make real money. The sooner you start doing what you are good at, what you love doing, what helps others, the sooner you will attract money and everything you need.

I hope you found this book interesting and useful.

Burke Franklin
President & CEO
JIAN

P.S. Inquiring Minds Need to Know

I gave a speech to the Entrepreneurship Class at the University of California at Santa Barbara in May 1995. I asked them what they thought it took to be successful in business. The words the students gave me were absolutely right. It occurred to me after I left what the true wisdom of the words could illustrate.

Their words described what a success looks like from the outside-in. I'd heard these same words for years, but now they had different meanings. How do you take what each of these words embodies and implant it into your psyche to function day in and day out with them as part of your own internal operating system? I suggest that you turn them inside-out. People will someday say that you too had a good idea, built a team, had talent, enjoyed some luck, persevered, had lots of customers, and made a ton of money.

It looks like an **Idea** from the outside looking in. . . but, from the inside looking out—You had a problem, solved it for yourself, and then created a product or service others could use to solve their similar problem.

It looks like **Perseverance** from the outside looking in. . . but, from the inside looking out—You are possessed with the notion that there has to be a way to make something work. There is a way, you just don't know it yet. You're going to do it no matter what.

It looks like **Talent** from the outside looking in. . . but, from the inside looking out—You've been learning, making mistakes, sorting out what works from what doesn't, practicing and perfecting your skills.

It looks like a **Team** from the outside looking in. . . but, from the inside looking out—You've figured out what talent you bring to your business and organized what else needs doing, the specific skill sets needed and then you hired the personalities that combine to form a productive company culture.

They look like **Customers** from the outside looking in. . . but, from the inside looking out—Certain people have a problem or an interest. You have developed a unique or better way to give them what they want and need.

It looks like **Luck** from the outside looking in. . . but, from the inside looking out—Preparation meets opportunity. When you can apply your background, interests, skills, and vision to the solution of a problem, and you know who else has the problem, luck can be created.

It looks like **Money** from the outside looking in. . . but, from the inside looking out—What do you need the money for? What if you could have whatever it is you want without cash? What can you trade? When I first ran my advertisements, I convinced a couple of magazines to give me credit. That way I could pay for my ad after I sold my products. That was much easier than finding money to first pay cash for the ads. This is called **Creative** in business.

Do not seek to follow in the footsteps of the wise.
Seek what they sought.
—Basho

Business *Builder*

Software Tools for Entrepreneurs, Business Owners & Managers

New Products Help You
Do Business Better

Tips for Staying Focused
and Getting Things Done

Managing and Tracking
Your Employees

How to Get the Financing
You Want

Creating Easy-to-Sign
Agreements

Measuring the Black Art
of Marketing

Tech Tips: Get the Most
From Your Software

Where to Look for Ideas
and Answers

For our latest
color catalog:
800-346-5426
650-254-5600
650-254-5640 fax
www.jian.com

JIAN

Business Planning Today:
The Ultimate Key to Success

100 essential software tools add structure and efficiency to your business

Expert Resources at Your Fingertips

If you ask business owners what they need most, they'll tell you more time, more money, and more resources. They want professional business expertise and proven tools they can use quickly and easily to accomplish important day-to-day projects.

Powerful Software to Build a Start-Up as well as Any Established Business

Whether you're about to start a new business or you've been building one for several years, here are 100 carefully prepared letters, documents, agreements, spreadsheets, checklists, forms, and templates in the four areas business owners need the most help:

A handy desktop directory provides a brief description of all documents and where they can be found. Although a rich collection, JIAN Business*Basics* is priced to be affordable for any business—large or small. JIAN Business*Basics* works with any Windows 3.1, Windows 95, or Macintosh word processor and spreadsheet software. There are no new programs to learn..

Takes the Guesswork Out of Doing Business

Launching a new product or service? Need vendor contracts or employment applications? Want to put together a cashflow statement or an operating budget? Now there's no need to start from scratch or hire an expensive accountant, attorney, or consultant. All documents can be used "as is" or can be quickly and easily customized for *any* business. Yet the cost of the entire collection is less than what typical consultants charge for an hour of their time.

This is a collection of our most popular ready-to-use business contracts, letters, checklists, spreadsheets, forms and other frequently needed documents to build consistency and effective practices into your business.

The Business Plan that started it all...

The world's best selling and most successful busines plan software now takes full advantage of Window 95. BizPlan*Builder* now uses the integrated Power*Prompt*™ question and answer process and Interactive Document Assembly Engine to guide you through organizing, writing, and publishing a pol ished and compelling business plan. With ove 400,000 copies sold and millions in capital raisec through venture capitalists, investors, banks, the SBA and corporate management, BizPlan*Builder* is the proven leader. It's a complete business plan on dish with more than 90 typed pages of carefully scriptec example text—ready for you to customize for you business in your own style. New navigation menu let you choose as much or as little as you need. Wore processor and spreadsheet included—or use you own. Self-directed format guides you through the entire process. Experts' comments throughout explair issues and give clear, sensible advice on business plan ning as well as ways to set up your business.

This is the business planning software recommended by more investors, bankers and consultants than any other. It's been refined through the experience of professional advisors and thousands of customers who've used it successfully to develop new strategies and raise money.

> **"BizPlanBuilder employs a refreshing combination of the philosopher and expert mentor approach."**
> – Gerald Herter, CPA, MBA, Accounting Technology Magazine

> **"I bought 2 other software programs. After reading all three, I went with yours."**
> — Chuck Stasny, Missouri City, TX

> **"BizPlanBuilder is the number one recommended software by our CPA, attorney, tax specialist and others."**
> — Robert Crawford, Jr., ROE Associates, Atlanta, GA

Whether you are self-financed or need capital, here's the help you need to build a persuasive presentation to get going now

Quickly and easily articulate your vision and mission analyze your market, describe your product or service develop your marketing strategy, and outline promo tional and sales plans. Expert guidance helps you se goals, and better understand financial statements, dis tribution channels and strategic alliances.

Easily calculate cash requirements

BizPlan*Builder* works with your own spreadsheet soft ware so there's nothing new to learn. You also enjo unlimited flexibility. Enter projected sales, expens and growth assumptions and this powerful softwar automatically calculates totals, percentages and ratios You can see at a glance how much money you'll nee (and when) and even how soon you'll realize profits Use "What if?" analysis to test different financial sce narios. You'll quickly be able to understand an answer the toughest financial questions.

> **"As an experienced financial consultant, I was amazed at the depth of the package and its ease of use."**
> — Tom Devine, The Clayton Group, New York, NY

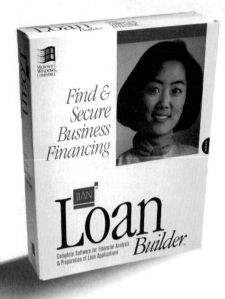

Find &
Secure
Business
Financing

JIAN
Loan *Builder*

Complete Software for Financial Analysis
& Preparation of Loan Applications

Which lender will loan money for your needs and use the tools to satisfy their criteria. Don't waste valuable time chasing rejection.

"The program can be a welcome addition... and it is not only easy to use and intuitive, but well documented."
— Bill McCabe, Accounting Technology Magazine

LoanBuilder has helped our clients create instant credibility with lenders. Being organized and prepared are characteristics every lender wants to see in an applicant, and since, LoanBuilder creates a complete plan package, it's an excellent tool for small business owners seeking financing. We use it all the time to help people put together SBA loan applications. I thought it was very thorough and logical.
— Kelly Bearden, Director, Valley Sierra Small Business Development Center, Modesto, CA

Open the door to 25 sources of financing for your business... including the SBA

Although they have strict guidelines to follow, lender want to loan you money. It's much easier when you work their system. Just use our sample Loan Proposal Summary as your professional cover document to introduce yourself, briefly describe your business and how it works explain your reason for requiring a loan, and provide you plan for repaying the debt. Complete analysis spreadsheets help you generate the percentages, ratios and credit scoring lenders use to make their decisions. We also provide ideas to streamline your way to getting the money you need more quickly and easily.

Loan*Builder* covers the 25 sources of business loans and has a unique "Loan Option Tree" which quickly lets you determine which loan, or loans, are viable for you business. By going after the right loan, you help ensure success and avoid wasting time with lenders whose approval requirements exclude your situation.

Automatic SBA forms shrink the process

We've captured the paperwork and automated the process for completing the forms to comply with Small Business Administration loan guarantee programs:

- 7(a) Loan Program including LowDoc
- CAPSLine revolving Line of Credit
- The Microloan program
- 504 Loan program

An accurate, complete and professional loan package makes it easy to get approval for your loan the first time The fill-in-the-blanks feature of Loan*Builder* automatically generates the forms you need and fills them in for you. We've incorporated advanced JetForm technology to make this easy. We've also included a cover letter, personal financial statement, board of director resolution—everything you'll need to put together professional looking loan application package to get th money you need. In the event you have to go to anothe lender, simply change the lender's name, and print. Use Loan*Builder* over and over whenever you need cash to build your business.

Win customers and build sales with these sophisticated selling tools and techniques

There's more to marketing than just writing a plan creating a few ads and printing a nice brochure MarketingBuilder provides the tools to organize, develop track, measure and control your marketing and advertising. You'll find numerous customized spreadsheets, schedules, forms and reports... everything you need to make informed decisions, and create and run a successful marketing campaign to build sales.

Turn a thorough market analysis into powerful promotional programs and profitable sales strategies

Dissect your competition. Plan and organize advertising brochures, direct mail, merchandising, sales promotion and trade shows. Use the custom spreadsheets to project track and analyze your advertising and direct mail campaigns so you can learn what's worked and what hasn't. When you understand what brings in your customers, you'll know what to do and how to invest your marketing budget to get the best results.

Refine your customer profile, target markets, pricing, positioning and promotions

Translate your marketing strategies into a powerful sale plan. Create sales forecasts by revenue goals vs. expenses by product or by sales channel. Use the hints and tips within the spreadsheets, documents and reports as expert guides to maximizing the return from your marketing and sales investments. Analysis worksheets are already set up to add, calculate percentages and produce ratios, so all you have to do is plug in the numbers. Works with most word processing and spreadsheet software—there are no new programs to learn. You can get going right away.

The #1 Marketing Software – with good reason.

Unlike other programs based on the opinions of just one or two people, we've compiled the best advice from a wide range of experts. MarketingBuilder offers an easy effective way to analyze your current marketing and improve its effectiveness. This powerful software provides you with a collection of handy and useful tools time-saving pre-formatted documents, and answers to your marketing questions.

This may be your best chance to achieve this level of marketing savvy and to compete effectively against larger companies with more people and resources devoted to marketing.

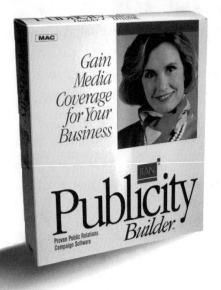

Most magazine articles, reviews, and TV feature stories highlighting products and companies are the result of good PR.

"PublicityBuilder amounts to a course in how to win editors and influence reporters. Every public relations person could benefit from the wisdom..."
— Larry Shannon, New York Times

"If you have a product, service or announcement you think belongs in the media and a budget you know won't stand much expense, consider PublicityBuilder..."
— Larry Blasko, Associated Press

"Well-written and organized, this software offers excellent ideas on getting your company name or product noticed."
— Andrea Hille, Buyers Laboratory, Hackensack, NJ

Turn your computer into a powerful public relations machine

Newspaper, magazine, radio and TV news editors are always looking for stories and interesting subject matter. But they are not interested in selling your product for you. So how do you get your product or service in the news? The secret is story power, or "angle." Plus, knowing what's news is the key, along with that all important element—timing. If you don't have these elements, your PR efforts will probably be unsuccessful. By taking advantage of them, there's no limit to how much publicity you can achieve. Publicity*Builder* teaches you to maximize your exposure by using the principles of angle, newsworthiness and timing, and shows you how to apply them to promoting your product or service.

How to grab headlines

Publicity*Builder* helps you interact effectively with the media. Use this contemporary and unique product to reach and attract reporters, and help them tell the world about your product, service, organization or event. Apply proven, creative approaches to get reviewed in business journals, consumer magazines, newspapers, radio, TV and trade publications. Give editors what they want, the way they want it. And demonstrate that you, your company, product or service are interesting to their audience.

Generate *free* advertising

Publicity*Builder* includes 40+ templates in all—Including 15 sample press releases, company and product positioning worksheets, company backgrounders, thank you letters to reviewers and editors, a checklist of tradeshow tactics and follow-up tasks, press kit materials, telephone contact guidelines and more. Just edit the worksheets and sample documents using your word processor. Model press releases eliminate the guesswork:

• Introduce a new product, service or company
• Promote the opening of your store, restaurant, etc.
• Publicize an event, service program, or fundraiser
• Announce a new contract, breakthrough or award

Complete PR reference guide included

Publicity*Builder* also includes a thorough public relations reference guide that provides the background and insight you'll need to handle your public relations like a pro.

People are more selective today than ever and they're looking for the right place to work. You can add much to your professional image as well as boost satisfaction and morale among your people.

"Hesser College is a two year college with approximately 100-plus full-time employees. The EmployeeManualMaker has been a tremendous help in organizing our policies and procedures, a time saver, as well as a money saver."
– Berna Berglund, Assistant to the President, Hesser College, Manchester, NH

"Well worth its modest investment. We use it to compare our existing policies with the latest employment practices in the personnel field, and also to assist us in developing new policies."
– Mort Smedley, Administrator, Carbon County, PA

Communicate your company policies, and expectations

Instant policy manual is a powerful management tool

If you're spending more time on employee problems than on running your company, you need EmployeeManual*Maker*. It can save you thousands of dollars and many hours of valuable time. Why reinvent the wheel? Choose from 120 of the latest employment policies and 30 different employee benefits.

Build productive relationships—minimize people problems

Experts agree that a carefully written employee handbook can improve morale, increase productivity, prevent disagreements, and even keep you out of court. By setting clear standards, you can make sure that all employees are treated fairly and consistently. No more misunderstandings, misinterpretations, or miscommunications that can cause you legal problems down the road. EmployeeManual*Maker* will keep your employees informed, and define your company culture. Plus, your manual will be written in warm, friendly, plain-English that will build and support a productive working environment.

Developed by a team of experts to cover all of your HR needs

Established practices enable you to hire and fire without fear. This is where most managers get into trouble. EmployeeManual*Maker* includes valuable insights, helpful tips and advice from a variety of top legal experts and practicing HR professionals including a personnel psychologist and several trade publication editors.

Comprehensive documentation on current labor laws and benefits is provided, along with the most popular employment checklists, memos and forms you'll need. We've included feedback from thousands of successful customers who've used EmployeeManual*Maker* throughout the years so you'll benefit from their direct experience.

Update an old employee manual? Changes on-line.

If you already have an employee handbook, but haven't revised it lately, given all the new changes in the law, it may have become outdated. An obsolete manual can be a real hazard to your company. Now it's easier than ever for you to update your manual as your business grows and as legal requirements change. You can get timely updates on important employment issues online.

Easily
track &
manage
employee
records

JIAN
Employee File *Builder*™
Your Instant Employee
Information System

Simplify & substantiate management decisions with this electronic personnel filing system

Replace your employee file cabinet and easily manage every employee's time-off, job and salary history, training experience, plus everything else you'd want to track.

Reduce your legal exposure, monitor your employees, and create customized reports... with full security... all from one simple menu-driven Windows program that's point-and-click simple to use.

No more bulging file cabinets, dog-eared files or lost notes

It's easy to handle personnel paperwork and better manag your employees' job & salary history, time off, vacation, sic leave, training experience and other personnel information No need to worry about misplaced file folders, loose paper or crucial lost information. EmployeeFile*Builder* is Windows-based database with intelligent reporting an analysis that gives you a powerful new tool to help you ru and build your business using your own computer.

Effortlessly track employee information

A relational database has never been so easy to use. Onc you enter your initial data, then keeping all of your record up-to-date requires only minimal effort. The system man ages the rest. File folder design and "on-the-fly" documen tation is user-friendly and lightening fast. Custom Viev function features a report generating wizard to help you cre ate exactly the reports you need. You have to put the infor mation in only once, and it will be automatically reflecte throughout your spreadsheets, graphs and reports.

Record keeping and tracking made easy

- Anyone can easily harness the power of Windows 95
- Quickly set up, maintain and update employee files on your computer
- Keep records in one easy-to-use centralized file folder
- Make changes "on-the-fly" with just a mouse click.
- Free up managers for more productive projects
- Create logs for employee activities planning & evaluations
- Instant access for multiple authorized managers
- Effortlessly track licensing, certification and training deadlines

Create a safe and healthy workplace. . . Quickly and easily comply with OSHA, and *avoid lawsuits!*

Here's everything you need to create a complete safety and health management plan. With a published injury and illness prevention manual for your business, you describe a formal system of record-keeping, inspections employee training, correction of unsafe conditions documentation and investigation of accidents. (Also, take a look at EmployeeFile*Builder* because it's ideal for maintaining many of these records.

Hundreds of Dangerous Work Practices covered to protect you and your people

Just select your state, industry, and Safe Work Practices from the comprehensive menu-driven system and SafetyPlan*Builder* will custom assemble your entire safety manual in just a few minutes. It automatically supplies recommended paragraphs for Agriculture, Construction, Food Service, Grain Handling Facilities, Trucking, Mining, Oil & Gas, Office Work, Paper & Paperboard Mills, Petro-chemical, Retail Sales, Sawmills, Shipbuilding, Logging and Warehousing. Then, you can easily edit and desktop publish your manual with any PC/DOS or Windows word processor.

Over 250 pre-written pages of industry-specific Safe Work Practices are included, plus paragraphs covering: Bio-Hazards, Chemicals, Construction, Electrical and Environmental Hazards, Explosives, Fires, Infection Control, Materials Handling, Power Tools, Sanitation, Seismic Safety, Transportation and many more.

Be Ready When OSHA Visits...

- Draft Federal or State OSHA-required Injury & Illness Prevention Plan
- Comply with California's tough SB-198 (which is likely to become standard nationwide)
- Avoid stiff penalties and even criminal charges!
- Revise and update as legal requirements change (Check our website for updates.)

Safety plans for businesses are required by law in many states. Here's everything you need to draft your company's federal or state OSHA-required Injury & Illness Prevention Plan.

> "This is a great product. I was able to create a safety plan for my company in no time at all. Thanks!"
> — Daniel Vance, Owner, Kimberly Nurseries, Elko, NV

> "Well done!...emphasize the speed and 'anyone can do it' nature of the program. I think it's a great product and I think it is a great step forward in our ability to provide safe and healthful places of employment."
> —Jack Wright, Certified Safety Professional, Chattanooga, TN

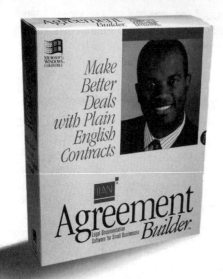

Any one of these legal agreements can easily be worth 10 times your investment. Think of AgreementBuilder as your legal tool kit. We've even provided you with a mini-course in contract law to give you a grasp of the basic principles involved.

> "I had a non-disclosure agreement drafted by my lawyer, but it was too scary to sign. With AgreementBuilder, the text is down-to-earth and everyone can agree on it."
> — S. Haugen, Chicago, IL

> I was immediately able to use the exclusive distribution agreement to establish one of the largest contracts of the company."
> — Andrea Sanchez, Owner, International Financial Services, Oxnard, CA

100+ comprehensive, *plain-English* business contracts

We've gathered and assembled some of the finest business contracts and translated them from legalese into everyday language for you to make deals with customers, suppliers, reps, employees, (and anyone else).

Excessive legalese removed

Before Agreement*Builder*, understanding complex, lengthy legal agreements wasn't always easy. We've done away with words like *hereof, whereas, hereto, hereinafter, set forth, pursuant to, thereof,* (and our favorite) *notwithstanding the foregoing.* (It means 'no matter what.') Use these agreements in negotiations to avoid forgetting an important point, unintentionally promising something, or making a mistake because a sentence was ambiguous. Establish clear terms and don't put yourself in the position of letting the court decide what you meant, what you and the other party did (or didn't do), and what it's worth.

As if an attorney were sitting next to you

Teaming up with real-world business attorneys and business deal makers, we have created thorough, legally binding contracts that support business deals rather than kill them. Each agreement includes expert comments on-screen between each section to explain the meaning and purpose of the text. Each agreement also includes a friendly, professional cover memo introducing the contract.

Instant contracts are perfect for making your next deal

Each agreement contains pre-formatted text for your convenience, but you have complete control over what goes and stays... and how it looks. Just fill-in and edit using any popular Windows or Macintosh word-processing software. Save money by having your attorney review your contracts rather than draft them from scratch. Agreement*Builder* will help you establish clear terms and develop sound contracts for your important relationships.

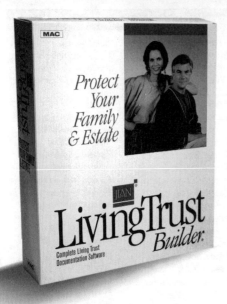

Protect Your Family & Estate

JIAN®
LivingTrust *Builder*

Complete Living Trust Documentation Software

There is a lot you can do to avoid estate taxes and the nightmare of probate court. You can even take steps to protect your business interests. Here are the documents you need. They're complete and easy to understand and use.

If something happens to you... who will run your business?

A living trust means security—it puts you in complete control so your wishes can't be changed by courts, greedy heirs or legal technicalities.

Plain-English documents

LivingTrust*Builder* was developed by experienced estate planning attorneys who've been preparing living trusts for 30+ years. It includes a choice of 5 trusts, an estate calculation worksheet, plus what you need to know about gifting, along with all the crucial supporting documents you need to complete your trust. Everything has been translated from "legalese" into plain English so you'll easily understand what you're reading.

The trust software for business owners

Unlike other living trust software programs, LivingTrust*Builder* is designed especially for business owners. In addition to trusts, deeds, powers of attorney, it contains an insurance trust, including the expert advice you need to assure a smooth continuation of your business without heavy taxes and legal hassles. Your insurance policies may cover you financially, but to assure the uninterrupted continuation of your business, you must formulate a succession plan. Even if you were only temporarily incapacitated, your succession plan would assure that your instructions are followed to the letter. We include a succession plan primer to help you map out your wishes and get all the paperwork in order. We've also added general partnership and "Buy-Sell" agreements to help you protect your partnership interests from personal problems. What if your business partner's ex-spouse wants to take over your business...?

Control your legacy

A living trust means more than just tax and probate savings. It also provides control over what happens to your business. It even gives you more control when you're alive, by providing specific provisions on how you want to be cared for in the event of serious illness or incapacity, and how you want your affairs to be managed during that time.

THE JIAN STORY

Burke Franklin, Founder & CEO

Burke has an extensive background in sales, marketing and business development with both technology and consumer products. He worked for companies like Texas Instruments and CPT as well as a number of start-ups and The Sharper Image catalog.

JIAN (originally named Tools for Sales) was founded in July 1986 to develop sales promotion materials. Burke used his experience as a successful field sales representative and marketing manager together with his ongoing study of psychology and communications to produce ads and brochures. These marketing materials helped increase clients' sales by 140%. He also applied this experience to number of business plans he worked on. The result was a more descriptive, concise and easy to understand proposal—more likely to be read and approved for funding.

Burke decided to take the best materials from each of these projects and put together the "ultimate" business plan. And that's what became BizPlan*Builder*. That was in March 1988, and since then we've received countless calls and letters from customers who've succeeded using BizPlan*Builder*.

Burke was elected delegate to the White House Conference on Small Business held in Washington, D.C. in June, 1995. In April, 1996, he was nominated for Ernst & Young's Entrepreneur of the Year Award. In May 1996, and again in April 1997, the Brazilian software council flew him to Brazil to teach business planning to Brazilian software entrepreneurs.

While a Black Belt is a master of the martial arts, "jian" (a real word pronounced: jee'on) is a master of every art—the ultimate human with extraordinary acumen, power and resourcefulness. JIAN is a contemporary American software company focused on applying modern techniques to the art of building businesses. We chose this unusual name because it reflects our goals as well as those of our customers.

Over the years, we at JIAN have come up with a few things you can use right now to make your life a little easier and your business more productive. Writing an excellent business or marketing plan, a bullet-proof employee or safety manual, drafting an important agreement—these used to be boring projects to be avoided at all costs. . . Frankly, I'd rather spend my time talking with customers, developing and improving our products and services, and still have enough time to enjoy my life. But these things must be done. I talked with friends and other entrepreneurs and discovered that I wasn't alone. I wasn't the only one who needed a better solution. I hated the business plans I read. I was burned-out working for companies that treated employees like cattle. I was tired of reading documents I couldn't understand without professional help. So, I took matters into my own hands. I wrote the original BizPlan*Builder* back in 1988 and, since then, our other products have evolved.

We didn't just fall off the turnip truck

Just because we sell software doesn't mean you get something a young, inexperienced propeller-head cooked up or limit you to the thinking of just one individual. We've sold more than 450,000 copies of our software worldwide since 1988, and every day we receive success stories and input from our customers who tell us we've done it right and how to do it even better next time.

It's a good thing I had Wilfred T. Grenfell for a professor way back because he blasted every report I wrote. . . *What do you mean by that? Prove it! Who? When? How do you know that? Give me an example! Like what?* It was hell, I hated him, but he taught me to write. And I hear his voice when I review our products. Now I even sound like him to our employees. As a result, our software is complete and will make sense to you, and definitely help you get your work done.

So, try any of our products and you'll discover feature-rich, productivity-enhancing tools that will revolutionize the way you work. It's an unbeatable combination of ideas, direction and examples you can use right now. And, if for any reason our software doesn't work for your business, you've got 60 days to send it back. With JIAN software, you'll successfully complete these business projects and enjoy time for other activities that will make you money. (Or go play.) Thanks for doing business with us.